STUDIES IN HISTORICAL GEOGRAPHY

Climatic Change Agriculture and Settlement

STUDIES IN HISTORICAL GEOGRAPHY

Editors: Alan R. H. Baker and J. B. Harley

Also published in this series

Southern Africa
A. J. CHRISTOPHER

Finland
MICHAEL JONES

Rural Settlement in Britain
BRIAN K. ROBERTS

Mirrors of the New World
J. M. POWELL

Forthcoming title

English Towns 1500–1700
JOHN PATTEN

STUDIES IN HISTORICAL GEOGRAPHY

Climatic Change Agriculture and Settlement

M. L. PARRY

DAWSON · ARCHON BOOKS

First published in 1978

Wm Dawson & Sons Ltd, Cannon House
Folkestone, Kent, England

Archon Books, The Shoe String Press, Inc
995 Sherman Avenue, Hamden, Connecticut 06514 USA

British Library Cataloguing in Publication Data

Parry, M L
Climatic change, agriculture and settlement.
– (Studies in historical geography).
1. Climatic changes – History 2. Agriculture
– Economic aspects – History
I. Title II. Series
338.1'5 S439 77–30583

ISBN 0 7129 0794 7
ISBN 0308 6607

Archon ISBN 0–208–01722–4

Printed litho in Great Britain
by W & J Mackay Limited, Chatham

To
J.K.P.

Contents

List of Figures

List of Plates

List of Tables

Foreword

In many parts of the world there is evidence of agricultural decline and dislocation of the economy, of cultural change and political unrest, in the late Middle Ages. In Europe this has been traditionally attributed to the ravages of the Black Death in 1348–50 and subsequent recurrences of this plague. In recent years, however, the beginnings of the troubles have been traced back several decades earlier, particularly to the harvest failures and famines around 1315 and to the cattle diseases and death that were produced by the same soaking summers. Many other studies have established beyond doubt a significant disturbance of the climatic regime – which for some long time previously had been remarkably benign – about that time.

Some years ago, when studying for his Ph.D. degree in Edinburgh, the author of this book made a close study of the record of abandonment of farms and cultivated land on the Lammermuir Hills. His study revealed a remarkably close association between the stages of this story and what is now known of the history of the climate of the times – a long, fluctuating downward trend of temperature. He devised ways of estimating not only the length but also the accumulated warmth of the growing season at each stage – and at all the heights concerned – and the probable frequency of harvest failures. The connections between these things are so securely demonstrated in this book, with illustrations of their impact upon the population and their way of life, that it is clear they must have played a central part in Scottish history and, as the author shows, in the history of many other lands besides.

This book is therefore an important contribution to the agricultural history of the last thousand years or more as well as to the writing of Scottish history. There is a farm in central Norway at the upper limit of agriculture which has been abandoned three times since it was first established around A.D. 400, each time during a period of deteriorating climate (i.e. summer warmth and raininess), and left for one or more centuries before being opened up again when the climate allowed. The last time it was abandoned was in or around the 1690s, to be first brought back into use in the 1930s. Dr Parry has rightly concentrated his greatest attention on such marginal places, because the impact of climate is clearest there; but he also shows how extensive the vulnerable areas are, as well as the links with human and animal health and well-being. Another of the book's virtues is the way Dr Parry helps the reader to see in perspective the partly separate workings of the short-term climatic fluctuations and shocks and the long-term trends.

This whole subject is extremely relevant to today's problems in a world where the teeming populations can be fed by maximising agricultural output and guarding against the impact of the inevitable climatic fluctuations and changes. Wise policies demand understanding. Dr Parry has focused on an aspect of history, particularly where long-term trends have acted as a deadweight to halt the recovery from individual bad years, that has been shockingly omitted from the history books in most countries outside Scandinavia where its importance can hardly be overlooked. His survey embraces Scandinavia and the same problem in the world's greatest grainlands in the United States Midwest as well.

In commending this book to a wide readership, I can only regret that this particular advance in knowledge did not come many years ago. I hope it will be read – with some fascination – not only by agriculturalists and historians but by politicians and planners in many fields, by students and a wide public besides.

H. H. LAMB
Director
Climatic Research Unit
School of Environmental Sciences
University of East Anglia
Norwich.

Preface

It was the orthodox view that studies of climate and of culture mix about as well as oil and water. Early attempts to assess the influence of one upon the other did not meet with conspicuous success; indeed, the subject has been poorly served by those highly generalised and wildly inaccurate prognostications on climate and history that were common in the 1920s and, unfortunately, seem to be common enough today.

This book aims to narrow the area of continuing speculation and uncertainty that surrounds the role of climatic change in agricultural history. It does so by focusing sharply upon particular types of climatic change occurring in particularly vulnerable areas. The specific means that are developed here for closely observing the link between climatic and economic changes should be useful elsewhere, and I hope that these will be adopted and improved upon by others. My intention has been not to attempt a definitive statement on the subject but to point to ways in which we can make steady progress towards one. This detailed approach will ultimately be far more productive than the broad-brush treatment of earlier approaches.

Martin Parry
University of Birmingham
January 1978

Acknowledgements

A number of people kindly commented upon part of the early draft of this book: Professor H. H. Lamb, Professor G. Manley, Dr E. T. Stringer, Dr Susan Limbrey, Dr J. W. R. Whitehand, Mr C. C. Dyer and Dr R. N. Gwynne; to these I am very grateful, but alone remain responsible for the content.

I am grateful to the late Professor Harry Thorpe and Professor P. H. Temple for their encouragement and for the use of reprographic facilities at the University of Birmingham; to those at Birmingham who helped prepare the final draft: Judy Astle, Jean and Geoff Dowling, Pat Short and Ron Swift; and to Cynthia Parry for assistance throughout the work, from research to proofreading.

Figures have been reproduced with the permission of: Dr J. W. King and the Editors of *Nature* (Fig 1), the Royal Society (Fig 8), Professor G. Manley (Figs 2 and 8), Dr J. A. Matthews and the Editors of *Nature* (Fig 7), Professor H. H. Lamb (Figs 3, 11, 12 and 13), Professor L. A. Lliboutry and Masson Press (Fig 4), Dr P. Bergthorsson (Fig 5), Dr W. Dansgaarde (Fig 6), Dr L. Lysgaard and the Editors of *Folia Geographica Danica* (Fig 9), Dr V. C. LaMarche and the Editors of *Science* (Fig 10), Dr J. D. McQuigg and the US National Oceanic and Atmospheric Administration (Figs 14 and 15), Professor R. A. Bryson (Fig 29), Universitêtsforlaget, Oslo (Fig 30), Professor S. Thorarinsson (Fig 35), Dr S. Fridriksson (Fig 36), Dr H. Salvesen (Fig 37), Dr J. Sandnes (Fig 38), Professor A. Holmsen (Fig 39), Professor M. M. Postan, Dr J. Z. Titow and the Editors of *Economic History Review* (Fig 40), Dr K. Beltzner (Fig 41), Dr W. R. Wedel (Fig 42), the Regents Press of Kansas (Fig 43).

Table 1 is reproduced with the permission of Professor G.

Utterström, and Table 3 with the permission of Dr S. Fridriksson.

The quotations in Chapter 3 and Chapter 6 are reproduced with the permission of Dr J. D. McQuigg and of Dr W. R. Wedel.

Finally, I am grateful to Professor Emmanuel Le Roy Ladurie and to the Flammarion Press for making available the photographic prints used in Plates 2, 3 and 4.

1

New Evidence, Old Attitudes

It was, in one sense, unfortunate that the climate of north-west Europe in the late nineteenth century displayed a return to the lower temperatures prevailing about a century earlier. This seems to have encouraged the belief, which may now seem curious, that climate is essentially constant and that the averages of observations taken over a length of time will truly reflect climates both of the past and in the future. It is the more unfortunate that we should have continued for some time in this belief because the period of widely used climatic 'normals' (1931–60) may have had the most abnormal climate of the past 500 years, and perhaps of the last 1000 years.[1]

Over the last fifty years climatologists have been piecing together the history of climate since the end of the last Ice Age – about 10,000 years ago. The history that they have written has, of course, been frequently altered, corrected and improved with the arrival of more detailed evidence for climatic change. Indeed, over the last twenty years, the development of new and independent sources of evidence have quite markedly extended our knowledge of the nature of climatic change. From this variety of independent evidence it is safe to say that, for north-west Europe at least, the general chronology of change over the last 2000 years is firmly established. Of course, there remains much to be learned about the details of shorter-term changes, but we may be reasonably certain of the secular trend – that occurring over centuries rather than over decades.

Two points relating to this secular trend deserve special mention. First, the scale of climatic change in north-west Europe – for example, the range over which mean decadal temperatures have fluctuated – is substantial; it is certainly large enough to have affected the long-term productivity of most types of agriculture and the ecological balance of many communities of plants and animals. There is a growing awareness of these agricultural and ecological implications, particularly with respect to land-use management at the present time and to land-use planning for the future. It is the more curious, therefore, that until recently historians have not seriously considered changes of climate as an important aspect of the 'environment' of history, particularly of agricultural history.

Secondly, as the understanding of climatic change has grown, early chronologies have undergone substantial revision. It is most unfortunate, then, that in the few cases where historians have investigated the implications of climatic change they have sometimes referred to chronologies which the majority of climatic historians now believe are incorrect and which have been superseded.

There may be two reasons for this imperfect appreciation of the scale of long-term climatic change and for the continued adherence to out-dated chronologies. Firstly, historians have in general given more attention to short-term fluctuations rather than to secular trends in climate, believing that the former are the more likely to have been of social or economic consequence. Secondly, most historians have been unable to evaluate fully the agricultural significance of climatic change because they are not familiar with those various climatic factors to which different types of agriculture are especially sensitive.

It is the purpose of this volume to summarise existing views on the scale and direction of climatic change in Europe since about A.D. 1000 and to evaluate its impact on past agricultural economies. The focus of the evaluation is firmly on 'marginal' areas, the thesis being that changes of climate are here most likely to have had a lasting economic impact; and underlying this thesis is the assumption that only long-term climatic changes are likely to have had long-term economic effects.

New Evidence

An increasing awareness of the tendency of climates to change has been recently impressed upon us by a remarkable sequence of extremes, of one kind or another, that has occurred since about 1960. Amongst these Lamb has listed for the British Isles the coldest winter since 1740 (1962–3), the driest winter since 1743 (1963–4), the mildest winter since 1834 (1974–5), the driest sixteen months on the 250-year rainfall record (April 1975 to August 1976);[2] in addition there is the warmest summer (June, July and August) on the

300-year temperature record (1976). Extremes such as these tend to be characteristic of a particular type of circulation of the atmosphere. They are probably linked with extremes occurring elsewhere, such as those droughts which occurred after 1968 in the Sahel and in India as a result of reduced northward penetration of monsoon rains.[3]

At the same time, and connected with the above, there has occurred since about 1940 a trend towards lower average temperatures, especially at higher and middle latitudes. The average length of the growing season has allegedly decreased by up to two weeks in England, and probably by a comparable amount elsewhere at high latitudes – on the Canadian Prairies, in parts of the Soviet Union and in northern Japan. The possibility of increasing climatic restraint on future production in agriculture, in spite of improving technology, is now seriously contemplated.[4]

A logical step has been to adopt these contemporary changes of climate as modern analogues of the past. Given that severe droughts occurred in the Sahel in the early 1970s and in midwest America in the 1930s, and that quite rapid cooling has occurred in northern Europe since the 1940s, then similar droughts and cooling could presumably have occurred in the past – possibly at a greater level of severity and over a longer period of time. Did they occur and, if they did, what was the response to them? The answers to such questions are important not only to the historian; the reconstruction of past changes of climate may help to forecast those in the future, and an understanding of the effects of climatic change should enable improved planning of those forms of economic activity that are open to influence from the physical environment. For example, the marked effect of weather on yields of most farm crops means that changes in weather may mean changes in productivity. In North America some recent studies have suggested that the consistently high productivity of the 1950s and 1960s has been due to a combination of improved technology and exceptionally favourable weather. A return to the more variable climatic conditions of earlier decades would probably produce far greater year-to-year fluctuations in agricultural output.[5] The cost is not easy to measure but would certainly be enormous.[6]

Increasing awareness of the significance of past changes of climate seems to derive from three factors which have only quite recently been demonstrated. Firstly, the scale of changes is substantial when measured in terms of a shift of regional climates. Lamb has suggested that changes of average summer temperature in central

England between the warmest and coolest decades of the past three centuries represent shifts between conditions typical for northern France and lowland Scotland; and changes of decade average winter temperature range from conditions typical for eastern Ireland to those typical for western Holland.[7]

Secondly, while climates were once thought to change slowly and steadily – for example, a gradual warming and cooling between ice ages – many climatologists now believe that they can change quite rapidly, in a step-like fashion between phases of relative stability.[8] The problems of adaptation are thus magnified and, while it would appear intuitively that in the long-run the effects of such changes (both adverse and beneficial) would balance themselves out in a phase of gradual change, in phases of rapid climatic change they would not – and the stress on environmentally-sensitive activities could be severe.[9]

Finally, it should be noted that economic and ecological stress may be heightened because its relationship with climatic change is not always linear, but it is sometimes almost exponential. The ecological response of some animal and plant communities to fluctuations in temperature or rainfall can be very marked and the chances of a failed harvest may, in particular circumstances, increase markedly with small changes in average summer temperature (see Chapter 3).

These three factors – in addition to the present trend of climate in high latitudes – have led some climatologists to forecast changes of climate in the future that will place real stresses on our agricultural systems.[10] It is difficult to reconcile this view with that commonly held by historians, even those interested in the history of climate, that the human consequences of long-term climatic change in the past were slight, and perhaps negligible.[11] If the possibility of stress from climatic change exists in relation to agricultural systems which have the support of modern technology, should not the possibility of similar, perhaps more serious stress, on early and more primitive agricultural systems deserve similar investigation?

Old Attitudes

In 1907 Ellsworth Huntington argued for the existence of climatic 'pulsations'.[12] He later proposed that the periodicity of these pulsations was perhaps the product of disturbances in the Sun's atmosphere (or sunspots) which, he believed, displayed an 11-year cyclic pattern of occurrence and which might be related to the planetary movements around the Sun.[13] Many of these ideas were subsequently rejected, sometimes ridiculed, although it is interesting to note that they are today receiving much more serious study.[14] The notion of climatic pulsations moved Huntington to investigate their links with the history of civilisations, which he saw as being sometimes closely connected with adverse or beneficial changes of climate. He suggested, for example, that Mayan migrations in central America, and the desertion of Roman settlements in Syria were in part a consequence of climatic shifts.[15] Huntington's excursions into cultural history were not substantiated by the data then available and were in time discredited.[16] In particular, they became unfortunately associated with a philosophy of environmental determinism – of which they were never truly a part – which was itself rejected in the 1930s.[17]

However, the notion of sunspot cycles did attract the attention of some economic historians, among them William Beveridge who, before his successful career as a social reformer, pointed to an apparent correlation between a periodic fluctuation in global barometric pressure at intervals of about 15·3 years and fluctuations of food prices. He inferred from this that a periodic crisis in climatic conditions on the earth as a whole tends to lower the general productivity of harvests.[18]

But any notions that may have emerged of a link between long-term rather than short-term climatic change and economic activity in the past were not supported by the existing chronology of climate. Before about 1950 one of the most comprehensive chronologies of early climatic change in Britain was a compilation by Britton, in 1937, of meteorological events up to A.D. 1450.[19] Included in this was a century-by-century index of severe winters, heavy snows, floods and hot summers which unfortunately took no account of the varying severity of the event, or of the changing comprehensiveness of the surviving record. The data were adopted in 1948 by Russell and, less critically, by Van Bath in 1963, to illustrate that economic decline in the fourteenth century was unlikely to be related to a 'deteriorating' climate since there was evidence of more frequent serious floodings over the period 1150–1300 – a period of economic buoyancy in north-west Europe – than over the period 1300–1450 – a period of more general economic decline.[20] To some extent this notion was reinforced by the findings of Brooks who noted the occurrence of a group of particularly wet years from 1087 to 1117, a run of hot, dry summers after 1275, and in general a greater 'raininess' over 1150–1350 than after 1350.[21] At the same time Brooks inferred from Easton's compilations for Europe a cold period around A.D. 1100.[22]

However, more recent chronologies, such as that first described in about 1960 by Lamb, contradict Brooks and indicate a phase of increasingly frequent wetness and coldness in the early fourteenth century. But the superseded chronologies are still alive and, mistakenly, reference is still made to the early medieval period as coinciding with 'one of Europe's cold cycles';[23] and the relevance of climate to the history of deserted villages in England is claimed to be minimal because few desertions occurred during or shortly after the period of supposed climatic 'deterioration'.[24] In fact the phase of most widespread desertion, 1370–1500, coincides broadly with a secondary nadir of average summer temperatures and a secondary peak of average summer rainfall.

The apparent lack of a 'fit' between the supposed chronology of climatic change and the chronology of economic growth was used by Russell to argue that short-term fluctuations of climate did not have an important influence upon the population of medieval England.[25] More recently Hoskins has admitted the important effect of year-to-year fluctuations of climate on the size of harvests and thus on food supply, but does not accept that more long-term changes such as that occurring in the second half of the sixteenth century adversely affected the size of harvest.[26]

Of course, the temporal coincidence of climatic and cultural events does not necessarily indicate that the one has 'caused' the other. The opposing views on this issue have been championed by Utterström and Le Roy Ladurie. Utterström has argued that – amongst other events – the decline of Norse settlements in Greenland, the transformation of the Icelandic economy in the sixteenth century, and the major medieval famines of Europe have been partly due to the 'changeableness of Nature'. Le Roy Ladurie believes that inferences such as these are not adequately substantiated by climatic data. Utterström has replied by noting that this difference of opinion seems to derive largely from contrasting views concerning the vulnerability of early agrarian societies to environmental change in general.[27]

There is also a curious contradiction of attitude, not only between scholars of the same discipline, but also within individual scholars. Some medieval historians, for example, have argued that peasant society in north-west Europe was particularly vulnerable to harvest fluctuations and yet that climatic changes – which were the major cause of such fluctuations – were unlikely to have been an important factor behind some of the economic difficulties of the late Middle Ages. The agrarian population is said to have expanded to a point of 'relative over-population' where the produce of the land was insufficient to sustain it through both good years and bad; the 'changeableness' of climate is thus implied while the relevance of climatic change is explicitly rejected.[28]

Several factors may explain this contradictory attitude. Firstly, many archaeologists and historians have in general an incomplete understanding of the ways in which climates change and how much they have changed during the historic or pre-historic past; and where they are familiar with the scale of change that seems to have occurred they may not fully comprehend its ecological or agronomic implications. Le Roy Ladurie, for example, has queried the importance of a long-term climatic fluctuation of 1 °C over western Europe which he has described as 'slight, almost intangible'.[29] Yet it is evident that in some maritime climates an overall reduction of 1 °C on mean annual temperature can have a marked effect on the length and intensity of the growing season.

Secondly, it is apparent that many historians do not generally appreciate that climatic fluctuations differ in scale and direction from one area to another, and that the areas themselves have very different average climates upon which a change of temperature or rainfall has very different effects. It will be evident, for example, that the growing conditions of summer in maritime climates are much more seriously diminished by overall cooling than those in more continental climates. Cereal cropping would, in this instance, be more markedly influenced in Iceland than in central Europe.

Finally, it is apparent that there is no complete understanding of the very different biological and agronomic effects produced by short-term and by long-term changes of climate.

Aims and Approach

This book is an investigation into how significantly the changes in climate over the last 1000 years have affected agriculture and rural settlement in north-west Europe and North America. Three themes in this investigation are closely related to the three areas of misunderstanding outlined above. First, there is a summary of existing information on the causes of climatic changes, the manner in which they occur and the evidence from which their chronology may be traced. The chronology that is presented is the most reliable available and is intended as a basis for subsequent discussion of the socio-economic significance of past changes of climate.

Second, there is the view that changes of climate are likely to have had their most profound effect in marginal areas. These areas may be broadly defined as those which barely give an adequate return to farming investment. We shall refer to two types of marginality; that which is the product of the entire range of natural and human factors that affect the profitability of farming; and a more specific notion of marginality where climatic conditions alone are barely suited to the range of crops grown and where farming systems are, in general, poorly adapted to climatic conditions. In speaking of this 'climatic marginality' we should not forget that social, economic and political forces will, in reality, modify our simplified crop-climate link. But it is helpful to hold these constant while first observing the climatic element alone. At a later stage this restriction can be relaxed. Climatically marginal areas will be the 'laboratories' of the present study; their special value in this respect was recognised by the Conference on the Climate of the Eleventh and Sixteenth Centuries which was convened at Aspen, Colorado in 1962.[30] In Chapters 3 and 4 climatically marginal areas in north-west Europe and North America are identified for particular study. These marginal areas are investigated for evidence of the changes in potential for crop growth that would have occurred as a result of climatic changes which are believed to have taken place over the last millenium. The emphasis is placed firmly upon crop, rather than on livestock, production because it is only for this sector of agriculture that adequate data are at present available.

Third, there is the contention that long-term changes of climate are more likely than short-term changes to have had long-term economic effects. These long-term changes may have altered the economic viability of marginal areas and it is hypothesised that they made marginal agriculture and marginal settlement particularly sensitive to social and economic events which touched upon their viability; had there not been this long-term change, the socio-economic 'triggers' of change would have promoted a less widespread and a less permanent response.

2

The Process and Chronology of Climatic Change

Since about 1960 a substantial improvement in our understanding of the circulation of the atmosphere has inevitably led to a greater comprehension of the probable causes of change in climate. In addition, the development of new methods of dating and measuring climatic change have added greatly to our knowledge of those changes in climate that have occurred in the past. As a result of these advances of knowledge, it has been necessary to rewrite much of the history of climate that had been pioneered by Brooks, Britton and Easton.

Understanding the Processes

The Climatic 'System'

The term climate usually brings to mind the idea of an average regime of weather; 'weather' refers to the condition of the atmosphere at a particular place and time. It is useful to view climate as a system comprising properties and processes which are responsible for its many types of variation, from yearly fluctuations to changes on a millenial time-scale. The most important influence on climatic change is the circulation of the atmosphere.

The rotation of the Earth causes the atmosphere to rotate about the Earth's axis. Both rotations are from west to east. In areas where the atmosphere is rotating more rapidly than the earth a westerly wind is observed, and where the Earth is rotating more rapidly than the atmosphere an easterly wind is observed. These winds blow almost along the lines of constant pressure, particularly when above the zone of friction of the Earth's surface. The main flow is a single 'circumpolar vortex' of upper westerly winds which occur in a deep layer in the atmosphere from about 2 to 20 km above the earth's surface. The strongest flow is generated where the horizontal temperature gradient between the Tropics (where solar radiation is most intense) and the Poles (where it is least intense) is greatest. This occurs over middle latitudes but migrates a few degrees towards the Equator or towards one of the poles according to the seasons. Superimposed on this seasonal variation are some geographical anomalies, produced by land, sea and ice, as well as shorter- and longer-term variations.

The barometric depressions and anticyclones that determine the prevailing surface weather are generated by disequilibrium of the upper flow, and it is apparent that two broad types of circulation have markedly different effects on surface weather systems. From periods of weeks to many years the flow of the upper winds may be predominantly westerly or 'zonal', while at other times it may display large north-south or 'meridional' excursions. Surface depressions are generally steered from west to east by the zonal circulation and bring alternating surges of colder and warmer air, with belts of cloud and rain sweeping over the middle latitudes. Anticyclonic conditions generally prevail over the subtropical zone and maintain a desert regime.[1]

At times of meridional-type circulation, however, the eastward movement of surface weather systems over middle latitudes is largely 'blocked'. The stationary patterns thus produced tend to maintain prolonged warmth or cold, and wetness or dryness in different areas in middle latitudes, bringing extremes of temperature and rainfall. For example, the extreme weather conditions experienced in a variety of forms in different parts of the northern hemisphere during 1976–7 – the very dry summer and wet autumn of 1976 in north-west Europe, the very snowy winter of 1976–7 in north-east USA – were characteristic of blocking by a meridional circulation. Indeed, an important concept of the climatic system is that changes of climate resulting from a change in atmospheric circulation, while being different in different places, are nevertheless likely to be strongly linked. This comprehension of the global behaviour of climate should enable climatic historians to piece together the general history of climatic change for any one place even where the local record of change is interrupted. We are less sure, however, of the more fundamental mechanisms behind the pattern of global behaviour.

Possible Causes of Climatic Variations

Several extra-terrestrial and terrestrial processes have been hypothesised as possible causes of climatic fluctuations. These have been discussed by Mitchell and Mason,[2] and have been conveniently summarised by Kutzbach.[3]

Theories of climatic change can be grouped into three types which are not all mutually exclusive. The first proposes that climatic changes result from random fluctuations about a long-term fixed mean; the second, that climatic changes result from internal feedback processes operating from the reaction of atmosphere, oceans and land surface; and the third, that climatic changes result from changes in extrinsic variables such as solar radiation, carbon dioxide content of the atmosphere due to industrial activity, and atmospheric transmissivity due to volcanic activity.[4]

The third theory is the most widely held, often with acceptance of the second – a recognition that feedback loops create a complex reaction by the atmospheric circulation to changes in an extrinsic variable. The extrinsic variables may be grouped as follows:[5]

(1) The intensity of sunlight reaching the Earth.
(2) The transmissivity of the atmosphere as modified by external factors, particularly by volcanic activity.
(3) The albedo of the Earth's surface and of the atmosphere as modified by external factors such as cloud, land use, snow and ice.
(4) The 'greenhouse effect' of varying amounts of water vapour and gases in the atmosphere.

Variation in solar radiation No long-term record of the total flux of solar radiation reaching the earth's orbit has been compiled, since most records were taken within the Earth's atmosphere and therefore have been affected by fluctuations in atmospheric turbidity. However, it seems (though it has not been proved to the satisfaction of some atmospheric scientists) that the variation in solar radiation is related to the incidence of solar flares or sunspots. Indeed a recent computation of global temperatures based solely upon sunspot frequency was seen to correspond quite closely with the observed general patterns of temperature variations since the seventeenth century.[6]

This apparent relationship between temperature and sunspot number is, some claim, reflected in the trend of crop yields. Figure 1 illustrates the similarity between the trends of crop yield, temperature and sunspot number in Britain during the two complete solar cycles 1937–57.[7] It seriously over-simplifies the complexity of the yield data, which are much influenced by economic production. It has also been criticised for the very short period over which the relationship is studied; over the fifty years preceding 1937 it appears that the relationship between sunspot cycle and potato yield does not hold.[8] However, the sunspot cycle has been related to other occurrences and, although it remains contested, the weight of evidence points to some kind of causal link.[9]

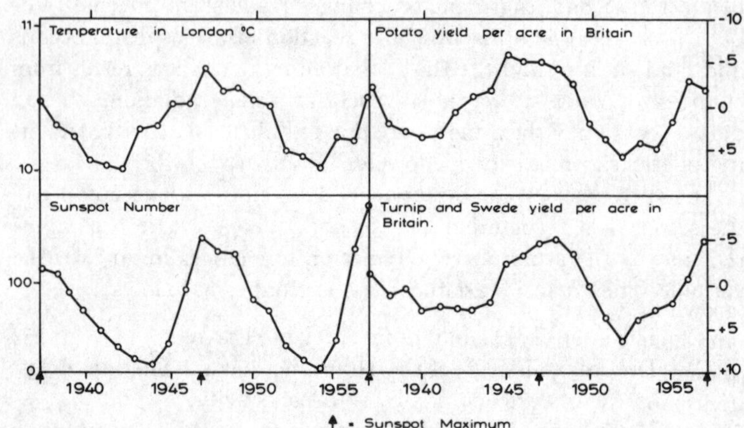

Fig. 1. Relationship between sunspot frequency, average temperature in London, and yields of major crops in Britain in 1937–57. The crop yield is shown as a percentage variation of the long-term average yield. After King *et al.* (1974).

The implication is that solar activity affects the weather on Earth, but the mechanism by which it does so is not fully understood. The incidence of sunspots may be determined by activity internal to the Sun,[10] or perhaps by the alignment of planets around the Sun which might have a tidal effect upon its gaseous surface and thus produce variations in solar activity.[11] Whatever the explanation, there is the possibility that consequent variations in the intensity of the 'solar wind' of charged solar particles produces disturbances of the Earth's magnetic field, similar to the disturbance in the upper atmosphere which we call the *aurorae*. Shifts of the magnetic pole may somehow be related to these disturbances; and, it has recently been suggested that the location of the magnetic pole has some influence on the position of the Arctic depressions, which would in turn influence the direction of Atlantic depressions – and thus the weather – over Europe.[12] At present this is speculation, but there remains the possibility that planetary alignments do – indirectly – influence weather, harvests and the supply of food on Earth.

Transmissivity of the atmosphere If the physical properties of the atmosphere did not vary, then about the only cause of climatic variation would be variations in solar radiation. However, the transmissivity of the atmosphere varies with time, due largely to changes in the quantity of particulate material.

The largest extrinsic source of particulates has been volcanic activity which has in the past created worldwide veils of finely divided dust which linger for years in the upper atmosphere reducing the admission of solar radiation. Volcanic dust veils have in fact produced a lowering of temperatures on a hemispherical scale (though more markedly in middle than in high or low latitudes); an estimated lowering of 1·3°C occurred in England after the two great eruptions in Iceland and Japan in 1783.[13] The lowering of temperature in middle latitudes is commonly 0·5–1·0°C for the year after a great eruption, as in 1815 on Sumbawa, near Java, and in 1835 in Nicaragua.

Increased injection of particulates into the atmosphere has also grown as a result of increased industrial pollution, extended slash-and-burn agriculture and wind deflation of soil disturbed by the plough. Indeed, Bryson believes that the resumption of volcanic activity in the 1950s and 1960s, combined with the strengthened anthropogenic factor since about 1940, has sufficiently increased the atmospheric loading to account for the average hemispheric cooling of about 0·3°C that has occurred since 1940.[14]

Albedo The reflectivity of the Earth's surface may vary with changes in snow cover and man-made changes in the vegetation cover. Such changes might produce a mean surface temperature change of 0·0001°C per decade, and do not appear to be comparable to other extrinsic factors behind changes in climate over the last two millenia.[15]

'Greenhouse effect' Solar energy that is absorbed by the Earth and atmosphere must be re-radiated outward if the global climate is to remain constant, but the rate of outward radiation is influenced by the composition of the atmosphere. In particular, increases in the atmosphere's content of CO_2 should have a warming effect on the lower atmosphere since, like the glass of a greenhouse, it is more

transparent to incoming solar short-wave radiation than it is to long-wave re-radiation from the Earth. Due to the burning of fossil fuels the concentration of CO_2 in the atmosphere has increased over the last century by 10 per cent from 290 to 320 parts per million, and about a half of this increase has occurred since 1945. If this was the only cause of climatic change, the mean global surface temperature should have risen, at an increasing rate, by about 0·25°C over the past twenty years.[16] It has, in fact, decreased by about that amount since 1940 and it is clear that other factors of greater magnitude are inducing global changes of climate.

There are also within the climatic system certain variables which may influence climatic change. Firstly, variations in sea-ice have an effect upon the heating of the overlying atmosphere and tracks of depressions may be displaced in parallel with the ice limit. This tendency is particularly marked in the North Atlantic where displacement of cyclone tracks south of Iceland tends to occur in summers and autumns that are characterised by extensive sea-ice, resulting in noticeably short growing-seasons in Iceland.[17] This link between sea-ice and climate provides us with a means of measuring long-term changes in Iceland's summer weather from early records of the amount of sea-ice that impeded navigation around Iceland's coasts.

Secondly, changes in mean surface temperatures of the sea have been observed to accompany changes in the atmospheric circulation – by as much as 1·5°C over wide areas of the North Atlantic.[18] The areas of greatest change occur where the westerly surface winds increased and decreased most, causing changes in rates of evaporation and upwelling. The sea-temperature anomaly has a feedback effect upon the atmosphere by generating an enhanced thermal gradient and thereby displacing the circulation.

The Pace of Climatic Changes

We should note that shifts of climate may occur over a wide range of time scales. Indeed, there is a growing belief that climate may change quite rapidly in a step-like fashion from one quasi-stable state to another, in contrast to the traditional view of slow and steady transitions. A worldwide study of radiocarbon measurements for significant climatic events of the last 10,000 years suggests that these events did occur at particular times and over short periods, perhaps in a few decades.[19] If this is true – and we cannot yet be sure because the historical record is incomplete – then the biological and cultural consequences may have been great.

Tracing the Chronology: The Evidence

Since about 1950 the means of measuring climatic change have been substantially refined both in terms of the variety of measures available and of their generally quantitative nature. It is important to distinguish between qualitative evidence of change, which often records only exceptional circumstances and may be subjective, and quantitative evidence which may not, indeed, be accurate but for which levels of accuracy can often be assessed. One may also make a distinction between direct evidence of climatic events, such as provided by instrumental records or weather diaries, and indirect evidence such as of harvest yields, tree growth, glacier movements or sediment build which cannot by themselves argue the nature of meteorological changes. But such indirect, or proxy, data are essential in extending the study of climatic history back beyond the limited period of direct instrumental records or direct (though qualitative) weather diaries.

Finally, it is important to distinguish between the data type or descriptor which carries the evidence of a changing climatic environment and the data source which itself records the descriptor. We may, for example, recognise glacier movements, or changes in the mean sea temperatures and in the frequency of drift ice as descriptors of climatic change, but we should note that estate papers, marine logs and saga literature are the sources in which the descriptors may themselves be found.

Direct Evidence

The instrumental record Surviving records of instrumental observations enabled the compilation of temperature records for several stations in Europe from the eighteenth century – for example, for Utrecht in the Netherlands from 1706, for Copenhagen from 1798, for Stockholm from 1757.[20] In the New World records survive for New Haven, Connecticut from the 1780s, and for Charleston, South Carolina from the 1820s.[21]

The longest temperature records survive, though in discontinuous form, in England, and these have been assembled by Manley into a table of monthly means for central England from 1659 onwards.[22] This was derived from the average of data recorded in Oxford and in Lancashire from 1815. From 1771 to 1815 it has been built up by averaging the departures for each month at a number of inland stations whose records are sufficiently long to be 'bridged' into the later run of data. Before 1771 data were bridged into the record from 1726 onward largely from the Midlands of England, with additions from London (from 1723), Upminster (from 1699) and from a variety of scattered observation points from about 1660.

The temperature record for central England is shown in Fig 2. It is thought to be reasonably accurate from about 1720 onwards, and

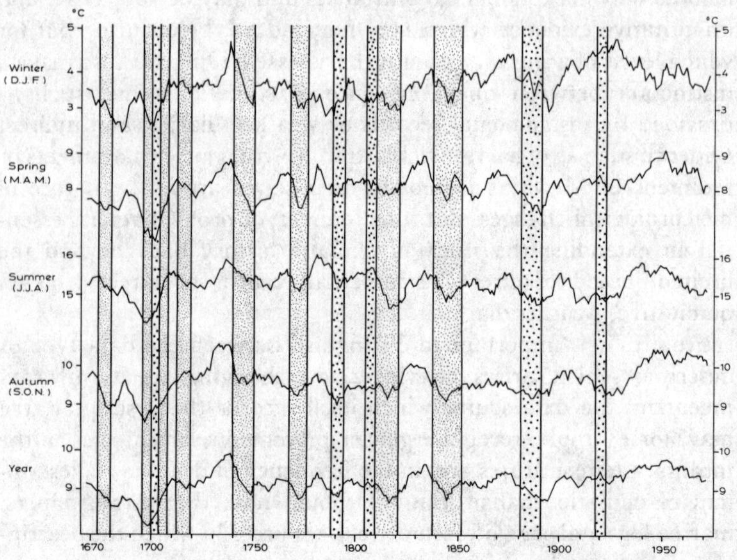

Fig. 2. Decadal running averages of seasonal and annual mean temperatures, 1659–1973, with periods of advance of European glaciers (stipple) since 1600. Lighter stippling indicates periods of less widespread advance. After Manley (1966, 1974).

probably represents an acceptable approximation from 1660 onwards. From this we have the picture of a general rise in mean temperatures (winter, summer and annual) from the late seventeenth century to the 1940s, with perhaps a slight dip towards the end of the nineteenth century. Within this general trend lie shorter-term variations of temperature, runs of perhaps four or five consecutively warm or cool years. Fig 2, for example, points to cold spells, in general occurring in all four seasons, in the 1690s, late 1740s, 1770s, late 1810s, 1840s and 1890s. Remarkable warm spells occurred in the 1730s, 1830s and 1870s.

Meteorological descriptions Less satisfactory are inferences drawn from early descriptions of weather, available in Europe for about one thousand years, mainly from annalists who wrote accounts of the most striking events of their times – for example, floods, droughts, frosts, and storms. These descriptions have been used by climatic historians on the assumption that, given confirmation of their date and authenticity, they give an indication of exceptional weather events. For example, a considerable number of droughts recorded in one century may suggest that the rainfall of that century was abnormally low; similarly, a large number of floods and storms suggest a heavy rainfall. It is important, however, to take account of the increasingly comprehensive nature of the record; it would clearly be misleading to compare – as did Van Bath – the number of records of, say, droughts for two different centuries, but it might be instructive to know the proportion of droughts to the total number of incidents recorded per century.

A further difficulty concerns the psychology of the annalists. Vanderlinden, in the preface of his compilation of Belgian records, has identified three types of annalist.[23] The earliest are concise; they merely state 'cold winter', 'dry year', etc., without any further subjective remarks. In the Middle Ages the records become lengthier and more fanciful, often the chronicler breaks into verse. In the fifteenth and sixteenth centuries there is some manipulation of the facts to conform with religious or superstitious beliefs, and it is not until the eighteenth century that the reports again assume a concise and scientific character.[24] Finally, it is likely that these descriptions are frequently comparative in nature. Conditions accepted as unexceptional during an exceptional period of years might well escape comment.

The most productive early source of climatic descriptions are chronicles, monastic charters and ecclesiastical histories. For England a comprehensive compilation of these has been made by Britton.[25] Many of the recorded statements remain uncorroborated by additional evidence and appear to relate to isolated events. However, some do refer to exceptionally frequent hazards that suggest an unusual period of weather. For example, the summer of 1198 seems to have been a stormy one; the following is one of three references to exceptional weather:

> In various parts of England in the month of July there were very great storms. The thunder and lightning terrified many men. Indeed the dreadful and violent lightning destroyed several villages with their inhabitants and herds. The crops, already damaged by lightning in the ear, were wholly laid low by the violent hail and the huge and hard hailstones. Birds of the air also, namely crows, and others of like kind, were killed, so that they were found scattered on the fields and roads.
>
> *Annals of Winchester* (from Latin)[26]

There are nine references to a late spring, cool summer and wet winter in 1294:

> In this yere fel the grettest snowe that evere was seyn before this tyme.
>
> *Chronicle of London*[27]
>
> From the feast of St. John the Baptist (June 1294) to the feast of Blessed Mary in March (1295), the frequent rain did not allow reaping in autumn or sowing in winter, as was necessary.
>
> *Annals of Worcester* (from Latin)[28]

Severe but dry winters that would have resulted from a blocking pattern of circulation are also well recorded, that of 1309–10 being an example:

> In the same year at the feast of the Lord's Nativity, a great frost and ice was massed together in the Thames and elsewhere, so that poor people were oppressed by the severe frost, and bread wrapped in straw or other covering was frozen and could not be eaten unless it was warmed: and such masses of encrusted ice were on the Thames that men took their way thereon from Queenhithe in Southark, and from Westminster, into London: and it lasted so long that the people indulged in dancing in the midst of it near a certain fire made on the same, and hunted a hare with dogs in the midst of the Thames: London Bridge was in great peril and permanently damaged. And the bridge at Rochester and the other bridges standing in the current of the waters were wholly broken down.
>
> *Annals of London* (from Latin)[29]

Scattered evidence of this kind, sometimes recorded long after the event, cannot on its own give a clear picture of climate through the ages. Apart from the variability in quality of the evidence, the variation in degree of extremeness of the meteorological event is rarely recorded for us. To merely tabulate century by century the number of severe winters or heavy rains, as was attempted by Van Bath,[30] without consideration of the exceptional quality of the event or of the changing quality of the documentary record, is likely to invite a spurious conclusion. We shall see later that a careful re-working of Britton's data, in conjunction with data from other compilations, has led Lamb to quite different conclusions about the relative warmth and wetness of the early Middle Ages.

Evidence from the chronicles may be supplemented by reference to more specific documents. For example, a detailed study by Titow of the account rolls of the estates of the Bishops of Winchester has revealed a large number of references to weather which can be arranged into a calendar of weather conditions.[31] The data are superior to those from the chronicles because they were recorded in the same year to which they relate although, once again, they refer only to exceptional weather. The evidence from the Winchester rolls, and from similar sources, provides us with a quantity of detail for the thirteenth and fourteenth centuries. For example, they point to particularly wet summers in 1315 and 1316 that seem to have had a disastrous effect upon the productivity of the Winchester manors. In 1315 the bailiff's accounts explained the changes in income for three different manors as follows.[32]

> *De venditione feni in prato nichil propter abundanciam pluvie in estate.*
> (From the sale of hay in the meadow, nothing on account of the abundance of rain in the summer)
> *(Exitus molendini:) Et non plus quia molendinum non molebat per dimidium annum propter inundacionem.*
> ((Profit of the mill) . . . no more because the mill did not grind for half the year on account of the flood).
> *De turbaria nichil pro tempore pluvioso.*
> (From the turbary nothing because of the rainy weather).

References of this kind are a valuable complement to the more general evidence of 1315 and 1316 available in the chronicles:[33]

> In the same year was a great inundation of rain for nearly the whole year and very great dearth, and lack of grain and all other victuals.
>
> *Annales Paulini* (from Latin) 1315
>
> Also in this same year there was such an inundation of rain in the summer and autumn.
>
> *Gesta Edwardi de Carnarvan* (from Latin) 1316

There is some confusion of dating on the many surviving accounts of abnormal rainfall and flooding between 1314 and 1317, but it is clear that there was at least one, and probably two abnormally wet years in the period. The reduced harvests brought a famine that was probably the most severe of the entire millenium, and we shall refer again to this period in a discussion of short-term climatic fluctuations in Chapter 7. Moreover, the variations in crop yields are recorded in detail in the bailiff's accounts for the Winchester manors and thus provide us with an important source of proxy data.

In addition to chronicles and account rolls, parish records may provide further information on early weather conditions. Utterström has quoted the register of Örslösa in the district of Kalland in western Sweden:[34]

> In 1596 at midsummer-tide the land was abundantly covered with splendid grass and much corn, so that everybody thought that there would be sufficient corn in the country. But at the time of the annual meeting of the clergy (i.e. the beginning of July), when the people were at Skara market, there came so much rain and flood that all the bridges floated away and people had great difficulty and anxiety how they were going to get home.

And with that same flood began the punishment for our sins, for the water went over the fields and pastures, so that the corn and grass were ruined and there was little of both grain and hay.

For slightly later periods reference has been made by Lamb to naval logs of wind and weather;[35] and Pearson has recently completed a survey of early Scottish newspapers to reveal the value of contemporary daily accounts of weather changes in the eighteenth century for areas in which instrumental records are not always available.[36]

This variety of direct meteorological descriptions is available in a number of compilations for different parts of Europe. These include Buchinsky's for the Russian Plain which offers special reference to the Ukraine, the Moscow region and Poland;[37] Hennig's, covering central Europe and Italy, but with some reference to other parts of western Europe;[38] Vanderlinden's for Belgium; and Britton's for the British Isles.

Lamb has made use of these compilations, complemented by amplifying evidence from vine harvests in Luxembourg and Baden and from ice on the Baltic, to construct for the period A.D. 800 to the present an index of winter severity and summer wetness for the whole of Europe from Ireland to the Urals.[39] The excess per decade of wet months in 'high summer' (July and August only) and the excess of mild months in winter (December, January and February only) was recorded from early descriptive statements in diaries, chronicles and accounts, and from instrumental records beginning in the seventeenth and eighteenth centuries in different regions of Europe.

A visual summary of the first stage of Lamb's work is presented in Fig 3. It indicates in a generalised form the probable types of summer and winter weather experienced, decade by decade, in different European longitudes near 50°N, (the latitude of Plymouth, Frankfurt, Prague and Kiev). While there are some minor contrasts between eastern and western Europe, the temporal trend is clear: the number of wet summers increased in western Europe in the fourteenth century, and there were probably long periods of wet years in the late sixteenth and in the seventeenth century. The trend in eastern Europe was approximately the same although the timing was different. Contemporaneous with the increased incidence of damp summers was an increased frequency of cold winter months with, once again, a peak of cold winters in the sixteenth and seventeenth centuries. Brooks has termed this cold phase in Europe the 'Little Ice Age'.

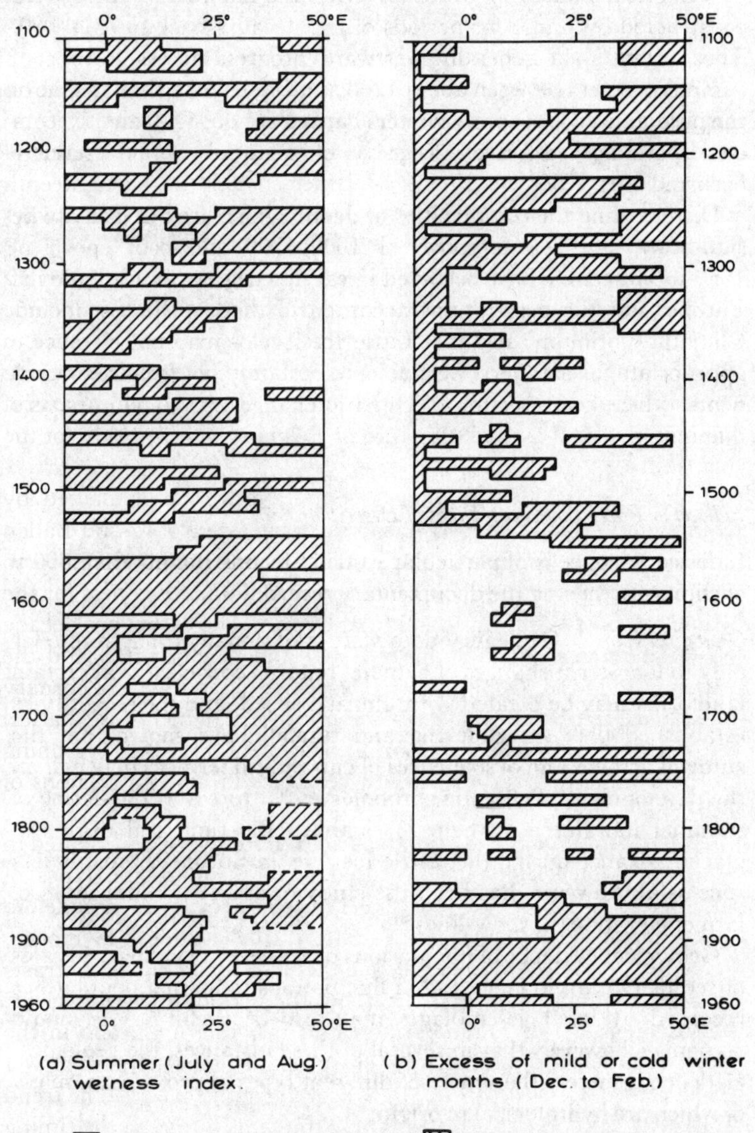

Fig. 3. Summer wetness index and winter mildness (or severity) at different European longitudes near 50°N by decades from A.D. 1100 to 1959. After Lamb (1966).

Numerical indices of winter severity and summer wetness were constructed by Lamb for periods of five decades back to A.D. 800. These point to a generally westward progress across Europe of summer wetness between about 1250 and 1400, and a similar shift of the predominance of severe winters between about 1200 and 1450. A corresponding eastward progress of reduced winter severity occurred after 1700.

Disregarding the complexities of detail, which are not likely to be significant, the warm epoch of 1000–1200 and cool epoch of 1550–1700 seem to have occurred in varying degrees over all parts of Europe. But the descriptions accorded to them – the 'Secondary Climatic Optimum' and the 'Little Ice Age' – may not always be appropriate for southern Europe, and certainly not for other continents, where the direction of climatic change was sometimes very different.

Indirect or Proxy Evidence: Types of Descriptor

Indirect evidence is of particular value in reconstructing the history of climate preceding the documentary record.

Geological evidence Geological data were traditionally thought to refer only to long-term changes of climate, but it is now clear that certain landforms may be created with unusual speed, and the recent links established between gulleying and rainfall have shown that the study of arroyos and of sequences of cut-and-fill terraces may help in the development of climatic chronologies.[40] Moreover, the dating of terminal moraines can help to establish the time and degree of glacial advance during the 'Little Ice Age' in Europe. Probably less successful, however, has been the study of cirques as indicators of former elevations of snow-lines.[41]

Geological evidence of fluctuations of sea-level, of changes in rates of sedimentation in lakes and of fluctuations in animal populations recorded by fossil assemblages may also be useful.[42] We should recognise, however, that in several of these instances, the geological evidence is merely the source of different types of proxy data, many of which are hydrological in origin.

Glacier movements The small mountain glacier, particularly in temperate latitudes seems to be sensitive to quite small changes of temperature. The Austrian glaciologist, Hoinkes, has shown that the two most important factors behind glacial advances in the European Alps are cool and cloudy summers which are unfavourable to ablation of the glaciers, and winters of heavy snowfall which favour rapid accumulation.[43] The combination of cool summers and snowy winters is the most favourable to glacial advance. But some glaciers, by reason of their shape, are probably much better natural thermometers than others, and we are far from certain as to which they are. Manley has therefore argued that we must be cautious in drawing deductions about climatic history from glacier behaviour.[44]

However, the chronology of glacier movements in Europe seems, *prima facie,* to provide confirmation of the history of climate already suggested by the documentary record. One of several studies is that by Le Roy Ladurie who has traced in detail the phases of Alpine glacier advance, noting a brief thrust from about A.D. 1200–1300 and a major advance from A.D. 1550–1850.[45] The years 1599 to 1600 seem to have seen the maximum of glacial advance throughout the Alps, and there are some signs that at this time high-lying settlements were destroyed either directly by ice or by glacially-ponded lakes. Ladurie quotes a judge's report from the Tyrolean valley of Schnals in 1601:

> . . . the people have much more difficulty than before in getting in the harvest, for every year more land falls into disuse; and because of the growth of the glacier many fields and meadows are abandoned and spoiled.[46]

Secondary maxima occurred in the 1640s, which were characterised by cool damp summers and a low rate of ablation, and also in about 1680. An arbitration report of 1642 for Chamonix declared that:

> Moreover the said glacier, called the glacier Des Bois . . . advances by over a musket shot every day, even in the month of August, toward the said land, and if it should go on doing so for four years more it is likely to destroy the said glebe entirely.

and

> . . . the said place of La Rosière (is threatened by) the glacier of Argentière which is the biggest of all, and which is greatly advancing, in danger of carrying away the said village, the avalanches which descend and fall from the said glacier drawing nearer each day to the said land and carrying away the cultivable fields and meadows; the people sow only oats and a little barley, which throughout most of the seasons of the year is under snow, so that they do not get one full harvest in three years, and then the grain rots soon after . . .[47]

Similar advances around 1700 and 1720 and in the 1740s appear to have overrun farms in Iceland and Norway, an occurrence which we shall study later in more detail. A later thrust occurred in the 1770s, over the period 1818–20 and, finally, over the period 1840–55. Thereafter, the Alpine glaciers saw a substantial retreat, which is illustrated in Fig 4. The contrast in location of the glacier fronts is remarkable (Plates 1 to 4).

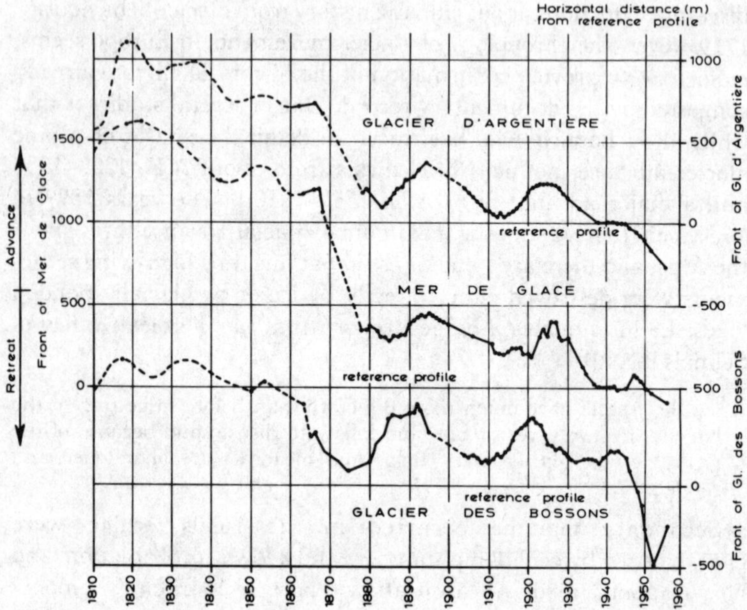

Fig. 4. Advance and retreat of the Chamonix glaciers, 1810–1960. Solid lines indicate recorded movements, broken lines indicate estimates. After Lliboutry (1965).

In fact, a rough comparison of Alpine glacier movements with known changes in temperature (Fig 2) illustrates that they are quite closely linked with temperature changes; and, since the general trends of recession apparent in Europe are evident in glaciers throughout much of the northern hemisphere,[48] it is evident that the study of glacier movements in the pre-instrumental period can help to extend our knowledge of early changes of climate, especially in areas poorly served by the documentary records.

Dates of freezing and thawing In the early nineteenth century, prior to the demolition of the old London Bridge which significantly reduced the upflow of estuarine salt water and encouraged the packing of ice above its narrow arches, the River Thames would freeze over once or twice in a Londoner's lifetime. When it did, frost fairs were sometimes held on the frozen river and these were sufficiently unusual to warrant a note in observers' diaries. From these we may surmise that from the building of the bridge (in about 1209) until 1400 the Thames was frozen only three or four times; but it was frozen six times between 1400 and 1600, about ten times between 1600 and 1700, and about ten times between 1700 and 1814. The largest frost fairs occurred in the winters of 1683–4, 1715–16, 1739–40 and 1813–14 (Plates 5 and 6).

Such data are of little use on their own, particularly if we wish to compare the frequency of freezing between different centuries for which there are historical records of very different quality. Probably more reliable are the dates of freeze-up and break-up of ice recorded in the work-books of trading companies which had a particular interest in the navigability of certain rivers or lakes. Table 1 indicates

Table 1: SUMMARY OF THE DATES OF THE BREAK-UP OF ICE ON LAKE MÄLAREN AT VÄSTERÅS, 1720–1859

Period	Mean date of break-up; decennial (and other) periods		Number of break-ups in each period in:		
	Month	Date	March	April	May
1720–29	April	14	2	8	—
1730–39	April	16	1	9	—
1721–35	April	14	3	12	—
1740–49	May	2	—	4	6
1745–49	May	8	—	—	5
1750–59	April	17	1	7	2
1760–69	April	27	—	6	4
1770–79	April	20	1	9	—
1780–89	May	6	—	3	7
1790–99	April	21	1	6	3
1800–09	May	2	—	3	7
1810–19	April	30	—	4	6
1799–1818	May	5	—	6	14
1820–29	April	23	1	6	3
1830–39	April	27	1	3	6
1840–49	April	24	—	7	3
1850–59	April	25	—	7	3

Source of data: H. H. Hildenbrandsson, 'Sur le prétendu changement du climat européen en temps historiques', *Nova acta regiae societatis scientiarum Upsaliensis,* 4th Ser., iv. 5, (Uppsala 1915), where particulars are given year by year, after Utterström, (1954).

Plate 2. The Rhônegletscher in 1966. Photo: M. Le Roy Ladurie.

Plate 3. The Argentière Glacier

Plate 4. The Argentière Glacier in 1966. Photo: M. Le Roy Ladurie.

Plate 5. Frost fair on the Thames, 1683–84

Plate 6. Frost fair on the Thames, January–February 1814. Photo: Radio Times Hulton Picture Library.

the dates of the break-up of ice on Lake Mälaren in Sweden from 1720 to 1859.[49] Both the mean decadal dates of break-up and the number of break-ups by month indicate the relatively low spring temperatures that characterised the period 1740–50 and the 1780s. The instrumental record for central England constructed by Manley reveals some close comparisons (Fig 2).

The longest run of such data relates to Lake Suwa near Tokyo for the period 1444 to 1954.[50] They are also available for the Neva at Leningrad from 1711 to 1951, Lake Kavallesi in Finland from 1834 to 1943,[51] and Lake Champlain in the United States from 1816 to 1935.[52] From these the general indication, at least for Europe, is of earlier autumn freezing and later spring break-up in the eighteenth than in the nineteenth century. It is not easy to be precise because much of the data have not yet been analysed in such a way as to elicit their full potential; and systems of content and contingency analysis discussed and developed further by Moodie and Catchpole for the Hudson Bay rivers would here seem to be of some utility to the climatic historian.[53]

Oceanographic evidence One of the most comprehensive descriptors of past changes of temperature are changes in the duration of drift ice which, because they profoundly affected the navigability of Icelandic coastal waters and were strongly linked to the growth rates of cereals and grass in Iceland, were often carefully recorded. The Icelandic geologist Sigurdur Thorarinsson has graphed the annual duration of sea ice from 1688 onwards,[54] and from these data Páll Bergthórsson has reconstructed a chronology of temperature changes for Iceland from A.D. 900 (Fig 5).[55] This reconstruction is based upon the comparison of known (instrumentally recorded) temperatures and the known incidence of sea ice from 1920 to 1969, which show a correlation that is significant at the 0.001 level. Pre-1920 temperatures were then extrapolated back to the sixteenth century on the basis of incidence of sea-ice, and were further extrapolated to A.D. 900 on the basis of a correlation (also significant at the 0.001 level) between the data on temperature/sea-ice and the incidence of 'severe years' recorded in the Icelandic sagas by mention of famine, drift ice and similar occurrences.

Bergthórsson's chronology tends to confirm the trends detected for northern Europe from other sources: a phase of high mean annual temperatures in the ninth to eleventh centuries was probably followed by late medieval expansion of the Arctic cold, which subsequently retreated in the nineteenth century. Within the phase of

Arctic expansion shorter-term falls in mean temperatures seem to have occurred in the late sixteenth and late seventeenth centuries. Indeed, the range of long-term fluctuation of mean temperatures in Iceland is substantial – about 1.5°C from the medieval 'optimum' to the 'Little Ice Age' – a range that will later be confirmed from other descriptors.

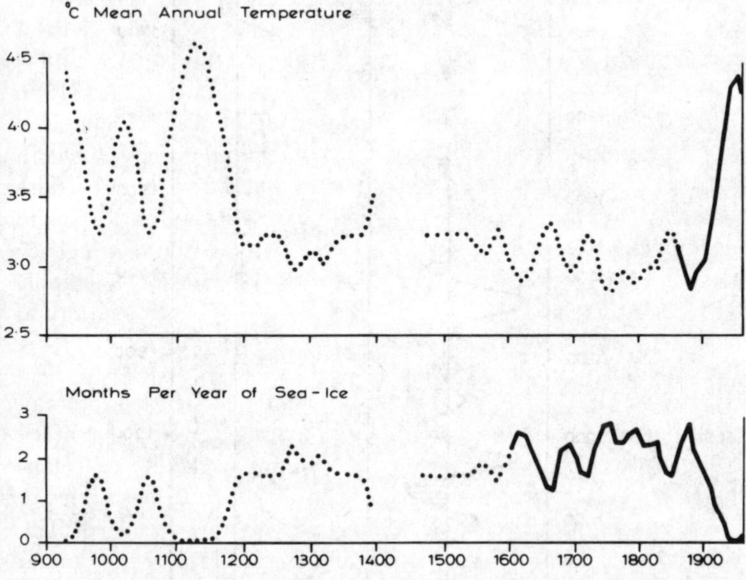

Fig. 5. Iceland: running 20-year means of temperature and incidence of sea-ice. Solid lines indicate instrumentally recorded trends. Dotted lines indicate estimates. After Bergthorsson (1969).

Isotope measurements Long-term variations of the oxygen isotope O^{18} are preserved for many tens of thousands of years in ice sheets. In a complex fashion, probably through fluctuations in solar radiation, the concentration of O^{18} in precipitation varies positively with temperature, so it is possible to detect former changes in temperature from long cores of ice, provided that the lengths of core can be dated by taking account of the annual rate of ice accummulation and the rate at which it has been compressed by successive layers of overlying ice.

In Greenland three ice cores, each of about 400 m, have provided data on climatic changes over the past two thousand years; a fourth core, from Camp Century, is 1390 m long and relates to changes which have occurred over the past 100,000 years. Figure 6 illustrates the inferred temperature trends from about A.D. 600: over the

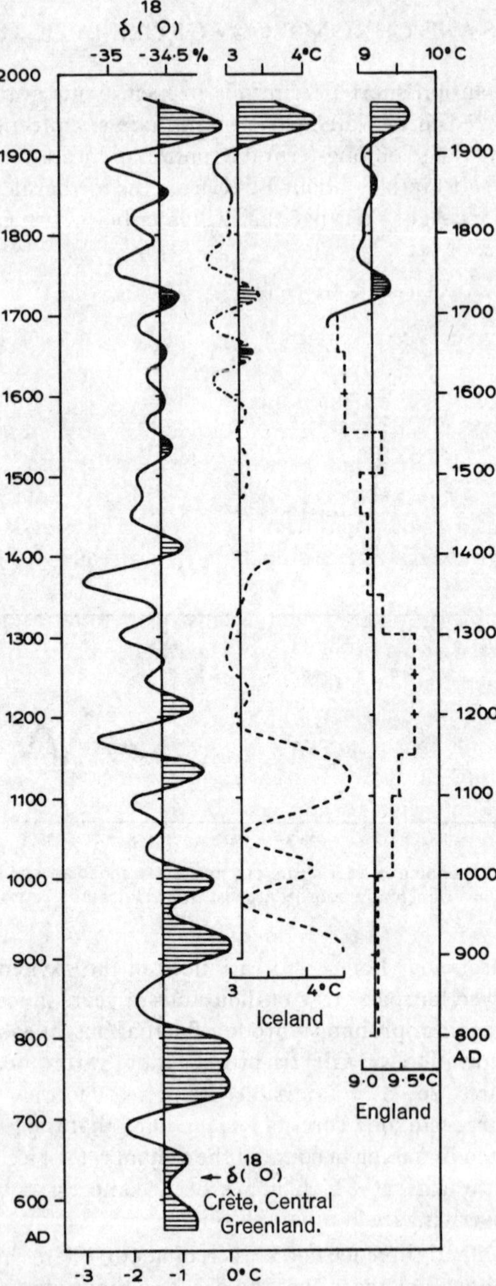

Fig. 6. Comparison between the O[18] concentration (left) in snow fallen at Crête, central Greenland, and temperatures for Iceland and England. The curves have been smoothed by a 60-year low pass filter, except for England A.D. 800–1700. Solid lines indicate a basis of systematic, direct observations; dashed-dotted lines indicate sea-ice observations; dashed lines indicate a basis of indirect evidence. After Dansgaarde, *et al.* (1975).

short-term these are very similar to the record of observed temperatures in Iceland and central England. Over the long-term, a warm phase between A.D. 800 and A.D. 1000 followed by cooling to a nadir in the fourteenth century seems to reflect the English trend, although it is distinctly out of phase. In fact, when a 250-year lag is discounted, comparison of the variation in temperatures in England from A.D. 1100 to A.D. 1950 with Greenland's O^{18} curve gives a correlation of 0·92.[56]

More recently, an attempt has been made to reconstruct the temperature record from a study of the variable concentration of similar isotopes in the annual rings of tree-growth. Isotope measurements in a Spessart Oak from Munich have pointed to warm spells during the 'Little Ice Age' (the 1570s, 1640s and 1730s), which Lamb has suggested broadly agree with his own data.[57] The advantage of this method of dating, if it could be improved, is that a means of tracing the dates of tree-ring patterns is already well established.

Dendrochronology Where there is a strong and simple correlation between tree-growth and certain climatic elements, such as rainfall and temperature, a study of the variation in width of the annual growth-rings of trees may enable a specific and precise climatic interpretation. This may be possible in areas where conifers are growing in conditions of environmental stress such as at the northern timberline in northern Europe or North America where summer temperatures exert a strong control over growth, and in arid habitats where moisture is the primary limiting factor. About sixty years of research at the University of Arizona – first by Douglass, and later by Schulman and Fritts – have now established dendrochronology as a very accurate means of reconstructing, season-by-season, the growing conditions of the past.[58]

Two major limitations, however, may restrict the use of tree-rings as indicators of long-term rather than short-term changes of climate. The first is that, even at the upper limit of tree-growth in northern Europe, it is rarely possible to establish a sufficiently high dependence of tree growth on summer temperatures. The second is that the calculation of standardised indices of tree growth, which is required in order to eliminate the influence of age on the rate of tree growth, can result in a bias of the long-term trend which is consequently unsuitable as a means for drawing inferences about long-term fluctuations of temperature. But it is possible to overcome these difficulties by building into the tree-ring record long-term adjustments from an independent source. In this way Matthews has successfully used long-term data on glacier movements to calibrate the short-term data provided by tree-ring measurements at the tree-line at about 2000 m O.D. in southern Norway.[59] The resulting temperature curve from 1700 to 1950 (Fig 7) confirms the impression of a general climatic recovery in western Europe from the mid-eighteenth century and illustrates that some, though perhaps not all, of the short spells of unusual weather – for example the cool spells of the 1740s and 1820s that occurred in central England, (see Fig 2) – also occurred at very different elevations in other parts of Europe. On average it seems that temperatures in southern Norway in the first half of the eighteenth century were about 1·5°C lower than at present.

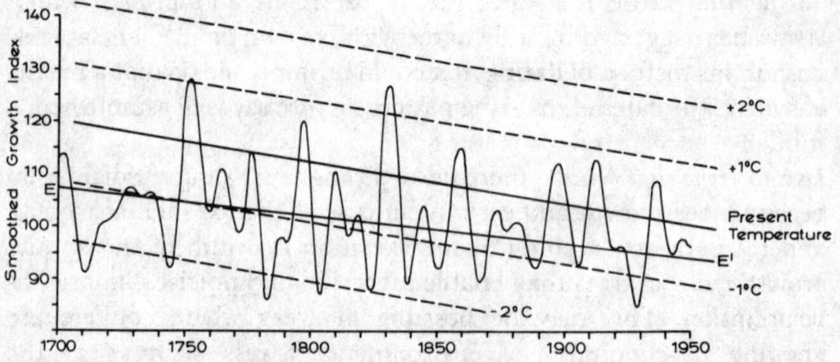

Fig. 7. Graphical representation of the variation of tree growth at 2000 m O.D. in southern Norway, 1750–1950. The curve, which has been smoothed by harmonic analysis, is calibrated using an index of summer temperatures and is expressed as a difference from the 1949–63 temperature average. After Matthews (1976).

Pollen counts Measurements of the extent of plant distributions – for example by counts of pollen preserved in peat – are more liable than measurements of rates of growth to bear the imprint of man's activity, and it is not easy to distinguish between the climatic, edaphic (soil) and anthropogenic factors that may all, in different proportions, lie behind a change in pollen spectrum. Indeed, there has been an increasing tendency among British palynologists to account for early changes of vegetation in terms of anthropogenic factors like cultivation, burning and grazing.

Pollen counts have, however, been of particular use in establishing the general trend of environmental change over several millenia.[60] Indeed they have provided the foundation for the chronology of long-term changes of climate, but over the shorter-term, as during the last two millenia, there is a limit to the preciseness of the interpretation of such counts engendered by such factors as differential pollen production and dispersal. The task of detecting minor climatic changes during the last millenium is not always well served by palynology owing to the lag in response of vegetation to minor changes and the degree of tolerance that many plants have for climatic stress. At the Aspen Conference in 1962 it was suggested that a solution to this problem might be the detailed analysis of 'tension zones', or ecotones, between two vegetation zones where stress, caused by environmental change, is heightened.[61] The advice has been followed by some American scholars in their attempts to evaluate the nature of the late medieval change of climate in the American Midwest and its effect upon contemporary Indian communities (see page 149).

Agricultural evidence There are problems in employing agricultural data to reconstruct a chronology of climatic change. Firstly, it is not easy to eliminate the strong economic and technological factors that influence agricultural production. Secondly, crop growth is responsive to very specific agro-climatic elements such as the length and intensity of the growing season that may not readily match our general measures of climate such as temperature, precipitation and windspeed. Finally, if it is our intention ultimately to evaluate the relationship between climatic change and agricultural change, we should be particularly careful to acknowledge the dangers of a circularity of argument that may develop from measuring climatic change by agricultural descriptors.

Given an appreciation of these problems in the use of agricultural evidence, it is possible to employ two broad types of evidence as indicators of climatic change: harvest date and harvest size.

Phenological studies have shown that there is a close correlation between the temperature of the growing period and the dates of blossoming and fruiting of certain plants. Historical records of blossoming and harvesting may thus be valuable records of early weather, and the records of two contrasting plants are of particular value in this respect: registers of the dates of wine harvests in Europe, and garden diaries of the dates of spring cherry blossom in Japan.

The date of the wine harvest in Europe was frequently selected by local experts of the community, fixed by public proclamation and recorded in village registers. Fortunately for the climatic historian many of these registers still survive, and it has been possible to trace the dates of harvest for certain areas such as Dijon in Burgundy, Kurnback in the Black Forest and Lausanne in Switzerland. Most of the reconstruction of these dates has been the achievement of three French historians – Angot, Duchaussoy, and Le Roy Ladurie.[62] In Ladurie's book *Times of feast, times of famine*, the dates of wine harvests in southern France have been tabulated from 1349 onwards.[63]

The dates of harvest are closely related to the mean temperature prevailing after the beginning of the growing season, although it is also determined by levels of sunshine and moisture. A comparison between Angot's harvest dates and Manley's instrumental data on mean spring and summer temperatures for central England reveals their closeness (Fig 8), and it is clear that the harvest dates can be of

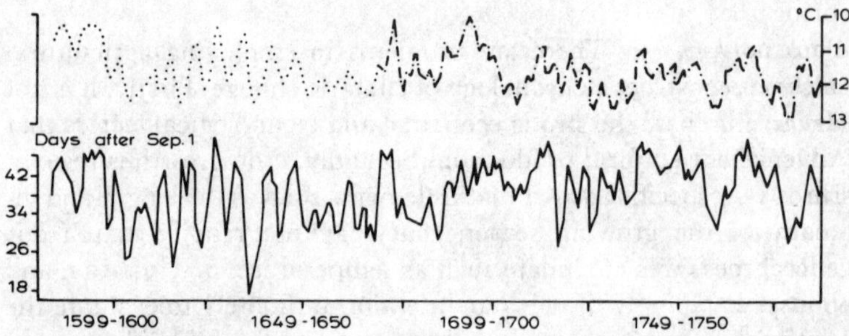

Fig. 8. Correlation between English spring-summer temperatures (2-year moving mean, 1 March to 1 September) and dates of wine harvest in France (2-year moving mean, days after 1 September). After Manley (1965).

particular use in extending backwards into the sixteenth century the record of year-by-year changes in weather that is not otherwise available until the mid-seventeenth.[64] For example, we now have confirmation of the pointers offered by the English chronicles regarding the sequences of exceptionally poor summers for the periods 1527–9, 1594–7 and for the difficult years 1648–9 already indicated by the isotopic and dendrochronological records. There is also evidence of cool summers in 1673 and 1675, in the 1690s and during the early 1740s. A sequence of poor years such as these resulted in famine and a rapid increase in food prices across north-west Europe. In Scotland the 1690s were years of starvation, widespread suffering and an accelerated death rate: this seems to have so hardened the hearts of the more fortunate survivors that the elders of one parish in the eastern Highlands complained that: 'The generality of the people had become so unchristian and inhuman that they would not so much as help to the churchyard with the dead bodies of the poor that were daily dying before them.'[65]

However, like the growth-rings of trees, the dates of wine harvests cannot be readily employed to measure long-term changes of climate. The adoption of new strains of vine and the changes in attitude to the quality of wine which itself is partly determined by the stage of ripening, led to decisions to harvest at different stages. For long-term measurements, therefore, the data need to be calibrated against other independent measures of temperature change.

A second phenological descriptor of weather is the flowering of plants. A great deal of folklore is woven around the relationship between the dates of blossoming and the average spring temperature. Thus in England a 'blackthorn winter' refers to a spring that is effectively delayed until after the blossoming of the blackthorn in April. In Kyoto, the former capital of Japan, annual celebrations accompanied the blossoming of local cherry trees (*Prunus yedoensis*) and records of these survive from the ninth century A.D.[66] Such records, in addition to those of the wine harvest in Europe, are our most detailed data source of annual variations of weather over the past millenium.

Records of the size of harvests are more generally abundant than those of harvest date, but they are not always the more useful source for the climatic historian. The link between weather and yield is certainly strong, but it is not always simple. In particular it is not always possible, without the careful study of particular crops cultivated under specific types of climatic conditions, to detect which elements of climate are the controlling variables of fluctuation in crop yield. Apparently similar falls of wheat yield in eastern England may be the result of entirely different types of weather – for instance, a wet autumn and spring which would prevent autumn ploughing and delay spring sowing, or a cool mid-summer and moist late summer, will both reduce the size of ear.

In subsequent chapters there will be a clearer definition of the precise nature of the effects of climatic change upon the yields of certain crops. If crop yields are to be regarded as good indicators of climatic change then this close scrutiny is necessary. Yet yields obviously do vary and records of their shifting levels often exist for early periods – a tempting source for the climatic historian; such data, covering the period 1209–1349, have been extracted by Titow from the account rolls of the estates of the Bishop of Winchester.[67] The long-term trends of such yields are arguably as much the product of changes in soil fertility due to mismanagement of the land or changes in the supporting technology of cultivation as they are of changes in environmental conditions, and it would be reckless to employ these data as primary climatic indicators.

Estimates of harvest yields are also available for Sweden for the eighteenth century, but the economic historian Gustav Utterström has pointed out that these were probably not drawn up until 1856 and were based upon contemporary qualitative descriptions taken from the reports of county governors.[68] For earlier periods the historian must rely on even less specific sources. For example the parish register of Örslösa continued its report for the cold, wet summer of 1596:

> Because of our sins the weather deprived us of God's gifts both on land and in the water. The clothes rotted on the backs of the poor. In the winter the cattle fell ill from the rotten hay and straw which was taken out of the water . . .
> The soil was sick for three years, so that it could bear no harvest.[69]

For Britain, we may resort to similar statements collated from surviving chronicles by Baker or Britton, but the exaggerated descriptions and the tendency to confusion of dates due to the delay between occurrence and time of recording should make us sceptical. Moreover, the authority for such statements is not always cited, as for example in this one for 1698 found by Baker:

> The first wheat cut in the middle of September, and much barley in swathe in December. In the north much corn ungot at Christmas, and in Scotland corn was reaped in January, 1699, and the snow beaten off it. Bread made of it fell to pieces and tasted sweet like malt.[70]

Finally, it is possible to point to archaeological indications of climatic change, although their disparate nature means that these can in general only be employed as supplementary evidence. For example, in 1921 the Viking graves at Herfoljness in Greenland were excavated from the permafrost – ground that was frozen all year round – in spite of the fact that the isotope measurements indicate a recent warming in Greenland. The permafrost must have been present for several centuries for the graves were so well preserved, and yet permafrost was evidently not prevalent at the time of burial, about 1450, since the roots of shrubs had, in subsequent years, penetrated the biers and skeletons.[71]

Tracing the Chronology: Convergence of the Evidence

The variety of evidence available to construct a chronology of climate also enables us to establish the unity of the trend of climatic change between different places by checking that the evidence is internally consistent. If there does, indeed, exist a unity of trend then this is likely to have been reflected by changes of climate that were concurrent or, at least, explicable in terms of time-lag. Concurrent changes, which probably have a common cause, would not necessarily be changes of the same direction. Some related changes might have resulted in warming in some areas, cooling in others.

Internal Consistency of Instrumental Data

Figure 9 shows running 30-year 'normals' of temperature in January at several stations in Europe and the United States.[72] It is evident that for many stations the curves resemble each other. The overall picture at middle and high latitudes in the northern hemisphere is consistently one of more frequently mild winters from about 1800 to about 1940 and, possibly, of more frequently cold winters since 1940. There are, of course, important regional differences – of direction, but not timing – such as those between, on the one hand, central and southern Europe (Rome, Vienna, Berlin) and, on the other, stations at higher latitudes (Edinburgh, Stockholm, Oslo). But at the more local level we find that there is a strong consistency of both direction and timing. For example, Manley has found that even the short-term anomalies of temperature in his reductions for the English Midlands are also evident in Mossman's series for Edinburgh, in Labrijn's series for Utrecht and in Liljequist's for Stockholm.[73]

Internal Consistency of Proxy Data

It has been shown that there is a strong similarity, firstly, between the trends displayed by Manley's instrumental record and those displayed by the movements of glaciers in northern and central Europe (Fig 2); secondly, between the same instrumental record and the curve of wine-harvest dates (Fig 8); thirdly, between the instrumental data for Iceland and the incidence of local sea-ice summarised by Bergthórsson (Fig 5); and, finally, between the records for Iceland, central England and the variation of O^{18} in the Greenland ice cores (Fig 6). The convergent nature of this variety of evidence is clearly quite marked.

We can also demonstrate the similarities between the trends exhibited by tree-ring data for bristlecone pines in California and the instrumental record for central England (Fig 10).[74] Features common to these curves are the medieval warm epoch, the fifteenth

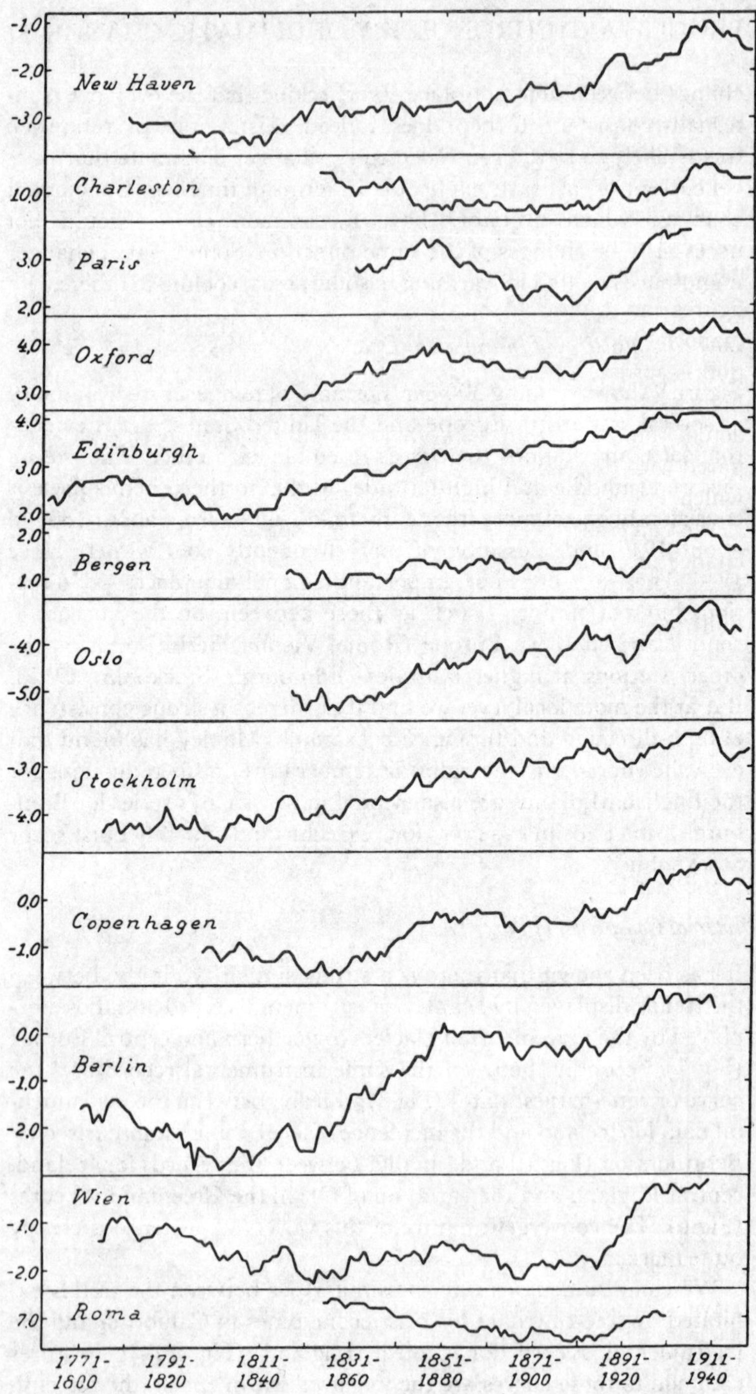

Fig. 9. Running 30-year means of January temperature in Europe and North America. After Lysgaard (1949).

and seventeenth century nadirs, the general increase in mean temperature from about 1700 and the return to generally cooler conditions since the 1940s.

Finally, from the discussions which took place at the Aspen Conference, it emerged that the high summer (July and August) wetness index values derived by Lamb for England for the decades between 1210 and 1349 showed a correlation of +0·77 with the figures for wet summers and autumns drawn by Titow from his manorial records, a source not employed by Lamb.[75] This correlation is statistically significant at a level approaching 1 per cent; a higher correlation probably would not have been achieved even if actual rainfall measurements for July and August had been compared with those for June and September (the additional months to which Titow's data also refer).

We can, therefore, be reasonably certain that the indications of change in climate presented by this new range of data, and drawn from a variety of largely independent sources, are likely to reflect quite closely those changes which did in fact occur.

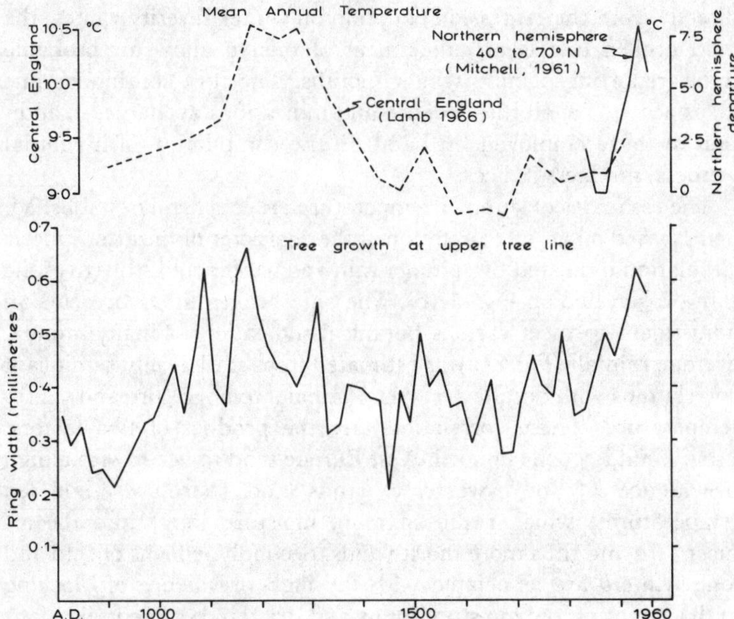

Fig. 10. Average ring widths (20-year means) in bristlecone pines at the upper tree line in the White Mountains, California, compared with regional and global estimates of mean annual temperature, A.D. 800–1960. After La Marche (1974). Copyright 1974 by the American Association for the Advancement of Science.

The Summarised Chronology for North-Western Europe

The longest temperature series for north-west Europe is that constructed by Manley for 1659–1973. For the period prior to 1659 Lamb has compiled the most comprehensive chronology based on a study of both the documentary, botanical, wine-harvest and sea-ice record; and was able to construct a decadal index of winter severity and summer wetness from about A.D. 800. On the basis of a correlation between these indices and decade values of temperature and rainfall recorded instrumentally since the seventeenth century, Lamb proceeded to establish average values of temperature and rainfall for the pre-instrumental era. These are given in Figs 11 and 12.[76] The margins of error shown are three times the standard error of the estimates, that is, they are 99 per cent confidence limits. Therefore only those major changes shown are firmly established, but it is apparent that these include a distinction between the cold epoch of the seventeenth century, the period of mild winters between 1500 and 1550, and the preceding period of more severe winters.

In Fig 11 (c) the thin broken line for winter temperature is derived directly from the regression equation on winter severity values; the bold broken line is an adjustment of this to allow for probable under-reporting of mild winter months. The thin continuous line takes account of all the evidence and indications available, in addition to those employed by Lamb in the compilation of his initial wetness/mildness indices.

The estimates of summer temperature are less firmly established, being based on an interpretation of the character of the atmospheric circulation indicated by summer rain and winter cold: this gives the thin broken line on Fig 11 (b). The bold broken line represents an adjustment to meet various botanical indications. Finally, annual average rainfall (Fig 12) was estimated from statistically significant correlations with decade averages of annual temperature and winter temperature. These correlations are the product of two factors. Firstly, mild epochs in north-west Europe tend to occur with a high prevalence of south-westerly winds and therefore high sea temperatures, which result in more moisture input into the atmosphere and thus more moist winds. Secondly, epochs of cold and long winters are associated with the high prevalence of blocking anticyclones of low moisture input and dry winds. The indications are, then, that the warm epoch between 1150 and 1300 was probably accompanied by a higher annual rainfall than now, whilst the high summer months were drier than now – despite a probable

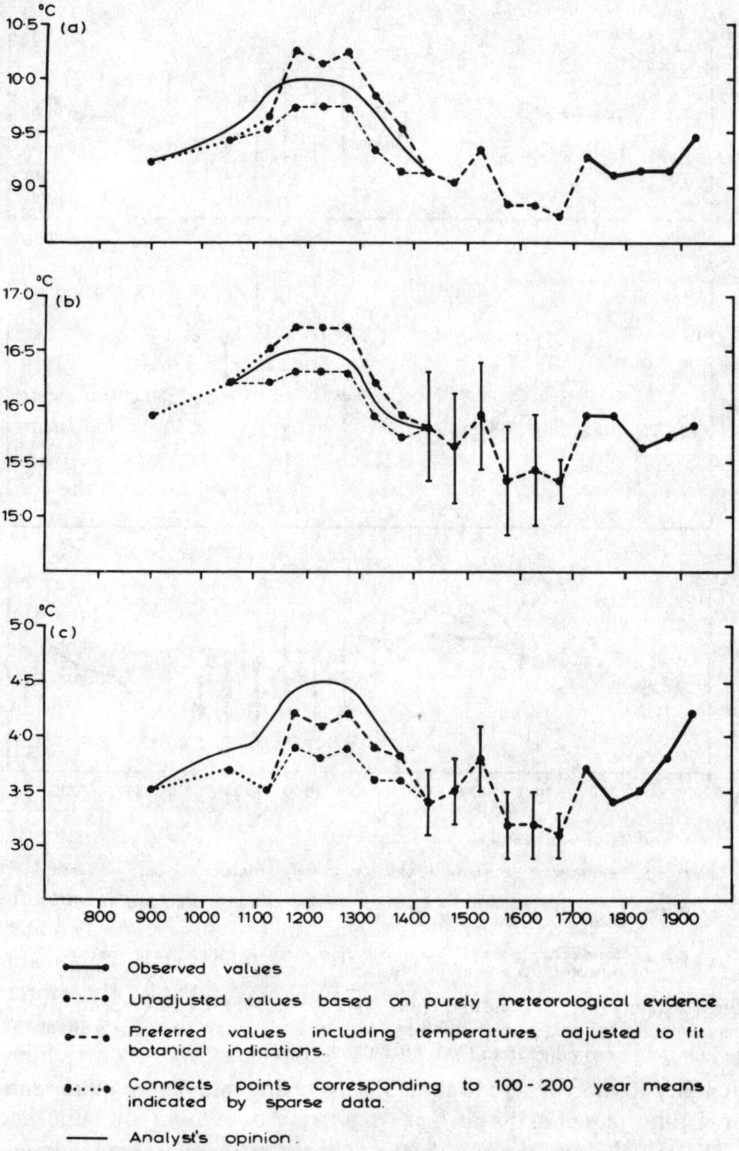

°C
10·5
(a)
10·0
9·5
9·0
°C
17·0
(b)
16·5
16·0
15·5
15·0
°C
5·0
(c)
4·5
4·0
3·5
3·0
800
900
1000
1100
1200
1300
1400
1500
1600
1700
1800
1900
Observed values
Unadjusted values based on purely meteorological evidence
Preferred values including temperatures adjusted to fit botanical indications.
Connects points corresponding to 100 - 200 year means indicated by sparse data.
Analyst's opinion.

Fig. 11. Temperatures in central England, 50-year averages, (a) year (b) high summer (July and August) (c) winter (December, January and February). After Lamb (1966).

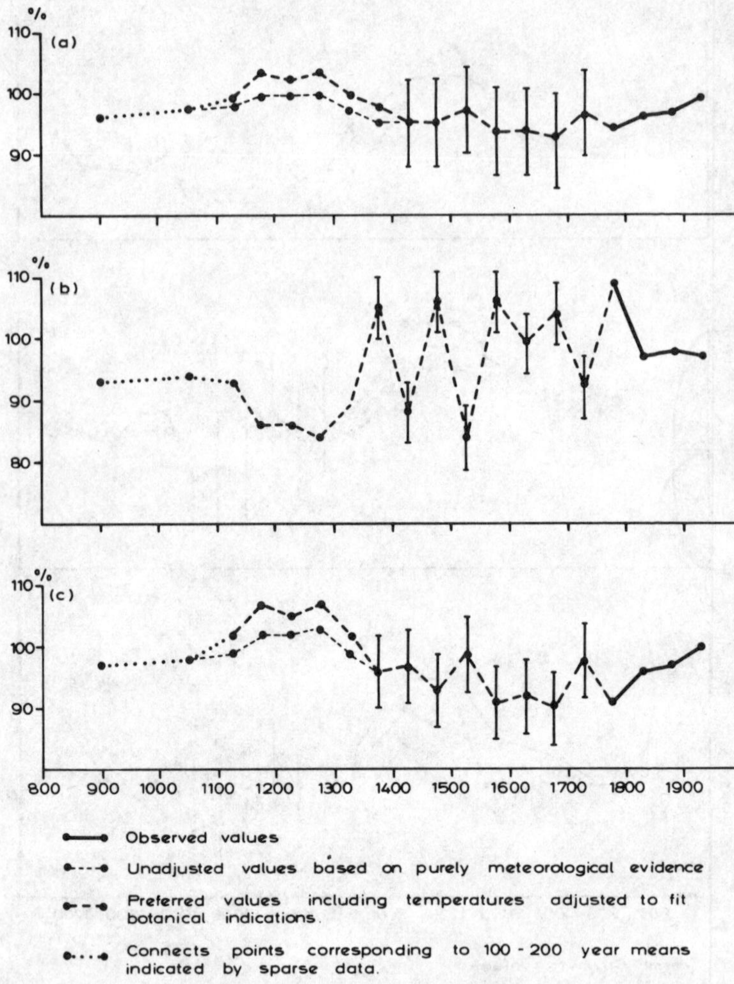

Fig. 12. Rainfall over England and Wales (as percentage of 1916–50 averages), 50-year averages, (a) year (b) high summer (c) cooler 10 months of the year (September to June), observed values from 1740. After Lamb (1966).

liability to more severe thunderstorms owing to a higher maximum moisture content of the air.[77]

Before eliciting the significant features of these trends, it is instructive to place them in their wider context. Thousand-year averages of temperatures which Lamb supposes have prevailed since about 10,000 B.C. are shown in Fig 13. The heights of the shaded ovals indicate the probable range of uncertainty of the temperature estimates, and their widths represents $\pm 2\delta$ margins of radiocarbon

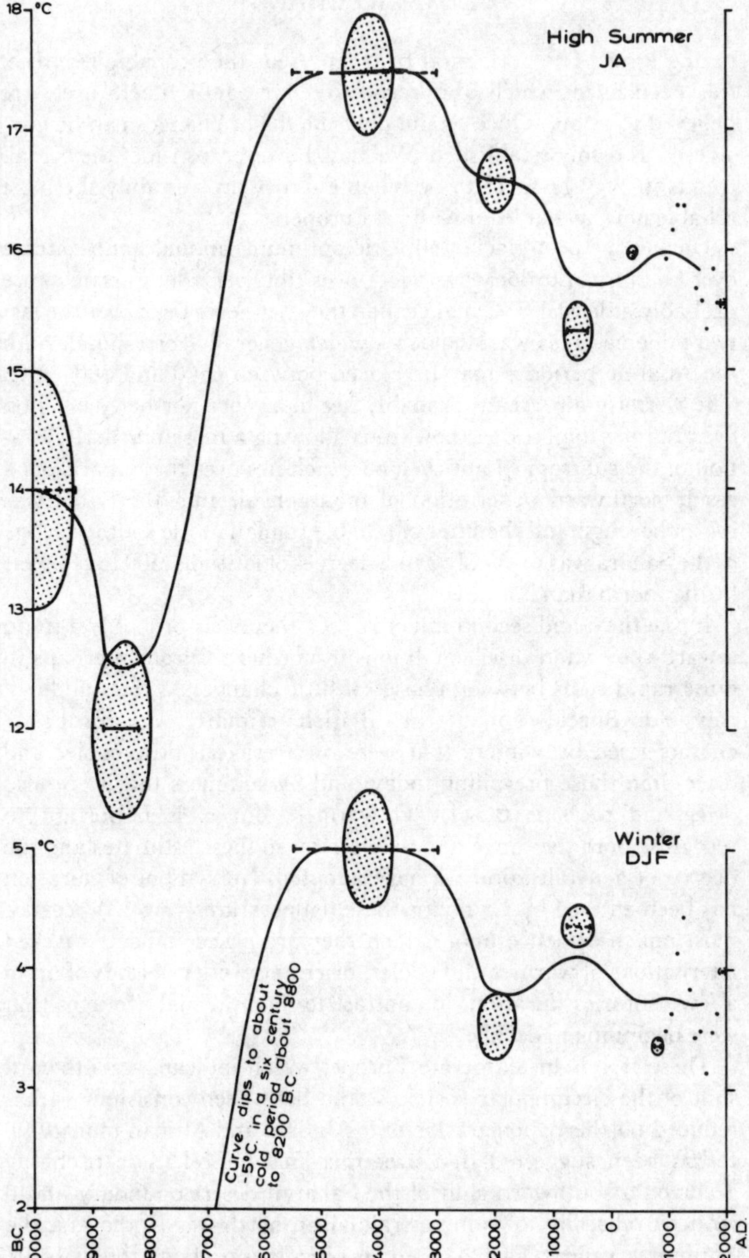

Fig. 13. Temperatures in central England, 1000-year averages. Dots indicate averages for individual centuries within the last millenium. For explanation of shaded ovals see text. After Lamb, Lewis and Woodruffe (1966).

dating error. The horizontal bars represent the probable length of the epochs to which the respective average temperatures are believed to apply. Once again, only the major changes can be considered as firmly established. We may, however, consider the overall trends in Figs 11 to 13 to be reliable – they are certainly the most reliable now available for western Europe.

During the post-glacial 'climatic optimum' annual temperatures over western Europe, averaged over the very long-term, were probably at least 1·5°C higher than they have ever been over the last two millenia. This warm epoch – which generally corresponds with the Atlantic period – may be placed between 6500 and 3000 B.C. The westerly air-stream probably lay in a more northerly position over Europe than it does now, thus allowing a more northerly location of the subtropical anticyclone which lies over the Sahara. As a result northward penetration of monsoon air into the Sahel was more thorough and the limit of reliable rainfall at the southern edge of the Sahara was probably 3 to 5 degrees of latitude (300 to 500 km) further north than it is now.[78]

In the third and second millenia B.C. there was probably a trend toward cooler and drier conditions in northern Europe, perhaps in quite rapid steps between phases of little change. At the middle of this Sub-Boreal epoch the British climate was probably characterised by winters that were on average a little cooler and drier than those prevailing today, and by summers that were also drier and perhaps 0·5–1·0°C warmer. But is is important to recognise both the range of possible error in these estimates and the degree of generalisation we have adopted. No symbol of duration has been entered by Lamb for these temperatures (Fig 13) because most pollen evidence upon which they are based indicate marked alternations of warmer and cooler, drier and wetter periods of up to a few centuries duration, in contrast to the millenial averages that were beginning to decline.[79]

These trends in temperate Europe, which indicate a southward shift of the circumpolar vortex, would have been consistent with a reduced northerly penetration of the Indian and African monsoons. It has been suggested that over this long period there probably occurred a southward shift of the Saharan desert boundary and a reduced reliability of summer rainfall in north-west India and the Euphrates valley. This has led to speculation about the possible climatic causes of decline in the Harappan and Sumerian civilizations.[80]

From about 900 to 450 B.C. there were frequent cyclonic circulation patterns and a highly maritime climate characterised by abnormal wetness and, especially in the western parts of Britain, by mild winters and wretchedly cool, damp summers. These trends are revealed by the signs of renewed bog growth which throughout north-western Europe are marked by a recurrence surface (or Grenzhorizont) in peat bogs.[81] In southern Europe and north Africa, we might expect at this time an epoch of more frequently moist winters and summers that would be consistent with a southward shift of Atlantic depression tracks.

From about 450 B.C. and into the Dark Ages the fragmentary information available points to a greater frequency of severe winters, especially over the period A.D. 600–800, and to warmer summers – a pattern which exhibits some similarity to the Sub-Boreal epoch. This trend would be consistent with increasing aridity of the subtropical desert margin in north Africa and the increased frequency of dry summers in southern Europe.

Moreover, we may now clearly define an early medieval warm epoch that occurred in north-west Europe between about 1150 and 1250 A.D. This seems to have been a period of frequently warm and dry, evidently anticyclonic, summers in temperate Europe, with quite frequent thunderstorm rains in the Mediterranean. In Britain mean summer temperatures, averaged over 50 years, were probably more than 0·5°C higher than they are at present, more than 1·0°C higher than they were in the seventeenth century. Winters were frequently moist and mild, being on average a little warmer than those from 1900 to 1950. However they seem to have been more frequently moist than is typical today, in contrast to summers which were on average 10 per cent drier than for the period 1916 to 1950 (Fig 12).

The cooling phase that occurred in the later Middle Ages was probably the result of a southward shift of the northern Atlantic depression tracks and reduced anticyclonic activity. The increasingly maritime climate, dominated by rain-bearing westerlies, saw an increased frequency of wet and cool summers: by A.D. 1500 these may have averaged more than 0·7°C less than those during the medieval 'optimum'. Winters became more frequently dry but cold – on average perhaps 1·0°C colder.

There has therefore been a radical revision of the trends described for western Europe by Brooks in 1925, apparently confirmed by Britton in 1937 and emphasised by Van Bath in 1963.[82] Rather than a phase of wetness and coldness in the eleventh and twelfth centuries, the new evidence points convincingly to a distinctly warm phase with low summer rainfall, and mild, moist winters.

The subsequent cooling phase was temporarily interrupted by a run of mild, wet winters and dry, warm summers over the period A.D. 1450–1530. Thereafter, the trend was renewed, with nadirs in the 1590s and 1690s, but through much of the seventeenth century the general pattern was that of dry and very severe winters and damp, cool summers. It was a difficult time for many communities. In the 1690s there were heavy losses of livestock in the winter snows and of cereal crops that failed to ripen in the cloudy summers. The Scots called them 'The Seven Ill Years' for they were years of widespread famine and starvation. In Finland the Great Famine, as it is called, saw a loss of one-quarter – perhaps even one-third – of the region's population. Of course, there were economic and social – not only environmental – factors behind these famines and in subsequent chapters we shall put these factors in their respective places.

This cold epoch lasted from about 1530 to 1700, and was followed by a general change toward higher temperatures in both summer and winter with, in general, more winter and less summer rainfall, though this trend was interrupted by occasional cold spells in the 1770s, early 1820s, 1840s and 1890s (Fig 2). Decadal averages of both winter and summer temperatures reached a peak from 1940 to 1950 and have since declined. Indeed, the indications are of a present trend of cooling on a hemispherical scale from the Yukon[83] to Iceland,[84] with increased pack ice in the Sub-Arctic and reduced surface sea temperatures in the North Atlantic.[85] Consistent with these trends are a southward shift of the jet stream with a consequent reduction in the northward penetration of the Indian Monsoon and a reduced penetration of the monsoon rains in the Sahel.[86] These anomalies, in addition to those such as the apparent increase in incidence of summer droughts on the Eurasian steppes and in California, seem to be part of an increased range of climatic extremes that are thought to be characteristic of the blocking type of circulation that is now prevalent.

From the variety of descriptors available, particularly from those like the isotope record that have been studied recently, it has been possible to reconstruct a history of changes in the climate of north-western Europe. The margins of error estimated for this chronology are often quite large, particularly for the period preceding about A.D. 800, and it is important that they be fully recognised. But it is possible to indicate the general direction and the general range of changes in temperature and rainfall that have occurred since A.D. 800. Over the past 1000 years in Britain the range of change of mean annual temperature has exceeded 1·5°C and that of annual rainfall has probably exceeded 10 per cent. This scale of change expressed in terms of temperature and rainfall certainly seems substantial, but how can we measure its significance for farming communities in the past?

3

The Significance of Climatic Change: Harvest Yield and Harvest Failure

So far the significance of past changes of climate has been considered only in terms of the descriptors which have recorded its influence. Most of these descriptors are biological and hydrological: some even make use of the sensitive relationship between weather and the farming calendar and care must be taken to avoid circular argument which discusses climatic change on the basis of evidence drawn largely from the harvest diary, and which then goes on to emphasise its significance to the existing farming economy.

It is instructive to place the established chronology of change more firmly in the context of its contemporary economic history; for it is not possible to assess adequately the historical importance of climatic change without an understanding of the sensitivity of contemporary economies to weather.

This chapter assesses the significance of past changes of climate by concentrating on two major spheres of weather influence – harvest yields and harvest failure. There are three sections. In the first it is argued that yields of certain crops are closely related to particular elements of weather and that changes in these elements are likely to have been important to a farming economy. In the second it is argued that such changes would have been of critical importance in marginal areas where, sometimes, agricultural systems were poorly adapted to climatic conditions. It was here that a farming economy, like that of the medieval peasantry in England, could be described as 'balancing on the margins of subsistence'[1] and it was here that apparently minor changes of climate tended to promote major responses in the natural and human environment.[2]

In the final section it is proposed that the probability of harvest failure was, as much as the average return to seed, the major way in which climate constrained subsistence farmers. Changes in climate can therefore be more realistically studied as changes in the probability of harvest failure.

Variable Yields and the Variability of Climate

There has been a notable failure by historians to comprehend the role of environmental processes in agriculture. Indeed, the seeming complexity of environmental interactions with farming systems has led some to dismiss any attempts to grasp these; for example one historical geographer has argued that the impossibility of distinguishing the effects of different weather elements on agriculture reduces our understanding to speculation about links between these and crop yields.[3] However, it is precisely these relationships that need to be more clearly comprehended before the agricultural significance of the variability of climate can be evaluated.

Of course, it is nonsense to suggest that the variability of climate is the sole agent of changes in agricultural productivity. But it is reasonable to argue that while long- or medium-term changes of climate may alter the range of potential crops that can be grown, short-term variations in climate that would be affected by such secular change would cause deviations from expected productivity and expected yield;[4] and such changes can be directly related to profits for the farmer, since costs per acre are virtually the same for low as for high yields. Even today the output of a technology-equipped agricultural industry varies enormously and uncontrollably from year to year.[5]

In this section consideration is given first to contemporary links between weather and yield so that these may be established on the basis of more reliable data than exist for the past. Later we shall consider those links occurring in earlier times. It is necessary, however, to comprehend and, if possible, to isolate non-weather influences on yield before proceeding to measure the influence of weather itself.

Non-weather Influences on Yield

Environmental factors, for example changes in soil quality, may have medium- or long-term effects on yields. Indeed soil impoverishment is increasingly used as an explanation of population movements in prehistoric Europe, and seems a plausible explanation of some vegetation changes and upland abandonment in Bronze-Age Britain.[6]

More important are the economic and institutional influences – the mix of technology and labour inputs that may change with time, and the managerial skills that arrange this mix. Even these do not work independently of weather; for while differences in managerial skills may be the source of farm-to-farm and year-to-year differences in returns, perhaps 15 to 30 per cent of the variation in productivity between farms of the same enterprise in Britain may derive from the impact of weather on farm management decisions, such as the timing of field operations and the skill in coping with adverse weather.[7]

The complexity of the causes is expressed in the literature of agricultural economics. For example a plausible production function for determinants of wheat yield can be expressed as follows:

$$Y = f(L, K, F, La, W)$$

where, Y = wheat yield, L = labour inputs, K = inputs of capital and technology, F = fertilizer inputs, La = area of basically fertile land used, W = weather effects and incidence of disease.[8] To this type of equation, some would add a random disturbance factor because the relationship between Y and (L, K, F, La, W) is rarely known exactly.

The link between yield and technology is a strong one: there is overwhelming evidence for a secular, sometimes even decadal, rise in yields with technological innovation. Perhaps the most remarkable is the post-war trend in the Corn Belt of the United States which has seen a doubling of corn yields since the 1930s (Fig 14). It is possible, however, to 'extract' technological influences from this rising trend in order to unmask the obscured influence of weather on yields. In effect, yield is the product of a weather-technology interaction in which favourable weather conditions allow technology to express its full potential. Viewed like this, the belief that technology reduces the influence of weather on agriculture is somewhat tenuous.

The Influence of Weather on Yield

The influence of weather may be manifested in several ways – in Britain it is revealed through the variation in soil preparation, in the length of growing season and in the nature of the harvested crop. There is, for example, an inverse relationship between autumn rainfall and autumn sowing of cereals, which is generally reflected in the total annual sowing.[9] Differences in summer temperatures have a major influence on the intensity and length of the growing season, and a variety of weather elements may reduce the final harvest by the lodging of the grain, by the sprouting of grain in the ear, or in prolonging the harvest period and delaying autumn preparation of the land.[10] In lowland Britain there is a particularly strong correlation between summer rainfall and cereal yield. For example, Milner has found that in Lincolnshire June-August rainfall accounts for 43 to 45 per cent of the variance in the yield of barley, wheat and oats;[11] and this is reflected in cereal yields in the United Kingdom as a whole although, in many upland areas both in Britain and Scandinavia, summer temperature takes over from summer rainfall as the dominant environmental control.[12]

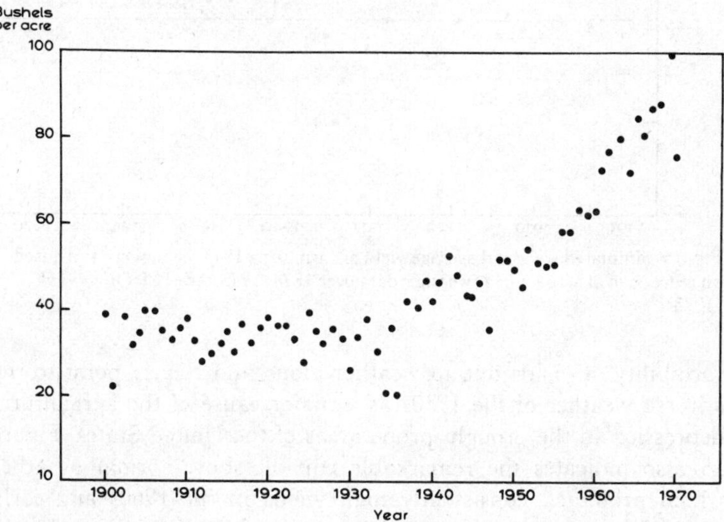

Fig. 14. Weighted average yield of corn in five Midwest states, 1900–70. After McQuigg *et al.* (1973).

Elsewhere, for example in the Midwest of the United States, the controlling variables are very different, but the consequences of changes in weather and climate are at least as great. By quantifying the relationships between large-scale weather variability and the variability of yields of corn in the United States Midwest, McQuigg and a team of meteorologists have been able to estimate the yield of corn expected with 'normal' weather.[13] This yield was established for technological conditions operating in 1945 and a simulated time series of yield data was then generated by using the observed (real) time series of weather data. This provided estimates of the specific impact of weather on crop yields as if technology and all other non-weather controls had remained constant at the 1945 level. The simulated yields for five Midwest states over the period 1900–70 illustrate the influence of weather alone in causing year-to-year differences in corn yield (Fig 15). They emphasise the great

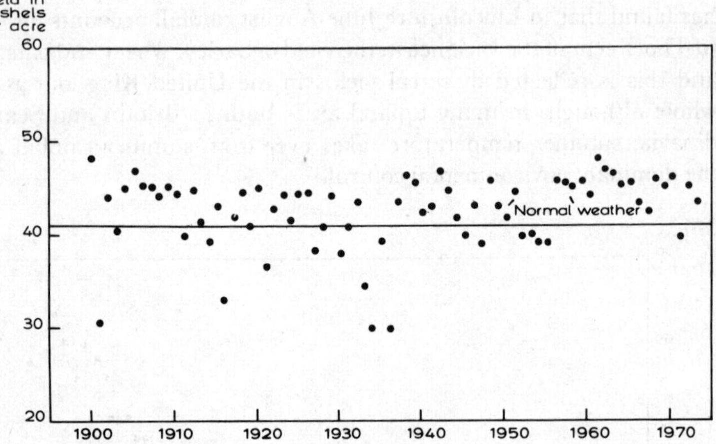

Fig. 15. Simulated weighted average yield of corn using 1945 technology and based on regression of actual yield/weather data over 1874–1945. After McQuigg *et al.* (1973).

variability of yields due to weather alone and clearly point to the adverse weather of the 1930s as a major cause of the agricultural depression in the drought-prone areas of the United States. Figure 15 also indicates the remarkable run of 'above-normal' weather which promoted consistently high yields in the 1960s and early 1970s. It is now clear that the rising trend of yields evident in Fig 14 in fact reflects a trend to less adverse weather. Indeed, since the range of yield values from year-to-year for 1945 levels of technology is very similar to those for 1973 levels of technology, the investigators concluded that:

> Technology has not influenced the susceptibility of crop yields to weather. The persistence of good yields in recent years is evidence of anomalously persistent good weather. There is no known reason why the variability that characterised the bulk of the 33-year record that has been examined should have disappeared. Therefore, we cannot expect the crop yields of the next several years to stay at these consistently high levels. It is imperative that we not be lulled into a dangerous and unjustified expectation that such fortunate circumstances will continue . . .[14]

Weather, then, is a major factor behind yield fluctuations, even in commercial cropping supported by modern technology; and the weather elements that account for most yield variability can be readily identified, thus providing the focus for an investigation of the agricultural significance of climatic change. This focus can be sharpened by giving attention to the special interaction of agriculture and climate at the margin of profitable farming.

The foregoing examples have illustrated the close relationship between weather and agricultural yields in non-marginal areas. However, in areas where the return to agricultural investment is marginal – for example in excessively cool or arid areas – this relationship is strengthened. Indeed, it seems that in cold-marginal areas the growth rates of plants and thus the yield of crops is almost a linear function of temperature. For example, Bryson has found that in Iceland a decline in summer temperatures of 1 °C will tend to reduce hay yield by 15 to 17 per cent. He concluded that the land-based economy of Iceland is therefore very sensitive to climatic change.[15] Moreover, it has been suggested that since hay yields in Iceland are partly determined by the level of winter-kill of grass, they are correlated with the duration of coastal sea-ice which, we have seen, can itself be used as a descriptor of past changes of climate.[16]

Those changes in yield that occur with increasing proximity to the physical margins of cultivation are less clear, although it is known that the growth rates of certain plants do exhibit a linear decline.[17] We can be more certain that growth rates and yields in cold-marginal areas tend to decrease linearly with elevation, in other words with reduced temperatures.[18] In many uplands, however, the variability of yield tends to increase greatly with elevation because the lowered temperature curves are liable to oscillate across the growth threshold of 6 °C, allowing only intermittent growth and bringing variable harvests.[19] Such a variation in yield emphasises the economic implications of weather and certainly makes marginal upland areas especially sensitive to changes of climate.

The Sensitivity of Marginal Agriculture

The sensitivity of marginal areas to fluctuations of climate seems to derive from three related factors. Firstly, there is a natural tendency for variability around average temperatures to increase where the average value is reduced. Thus the size of yields, the length of growing seasons and the intensity of warmth tend to increase in variability with elevation. In the same way, a temporal decrease in mean temperatures would also increase this variability, and would thus tend to compound the hazards to marginal farming. Secondly, marginal agriculture, which by definition gives a slim return to investment, does not generally allow the accumulation of a surplus to act as a buffer against hard times – it is in the nature of the marginal farmer and his marginal economy to be at risk. Thirdly, it is often true that systems of marginal agriculture are poorly adapted to their environmental conditions and are not as well able to tolerate environmental change as non-marginal systems.[20]

The consequences of climatic changes in the past were thus most likely felt by marginal economies, and it is in marginal areas that the change would have found most widespread and, perhaps, most lasting expression. These areas are thus the 'laboratories' of the present study, and the remainder of this chapter attends to the mapping of marginal study areas in north-western Europe and central North America. This is discussed as a sequence of three operations: Firstly, suitable parameters are established for those climatic elements that effectively restrain agriculture in some marginal areas. Secondly, the climatic limits to cultivation in such areas are defined on the basis of threshold levels of the parameters. Finally, the nature in which these climatic restraints operate will be discussed as a probability of crop failure which, it will be argued, is a more important consideration to the marginal subsistence farmer than the average return to seed.

Climatic Restraints on Early Cereal Cultivation

Attention is first focused on the identification of cold-marginal areas and the climatic constraints operating within them. It is these areas, widespread in north-west Europe, that most clearly exhibit a history of marginal economy – where the combined influence of elevation and latitude create a pattern of marginal and submarginal upland areas interdigitated with productive lowlands. This pattern is particularly marked in Scotland, especially in the Southern Uplands, where low relief and gentle slopes ensured that any response by the cultivation limit to temporal changes in climate occurred over a wide range of marginal foothill. We may, therefore, adopt upland Scotland as the study area in which we can establish hypothetical climatic limits to early cultivation. From here we shall extend our study to other uplands in north-west Europe.

In many of these uplands – certainly in Scotland, western Norway and in Iceland until the final abandonment of cereal cultivation sometime after the fourteenth century – early cultivation before 1800 was largely restricted to the cropping of barley, oats and rye. In Scotland before 1800 the upper limit of cultivation was the furthest extent of outfield oats cultivation. The moors above this limit were extensively grazed by sheep and cattle, an enterprise which, in view of the quantity of grazing available, would not have competed for land with cereal cropping. The limit of cultivation here was, therefore, not so much an expression of a change in the comparative advantage which tillage may have enjoyed over extensive grazing; it was the product of a cereal crop approaching the limits of its ability to tolerate an increasingly adverse environment.

The varieties of oats grown in upland Scotland before 1750 were commonly the 'black', 'grey' or 'small' oats which, in southern Scotland, were replaced before 1800 by the 'common Scotch' oat, and by the Red and Blainslie varieties in the early nineteenth century.[21] These early varieties were shorter in the stem and less liable to shaking than those now sown in Scotland, but there is no evidence that they required a shorter growing season or that they were more tolerant of soil wetness and acidity. Indeed, most recent varieties have been introduced with the aim of reducing the chance of failure in cool, wet summers. Similarly, improvements in husbandry, particularly in draining and liming, have tended to reduce the restraint of soil wetness. We may, therefore, estimate the climatic restraints on early oats cultivation by examining the physiological requirements of modern varieties of oats, but should note that these estimates may, if anything, err on the low side.

Selection of the Parameters

The climatic restraints may be distinguished from those of a physiographic nature. Of the latter, the influence of elevation and site, particularly with respect to the type of climatic regime, is the strongest.[22] Slope, aspect and surface roughness have been shown to be important features determining local levels of cultivation rather than its overall elevation.[23] Similarly, edaphic restraints, such as inadequate soil depth, water-logging or excessive acidity, are secondary influences. These are often the product of an upland climate, and are essentially local controls on the limit of cultivation. Since this study is concerned with synoptic rather than unique patterns these secondary restraints will not be considered in detail.

Altitudinal changes in the character of climatic factors are, however, the fundamental controls on the elevation of the cultivation limit. Insolation, exposure, warmth and wetness, especially during the growing season, are the major restraints to the uphill extension of oats cropping. Significant parameters of these factors can now be selected and their significance assessed by comparing parametric isopleths with the existing upper limit of cultivation. The aim is to establish values which are critical for cereal growth and which may be used as a basis for later discussion of the agricultural significance of a locational shift of the isopleths due to secular changes of climate.

Insolation In maritime climates the altitudinal increase in solar radiation is more than balanced by a reduction in the hours of bright sunshine due to an increase in persistent cloud and mist.[24] The result may be a roughly linear reduction with altitude,[25] but the rate of fall (about 5 per cent over 200 m in south-east Scotland) represents an insignificant decrease in potential for crop growth when compared with changes in exposure, wetness and warmth.

Exposure Altitudinal increases in windspeed and turbulence are severe in Britain, Norway and Iceland. In south-east Scotland average windspeed increases about 1 m/s every 70 m up to 200 m O.D. and 1 m/s every 80 m at higher levels.[26] In this upland region the isopleth of 4·4 m/s is remarkably coincident with the limits of cultivation existing in 1860, and apparently contributes to a pronounced southward down-tilt of the limit (Fig 16).[27] Indeed, over the western Highlands of Scotland as a whole a north-west shelving of natural vegetation limits may well be linked with variations in exposure.[28] The sensitivity of oats to windshaking strengthens the suggestion of a causal link between windspeed and the upper limit of early cultivation.

Summer wetness Oats are particularly tolerant of persistent wetting and high relative humidity.[29] However, lowered temperatures and reduced evapo-transpiration, associated with increased rainfall, promote a steep gradient of soil moisture increasing with elevation, and the greater sensitivity of oats to waterlogging places an absolute limit to the cultivation of oats at about 425 m O.D. in south-east Scotland. A study of temperature will show that absolute levels of inadequate summer warmth are reached well before those of excess

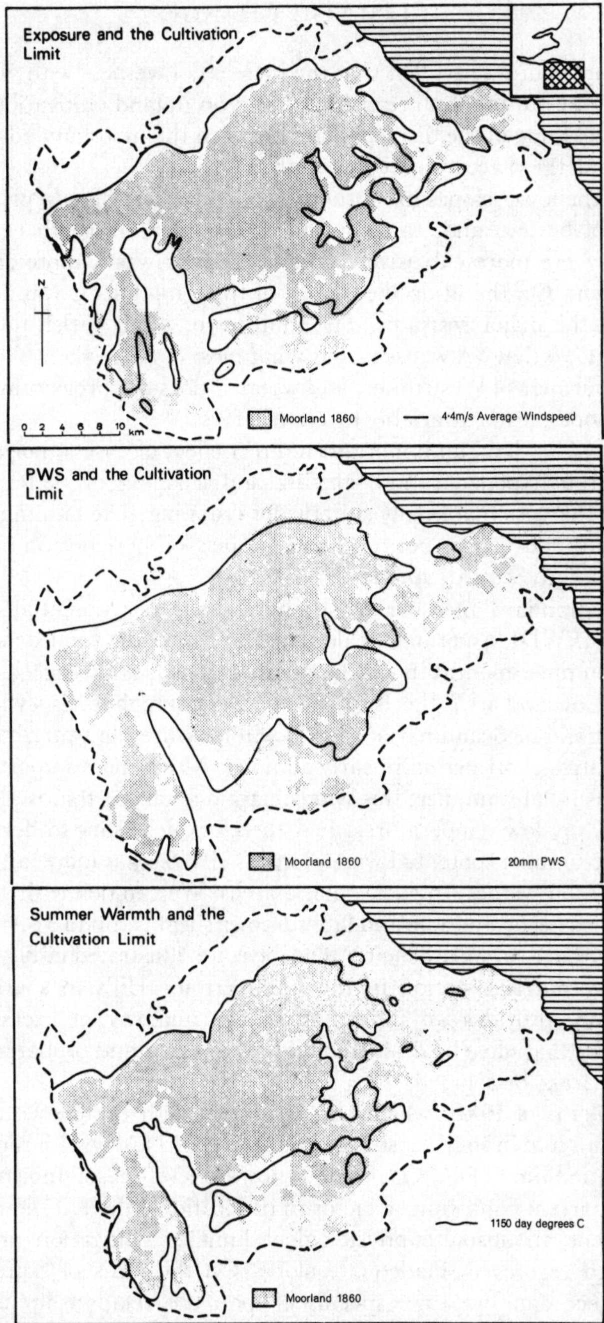

Fig. 16. Exposure, soil moisture (accumulated PWS), summer warmth and the limits of cultivation in south-east Scotland. For explanation, see text.

moisture; but it is evident that the increase of wetness with altitude contributes to the total restraint placed on upland cultivation, and explains some of the discrepancies between the moorland edge and the isopleths of accumulated warmth.

On the lower slopes in southern Scotland where bere (a primitive form of barley) and, towards the end of the eighteenth century, wheat were more extensively grown, wetness was a more specific deterrent. On the ill-drained areas of these foothills, it was singled out as the major restraint. The minister of a hill parish noted in about 1790 that: 'A wet season is what most of all awakens the fears of the farmers of Westruther; and where it does not prove ruinous to their hopes, leads invariably to a late harvest'.[30]

On higher land an important indirect effect of excess moisture is felt through podzolisation, gleying and leaching of well-drained soils, otherwise marginally suitable for cropping. The minimum pH value for oats, 4·3, is not reached in upper soil horizons on most of the southern Scottish uplands.[31]

The standard measure of summer wetness is potential water deficit (PWD), a parameter designed to assess the total deficit for those summer months in which potential transpiration exceeds rainfall. In lowland areas this is satisfactory, but at high levels – whether in Scotland or Scandinavia – PWD will measure the water balance over only a short period in early summer. Much more important is wetness in late summer; this will constrain a harvest that is already delayed by low temperatures. It is therefore necessary to devise an 'end-of-summer' potential water surplus (PWS) that more faithfully reflects soil wetness in cool, upland areas. We can define this PWS as the excess of a middle and late summer surplus (up to 31 August) over an early summer deficit.[32] The measure, illustrated in Fig 17 for a meteorological station in the Lammermuir Hills in south-east Scotland, provides an indication of the quantity of excess soil moisture that must be drained off if waterlogging and probable crop failure are to be avoided.

Isopleths of PWS, which can be drawn with confidence to the nearest 5 mm in south-east Scotland, correlate closely with the 1860 cultivation limit (Fig 16), and point toward levels of soil moisture as an important contributory factor in its location – though these may represent an absolute physiological limit to cultivation only in exposed regions of inadequate slope. On the basis of scant and imperfect data we may speculate upon the relationship of soil moisture to altitude: it seems not to be linear, but rather quasi-exponential. Up to the 30 mm isopleth (which in south-east

Scotland lies at 225–275 m O.D.) PWS is raised 10 mm every 30 m of elevation; above this by 10 mm over 15 m, and this curvilinear gradient has been detected in other British uplands.[33] The gradient is not so steep as to prevent the existence of a marginal belt of wet land on the fringes of the uplands, but it emphasises the increasing meso-climatic restraint imposed by altitude on successful cropping and points to the similarly large effects that a change in climate would have on this marginal fringe.

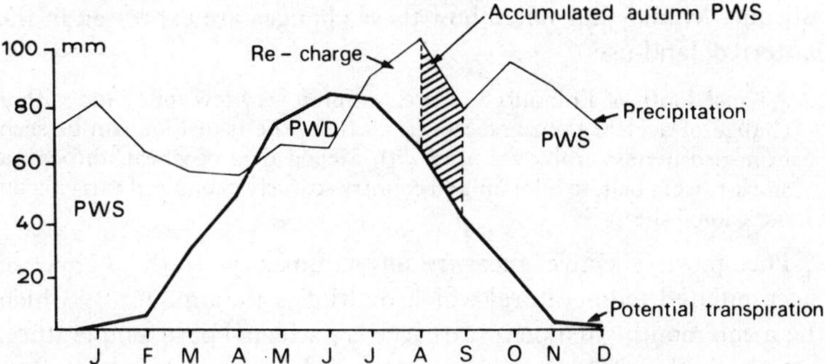

Fig. 17. The calculation of accumulated autumn potential water surplus.

Summer warmth In maritime climates the slow rise in mean spring temperatures leads to a retarded and low summer maximum. The shallow curve of the mean annual temperature regime results in marked falls in mean temperature with moderate increases in altitude.[34] These changes are compounded, because the greatest difference between mean temperatures of upland and lowland maritime sites occurs in Britain in late April and May.[35] Altitudinal foreshortening of the growing season is, therefore, particularly rapid in maritime areas. For example, Manley compares a ten-day reduction of the season over an altitudinal rise of only 76 m in southern Scotland, with a similar reduction over 230 m in the Harz Mountains.[36] A very similar reduction of growing season could occur from an overall cooling of the climate as would occur from an increase in altitude. For example, the very shallow temperature curve in Iceland means that a fall of only 1°C in the mean annual temperature would reduce the average growing season by two weeks and the number of growing days by as much as 27 per cent.[37]

Moreover, increasing elevation leads to a proportionally greater reduction of intensity of summer warmth in maritime than in continental climates.[38] This seems to be partly a result of the exceptionally rapid fall in maximum temperatures with elevation.[39] The consequent increase in annual variability of warmth contributes to the rapid altitudinal fall in potential for crop growth;[40] also important is the role of associated factors, such as a lowered cloud base, reduced sunshine and higher humidity, which exaggerate the effects of lowered temperatures by reducing evaporation and transpiration.[41]

The maritime temperature regime of south-east Scotland is, therefore, responsible for rapid changes in summer warmth with altitude. Manley has noted how these changes are expressed in the pattern of land-use

> . . . just south of Edinburgh where, within a very few miles and with a change of a mere thousand feet in altitude, the transition can be seen from prosperous arable farming with a good deal of wheat, through a stock-raising belt, to bare upland country scarcely capable of carrying an occasional sheep.[42]

The most effective measure of summer warmth is one of 'accumulated temperature' which multiplies the amount by which the mean monthly temperature exceeds a selected base temperature, or growth threshold, by the number of days in each month. The data are then expressed in 'day-degrees'. The measure has been criticised by some and improved upon by others; but, it remains sound and is well suited to the imperfect temperature data that we shall be using.[43] The selected base temperature, which relates to the onset of growth in cereals, is 4·4°C rather than the conventional 6°C which relates more closely to grasses.[44]

Using this measure it is possible to map the pattern of summer warmth as isopleths of accumulated temperature. This has been done for the Lammermuir Hills in south-east Scotland in order to examine the constraining influence of summer warmth on cereal cultivation. The temperature data used are those for the period 1856–95 since these are available for a dense coverage of stations.[45] The relationship between isopleths of warmth and the 1860 cultivation limit is illustrated in Fig 16. The plane of summer warmth is tilted in the same direction as the moorland edge and may impose a fundamental control on its location. Certainly, those parts of the moorland edge that are discrepant with the 1150 day-degrees C isopleth are coincident with patterns of exposure and wetness. The suggestion is that there is a local modification of air and earth temperature by variations in exposure, insolation and wetness.

We may, at this point, conclude that the early cultivation of oats in the marginal uplands of southern Scotland was particularly sensitive to three climatic factors: exposure, summer wetness and summer warmth. Average windspeed, PWS and accumulated temperature appear to be the most effective parameters of these restraints. We are now able to evaluate the minimum thresholds of these parameters which may have determined the location of the upper limit of cultivation. Having established these we can focus our attention on those secular changes of climate which may have shifted the location of such thresholds and thus radically affected the viability of cropping in marginal areas.

Absolute Climatic Limits to Cultivation

It is possible to establish a minimum level of warmth necessary for oats cultivation by reference to phenological data which, while not yet fully available in Britain, have been calculated for stations at the northern margin of cereal growing in Finland.[46] Minimum heat requirements for spring wheat at Alatornio (Lapi Province, 65°50′ N) and Rovaniemi (Lapi Province, 66° 30′ N) are 922 and 889 day-degrees C above a base of 4·4°C. These were adjusted for oats, which have a slightly longer vegetative period than spring wheat, and corrected by a photothermal equivalent to take account of differences in day-length between Finland and Scotland. These calculations suggest that the minimum heat requirement for oats in southern Scotland is about 1050 day-degrees C, a figure which is inevitably approximate because it fails to take account of the differences in humidity, regime of temperature and water balance between Finland and Scotland, but which is corroborated by evidence in the field.[47]

From a study of contemporary oats cultivation in the Southern Uplands maximum levels of PWS and exposure were established at 60 mm and 6·2 m/s. These levels of exposure, wetness and warmth may thus be considered critical to the ripening of oats in southern Scotland. The isopleth of these combined restraints stood at 320 m to 350 m during the period 1856–95.

By reference to the Finnish phenological data and to the pattern of commercial cereal cropping in south-east Scotland, it is also possible to establish the approximate levels of warmth, wetness and exposure critical to commercial cereal cultivation: 1200 day-degrees C, 20 mm PWS and 5·0 m/s average windspeed. These may be used to define the lower limit of subsistence cultivation, and thus point to a fringe of foothill that is climatically marginal to the cropping of oats. Isopleths of the upper and lower limits to climatically marginal land are illustrated in Fig 18. The location of the lower limit is, of course, largely the product of the economic or social incentives to cultivation operating at any one time. But the upper limit may be an absolute one, above which cultivation of oats would have been impracticable under most socio-economic conditions. Indeed, almost all the fluctuation of the moorland edge between 1850 and 1960 is contained in the area defined by the climatic limits to marginal land and, since the fluctuation between moorland and improved land is one indicator of land which is economically marginal, the suggestion is that the climatic limits of marginality have been correctly selected.

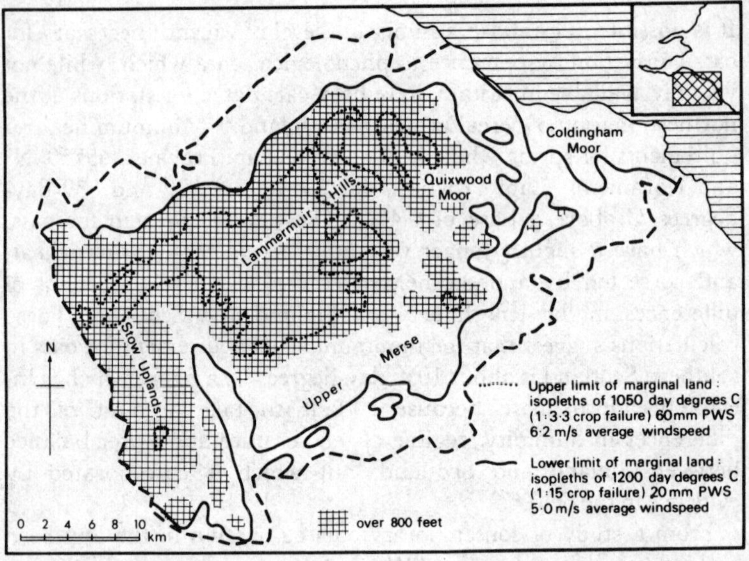

Fig. 18. Climatically marginal land in south-east Scotland. After Parry (1975).

In this manner it is possible to define those theoretical limits to cereal cropping which circumscribe climatically marginal areas – areas in which cultivation is particularly sensitive to changes of climate.

Mapping the Climatically Sensitive Margins

Climatically marginal land can be mapped in the same way over much larger areas, although it clearly will be necessary to alter the emphasis on various weather elements according to the type of climatic regime and the data available.

For example, the marginal foothill zone could be mapped, on the basis of summer warmth, summer wetness and exposure, for Britain as a whole. More rapid, though less accurate, mapping is possible from published data of accumulated temperature alone.[48] The result, Fig 19, is only approximate since consideration has not been given to summer wetness or to exposure; but, it does serve to delineate those upland regions in Britain that are probably marginal to cereal cultivation and likely to have been characterised by precarious agricultural economies that would have been sensitive, both in the long- and short-term, to changes of climate. These would

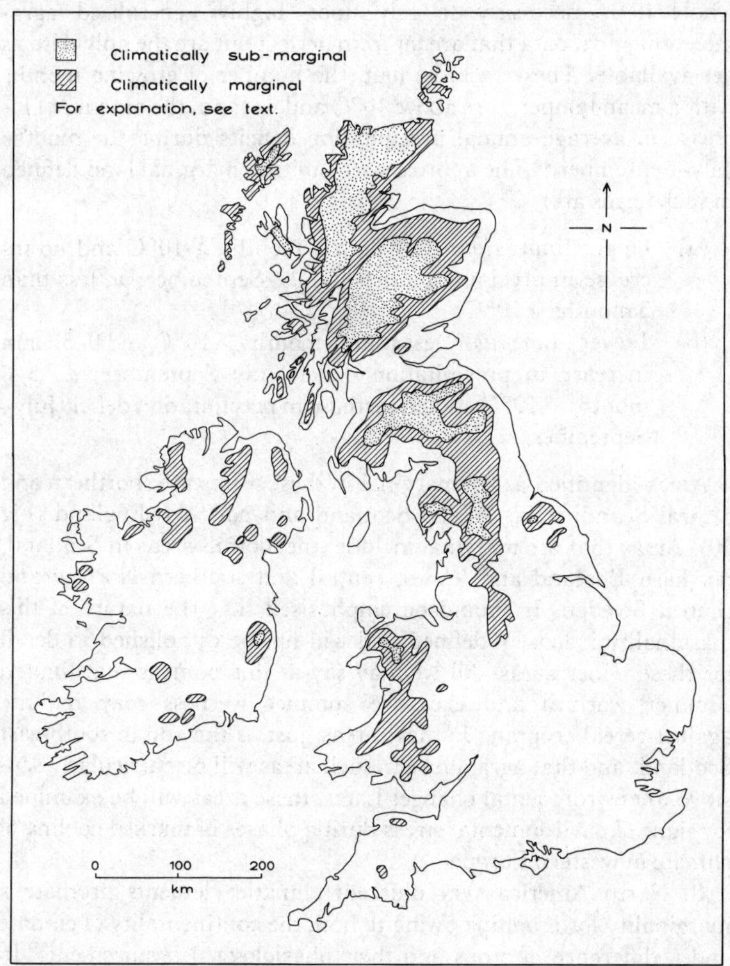

Fig. 19. Climatically marginal land in the British Isles.

appear to include most of Scotland north of the Highland Line and most of the elevated areas in its Southern Uplands, the uplands of northern England (the Pennines, Lake District and North York Moors), the higher parts of Wales, and the summits of Exmoor and Dartmoor in the south-west of England. About 2·75 million hectares, or 12 per cent, of the British mainland are marginal in terms of adequate summer warmth for cereal cropping, and about a further 15 per cent is submarginal – too elevated for cropping under almost any conditions.

To map climatically marginal areas in north-west Europe as a whole it is necessary to rely upon highly generalised agro-meteorological data that are far from perfect but are the only data as yet available. These include, first, the number of growing months with a mean temperature above 10°C and, second, the amount of increase in average annual precipitation deficits during the months July–September.[49] The approximate limits of marginal land defined in such terms are:

(a) Upper limit: *either*, less than 5 months > 10°C and no increase in precipitation deficit July–September; *or*, less than 3 months > 10°C

(b) Lower limit: *either*, less than 5 months > 10°C and 0–50 mm increase in precipitation deficit July–September; *or*, 5–6 months > 10°C and no increase in precipitation deficit July–September.

Areas identified as submarginal in these terms are: northern and central Scandinavia, upland Scotland and northern England (Fig 20). Areas that are marginal include: the foothill areas in Scotland, northern England and Wales, central and southern Norway and central Sweden. It should be emphasised that the nature of this marginality is loosely defined and will not be established in detail for these wider areas. All we may say at this point is that limited summer warmth and excessive summer wetness may militate against cereal cropping in these areas, just as they do in south-east Scotland, and that agriculture in such areas will be particularly sensitive to environmental change. Later, these areas will be examined for signs of environmental stress during phases of marked cooling of climate in western Europe.

In North America very different climatic elements promote a marginality for cropping owing to both the continentality of climate and a difference of crops and their physiological requirements. In the western parts of the Great Plains, pre-European Indian

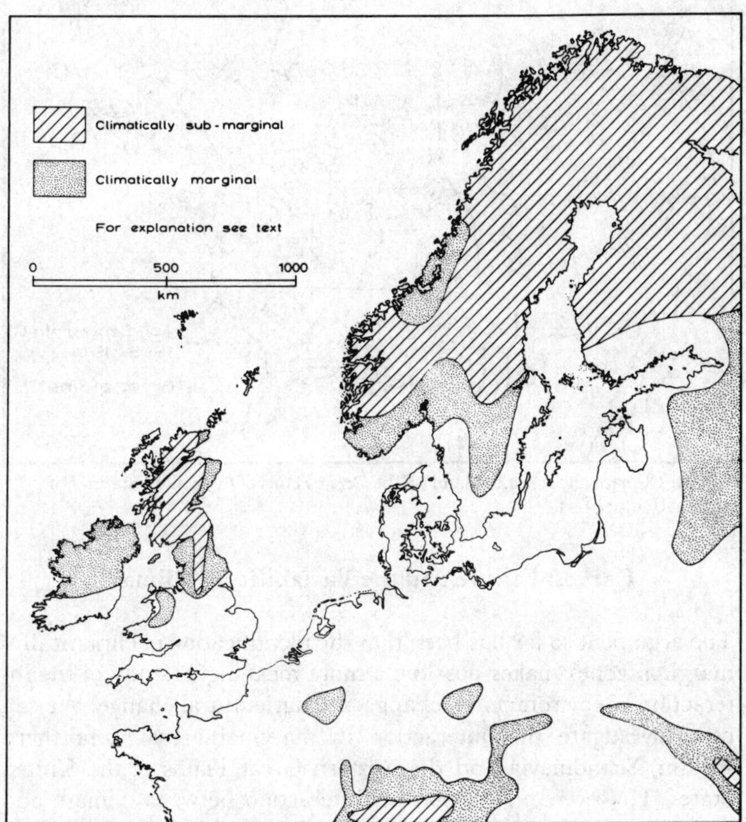

Fig. 20. Climatically marginal land in northern Europe.

agriculture was frequently based on corn (maize), which may have been especially sensitive to mean levels and to the variability of spring and summer rainfall. Indeed, it may be that the 40 cm and 30 cm isohyets of April–September rainfall mark the eastern and western borders of a 2500-km belt, running from North Dakota to southern Texas, that is marginal to unirrigated corn cropping (Fig 21). The distinctiveness of this arid-marginal zone is still suspect, but the notion may be treated as a hypothesis which will later be tested in relation to the pre-European history of peripatetic corn cultivation in South Dakota, Nebraska and Kansas.

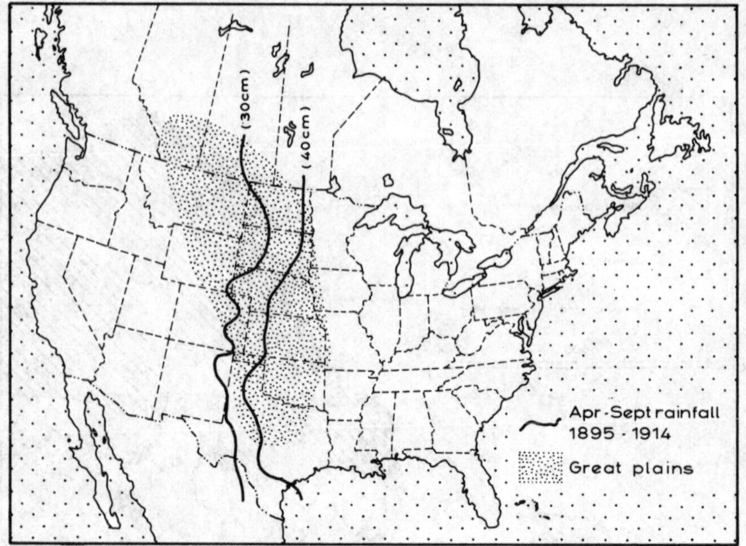

Fig. 21. Climatically marginal land on the Great Plains of the United States. For explanation, see text.

Harvest Failure and the Variability of Climate

The argument so far has been that the identification of climatically-marginal zones makes possible a more meaningful study of the interaction of environmental change and agricultural change. We can now investigate this interaction in marginal areas in northern Britain, Scandinavia and the western Great Plains of the United States. However, one important interaction between climate and agriculture has, up to now, been omitted and needs to be discussed.

We have suggested that the strongest influence of weather variability on farming decisions is felt through two conditions: the average size of yields and the likelihood of outright harvest failure. While variations in yields are strongly related to weather in marginal areas, just as important may have been variations in the probability of harvest failure, particularly in difficult environments, in remote locations and under conditions of a subsistence rather than market economy.

The Probability of Crop Failure

In marginal areas of early subsistence cropping a causal relationship between variability of weather and change in agriculture was determined by the farmer's appreciation of the climatic viability of cropping at particular locations. This appreciation was founded upon a number of considerations many of which cannot be assessed but of which the most important may have been the farmer's intuitive understanding of the likelihood of a particularly poor harvest. Failure of the harvest, particularly in two successive years, could have been disastrous.[50] The chance of outright failure may thus have been a more important factor than the average return to seed in the farmer's decision to reclaim or abandon land.

The farmer's estimate of this probability is likely to have been based on both the frequency of crop failure in living memory and on his appreciation of the average and the variability of the climatic characteristics of the region. If the location of cultivation limits and the shift of these limits were, in part, the expressions of decisions made by a number of farmers over a long period, then a more meaningful assessment of the role of climatic restraint in locating the limits, and thus of climatic change in inducing their movement, can be made by resolving the isopleths of critical climatic values into isopleths of the probability of crop failure. This study would provide an insight into the tolerance levels of early marginal farmers in respect of the frequency of poor summers, and into the importance of successive runs of poor years in promoting a retreat of cultivation. The significance of this variability of weather can be assessed by reference, once again, to the cultivation of oats in our study area in south-east Scotland and to our data for the period 1856–95. For the present we shall consider only variability of summer warmth in determining changes in the probability of crop failure.

The concept of crop failure in subsistence cultivation in Scotland is largely a hypothetical one since oats can be harvested in December, and, however small the return of grain, the straw was always valuable as fodder. Long delays in the harvest, however, reduced the amount and size of the grain and increased loss by wind-shaking. Thus, although the crop may rarely have failed outright, the yield was likely to be so small that the subsistence farmer was forced to use his reserve of seed. The crop of the following year was therefore reduced.

By reference to diaries and journals, it is possible to assess the weather conditions which may have led to long-delayed harvests. For example, a meteorological record noted that in the Edinburgh area in 1799, '. . . the period from 20th of March to the 20th October was characterised by a great depression of temperature, so much so that the harvest was not generally got in till the end of November, and in the high grounds till the end of December.'[51] Evidently, this was a year in which there was even a net loss of seed grain on land near the margin of cultivation. Similar conditions occurred in 1782 and in 1816.[52] A summer worse than these would probably have led to a greatly delayed and meagre harvest on high ground.

The accumulated temperature for the growing season of 1799 in Edinburgh (76 m O.D.) can be estimated from published mean temperatures to have been 1340 day-degrees C.[53] At the upper limit of cultivation in the Lammermuirs (320 m O.D.) the sum is likely to have been about 970 day-degrees C, and at the lower limit of marginal land (c. 215 m O.D.) about 1110. It can therefore be concluded that, at locations near the 1050 day-degrees C isoline or the absolute upper limit of cultivation, a summer in which accumulated warmth failed to exceed 970 day-degrees C would have led to an extremely delayed and reduced cereal harvest. At locations near the upper limit of commercial cereal cropping, the 1200 isoline, harvests in summers with not more than 1110 day-degrees C would have been delayed until late November and would not have sufficiently rewarded inputs of labour and capital.

The statistical probability of crop failure can now be calculated for different elevations and an assessment can be made of the frequencies of failure which marginal farmers were prepared to tolerate.

The Calculation of Probability

Little is known of the variation in the standard deviation of accumulated temperature that may occur with elevation, but it seems likely that below about 500 m O.D. this may not be great.[54] It thus seems reasonable to assume, for the present, that the standard deviation of accumulated temperature at Edinburgh for the period 1856–95 was broadly representative of that for stations elsewhere in south-east Scotland which lie entirely below 500 m. Given this assumption, a linear fall in day-degrees with elevation will give rise to a linear increase in the coefficient of variation of accumulated temperature (Table 2).

Given the further assumption that accumulated surface temperatures are not skewed in their distribution, it is possible to use the normal distribution function to calculate the probability of accumulated temperatures in south-east Scotland being less than the critical value 970 day-degrees C. Table 2 illustrates this probability and the resulting frequency of harvest failure for hypothetical stations at 50 day-degree C intervals. The probability increases with elevation, not linearly, but in an S-shaped curve that is characteristic of the accumulated frequency of a normal distribution (Fig 22a). There is a marked, indeed quasi-exponential, increase of probable harvest failure with elevation at the lower end of the curve. An increase such as this may be significant on marginal foothills where average accumulated temperatures lie between 1250 and 1050 day-degrees C and where the probability of harvest failure is thus already high.

Table 2: PROBABILITY AND FREQUENCY OF HARVEST FAILURE BY 50 DAY-DEGREE C INTERVALS IN SOUTH-EAST SCOTLAND, 1856–95

$\bar{x}$ average day-degrees C	Coefficient of variation	d	Normal probability of single harvest failure	Frequency	Probability of two consecutive failures	Frequency of two consecutive failures
1350	11.48	–2.4516	0.007	1 in 141	0.00005	1 in 19783
1300	11.92	–2.1920	0.017	1 in 60	0.0003	1 in 3610
1250	12.22	–1.8064	0.035	1 in 28	0.001	1 in 800
1200	12.92	–1.4839	0.069	1 in 14	0.005	1 in 210
1150	13.57	–1.1613	0.122	1 in 8	0.015	1 in 67
1100	14.09	–0.8387	0.201	1 in 5	0.040	1 in 25
1050	14.76	–0.5161	0.303	1 in 3	0.092	1 in 11

critical value (x) = 970 day–degrees C

standard score $(d) = \frac{x-\bar{x}}{SD}$

standard deviation (SD) = 155 day–degrees C

coefficient of variation $= \frac{\bar{x}}{SD} 100$

(from Parry, 1976)

It is clear, then, that the climatic restraint imposed on cropping by elevation increases markedly towards the upper limit of cultivation. At about 150 m O.D. in the Berwickshire Merse the theoretical frequency of a failure may well be less than one year in fifty (Fig 22b). But at about 250 m O.D., where accumulated temperatures average only 1150 day-degrees C, the average frequency is, *ceteris paribus*, less than one year in ten – a five-fold increase over 100 m. At the cultivation limit (300 m O.D.) the frequency is about one year in five and may double every 50 m. Perhaps this frequency of harvest failure can be viewed as the largest that could be tolerated by early farmers in Scotland. A change of climate that induced more frequent failure might lead to land abandonment.

Isopleths of accumulated temperature, resolved into isopleths of the 'frequency of harvest failure', reveal the spatial significance of

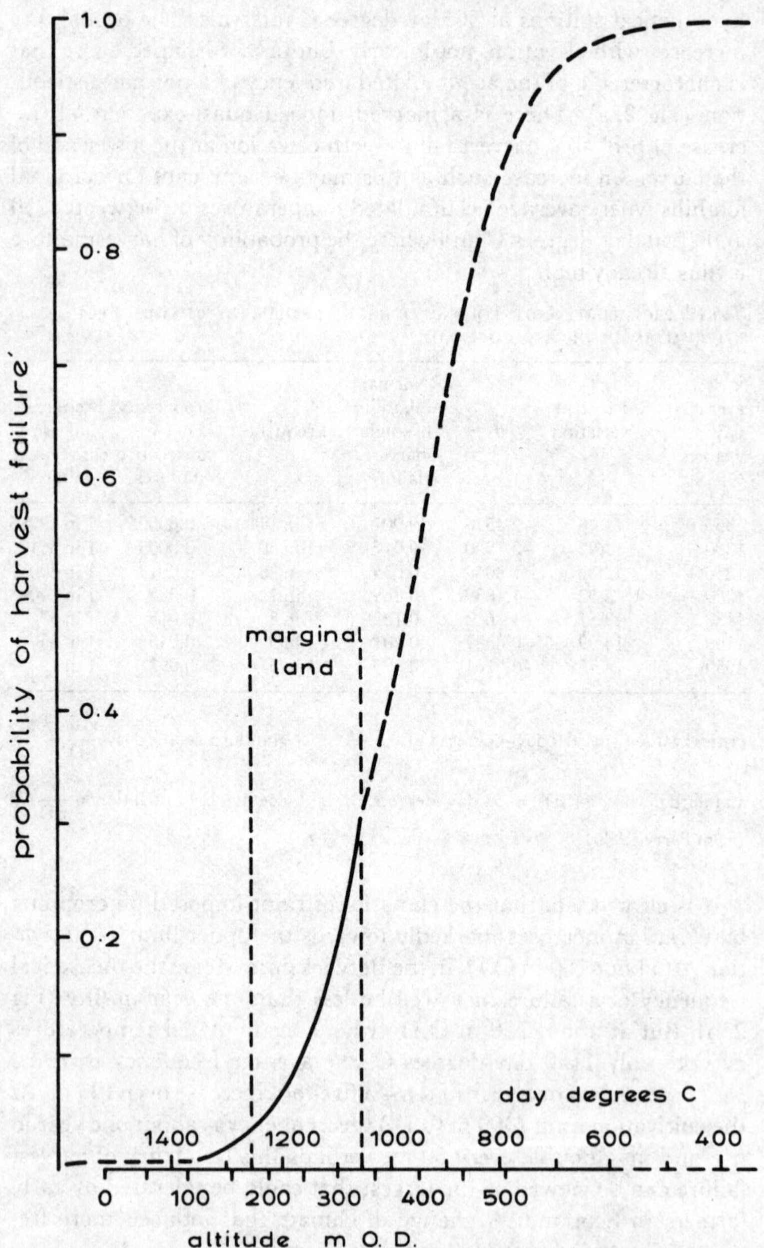

Fig. 22. Harvest failure and variable summer warmth: (a) Probability of 'harvest failure' in south-east Scotland, (b) frequency of 'harvest failure' in single and in two consecutive years in south-east Scotland. After Parry (1976).

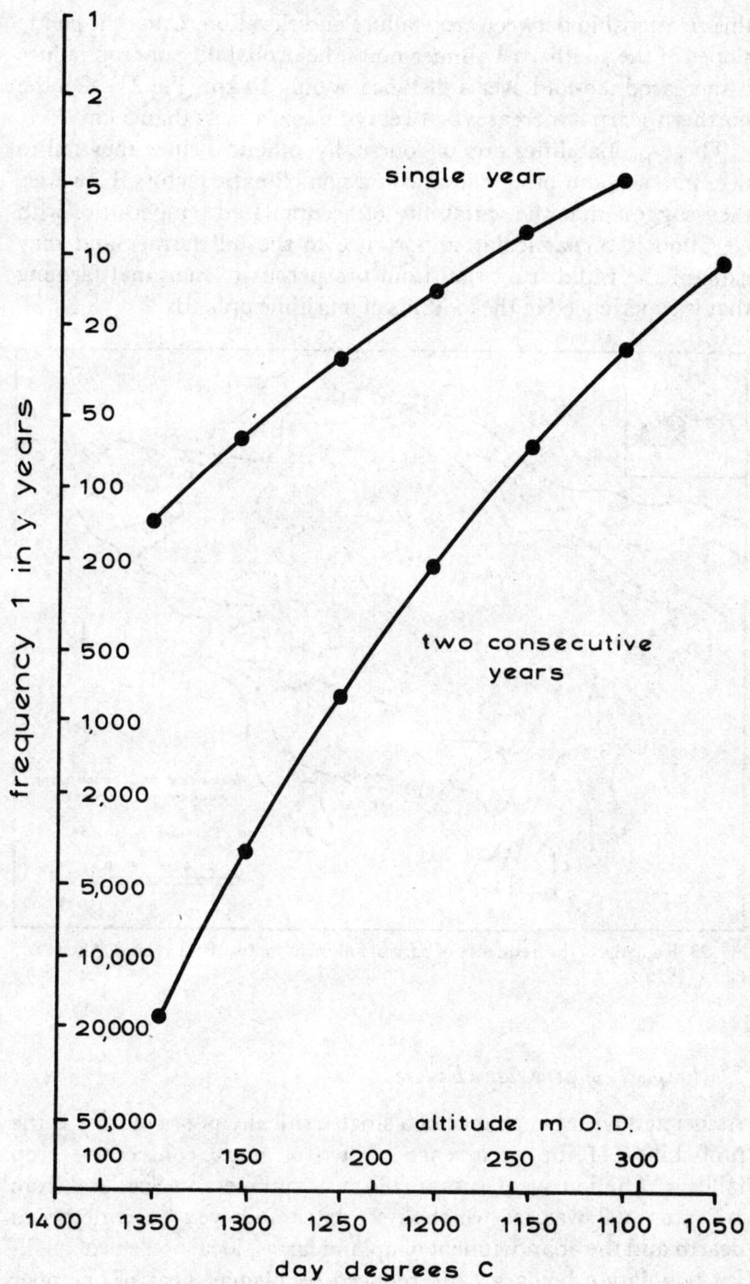
frequency 1 in y years
1
2
5
10
20
50
100
200
500
1,000
2,000
5,000
10,000
20,000
50,000
single year
two consecutive years
altitude m O. D.
100
150
200
250
300
1400
1350
1300
1250
1200
1150
1100
1050
day degrees C

this relationship between crop failure and elevation. Upon the gentle slopes of the southern Lammermuirs the probability of crop failure is increased ten-fold over a distance of only 10 km (Fig 23). On the northern scarp it increases by twenty times over less than 5 km.

These probabilities are, of course, hypothetical since they fail to take into account other climatic and non-climatic factors. However, they suggest that the variability of accumulated temperature with elevation is of particular importance to the hill farmer and may explain the rapid transition from prosperous to marginal farming that is experienced in the foothills of maritime uplands.[55]

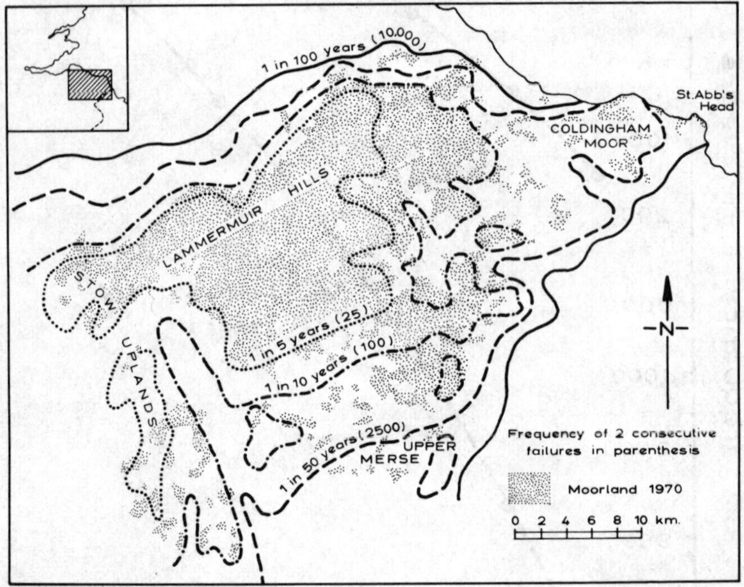

Fig. 23. Isopleths of the frequency of harvest failure in south-east Scotland. After Parry (1976).

The Frequency of Consecutive Failure

Associated with the chance of a single critically poor summer is the probability of the occurrence of two or more consecutive crop failures. The four-year run of cold, wet summers in Scotland from 1694 to 1698 was, as we shall see later, followed by widespread dearth and the abandonment of upland farms, local pockets of an ill-fed population being greatly reduced by plague. Fear of one poor summer following another must, therefore, have played an important part in the subsistence farmer's appreciation of the viability of farming marginal land.

Variations in accumulated temperature reveal a tendency toward the clustering of 'good' and 'poor' years.[56] However, if it was assumed that these were not clustered, but instead normally distributed, then a squaring of the probability of a single 'poor' year would indicate the probability of two consecutive 'poor' years (Table 2). In this case the relationship between harvest failure and elevation is strengthened (Fig 22b). In south-east Scotland the hypothetical frequency of consecutive crop failure increases 100 times with a 150 m increase in altitude. In reality, the clustering of poor years may increase the absolute frequency and may thus influence its relationship with elevation.

It can be concluded that in marginal maritime uplands such as those in Britain, Iceland and Norway the probability of harvest failure exhibits a quasi-exponential gradient. At the cultivation limit in south-east Scotland a rise of 25 m may reduce summer warmth by only 5 per cent. But this will lead to a 50 per cent increase in the frequency of failed harvests and a doubling of the frequency of two consecutive failures. It is clear, then, that small temporal changes of summer warmth, perhaps due to a more general cooling of climate, could have a marked effect on the viability of cropping at marginal upland locations. In a cooling phase, settlements on the upland fringes in north-western Europe would certainly have been placed in a position substantially more precarious than that to which they would have been accustomed. The maritime upland fringe is, therefore, one example of a marginal environment sensitive to climatic change.

But marginal zones can be readily identified in climatic regimes very different to that of north-west Europe. For example, in the Great Plains of the United States the risk of environmental hazards to agriculture is surprisingly high. The Plains farmer, generally, fails to fully appreciate these levels of risk as, indeed, do national agricultural authorities: in 1974 the statistical probability of a drought occurring before 1978, and being sufficiently severe to cause at least a 10 per cent fall in the Plains wheat harvest, was calculated to be as high as 29 per cent.[57]

In this example, as in those drawn from western Europe, it can be seen that changes of climate have two possible aspects: firstly, they involve changes in the probability of a particular occurrence at any one place, and secondly, they cause a shift in the location of frequency isopleths (e.g. crop failure) and quantity isopleths (e.g.

wetness and warmth). Such a shift may cause substantial ecological responses; for example the recent movement of the desert-steppe boundary in north-west India was due to changes in the reliability of monsoon rainfall. The probability of the monsoon bringing less than half its normal rainfall to north-west India fell from 0·116 before 1920 to 0·071 over the period 1920–60.[58]

This ecological response might be considered by the systems biologist as a homeostatic adjustment; but in a discussion of response in agriculture there is the implication of the operation of a 'theory of games' whereby farmers, confronted by uncertain conditions, make rational decisions and choose strategies that maximise the certainty and quantity of return in relation to time and effort.[59] The increasing uncertainty of a harvest determines that the rewards of reclamation in certain areas do not balance with the time and effort spent on cultivation which could be more profitably directed elsewhere. The level at which this balance fails to be achieved depends on the factors which contribute to the uncertainties of harvest and to the availability of land elsewhere.

Considered in these terms shifts of marginal agriculture, unlike shifts of vegetation zones, may be seen as the product of one, or a combination, of four causes:

(a) an incorrect appreciation by farmers, who reclaim land, of the suitability of an area for agriculture;
(b) a change in the levels of tolerance of low yields and uncertain harvests owing to the appearance of better opportunities elsewhere;
(c) changes in the farming systems, as a result of increased productivity of cropping in more favoured areas;
(d) climatic changes which reduce the suitability of once-marginal areas for agriculture.

This discussion has drawn attention to the fact that the fourth factor may be important. Temporal changes of temperature, while having a linear relationship with the intensity of summer warmth, and thus with crop yield, may have an exponential effect on changes in the frequency of harvest failure. In cold-marginal areas, at least, it seems that changes of climate could be more important a factor in agricultural change than we might, generally, have appreciated in the past.

4

Climatic Change and Changes in the Limit to Cultivation

It has been suggested that there is a range of environmental constraints on agriculture which, while operating within the context of a social, technological and political framework, may under certain conditions – conditions of extreme marginality – be a critical factor behind the location of agricultural limits; for marginal subsistence economies these constraints may determine the limits of the habitable world. However, if we accept the evidence for past changes of climate, then we must accept the possibility of shifts in limits to cultivation; and the historian of marginal communities, which were 'balanced on the margins of subsistence', should be prepared to investigate environmental changes which may have touched upon the viability of early economies.

The question arises as to whether past changes in climate occurred at such a scale, direction and time as to have created a significant movement of theoretical limits to cultivation, and whether this shift induced a real response by agriculture and settlement. This is answered by establishing the *a priori* argument for such a theoretical shift and presenting the *prima facie* case for a real response.

Shifts in Agro-Climatic Zones: The *A Priori* Argument

It is possible to assess the effects of secular trends in climate on the margins of agriculture by resolving known changes in mean temperature and rainfall into those elements of climate that have been established as critical to marginal agriculture – in upland Britain these are summer warmth, summer wetness and exposure.

Elsewhere these elements will be different, but for the present the plan is to focus upon the 'upland laboratory' in southern Scotland in order to establish the reasoning behind the argument. At a later stage it will be possible to extend the study to those other marginal zones already identified in northern Europe and in the Great Plains of the United States.

The trends in warmth and wetness will be translated into 'movements' of the theoretical climatic limit to cultivation. The area over which these limits have moved within the last millennium may then be considered as 'recurrently marginal' – here, at one time, land will have been supramarginal to cultivation and, at another time, submarginal.

Trends in Summer Warmth and Wetness

Data The trends established by Lamb and Manley for central England from A.D. 800 to 1950 are used since these probably represent the most accurate available. But it should be remembered that only the largest changes in 'high' summer rainfall and winter temperature can be regarded with a 99 per cent level of confidence; these include the particularly mild winters between 1500 and 1550, the severe period during the seventeenth century, and the 'high' summer rainfall in the late fourteenth and throughout the sixteenth centuries. Changes in annual temperature and rainfall are less firmly established, being based on an interpretation of pressure conditions indicated by summer rain and winter cold.

Regional variation The changes established for central England are accepted by Lamb as common to Scotland and the remainder of north-west Europe.[1] Moreover, Manley has found that even the short-term anomalies of temperature found in his reductions for the English Midlands are also evident in Mossman's (1896–8) series for Edinburgh.[2] Short-term trends in rainfall, even between the subregions of Scotland, tend to exhibit greater disparities, although almost all of these disappear when they are smoothed over ten-year means.[3]

Thus some of the doubts expressed over the use of English records, particularly with respect to the study of climatic change in upland Wales, are unfounded.[4] Both temperature and rainfall, considered over 50-year means, exhibit similar changes throughout the British Isles, and the general trends established for central England can, with some confidence, be used for south-east Scotland.[5]

Secular changes in accumulated temperature and PWS Lamb has calculated that both average 'high' summer and average mean annual temperatures may have fallen by more than 1·0°C over the period 1300 to 1600, and that there were corresponding changes in summer rainfall. The implications of these changes for upland cultivation can be assessed by resolving the trends into those of accumulated temperature and potential water surplus.

Estimates of the mean temperatures of 'growing months' were made by interpolating between 'high' summer and winter along a curve of régime typical for upland south-east Scotland. These were converted into a temperature accumulation and expressed as a deviation from the 1856–95 'normal'.

Changes in mean monthly rainfall and potential transpiration over the growing season were similarly established, transpiration rates being assumed to alter almost linearly with rainfall through humidity, cloudiness and radiation – the close correlation between summer temperature and summer rainfall in Scotland makes this assumption tenable.[6] The end-of-summer PWS was calculated for selected dates and expressed as a deviation from the 1856–95 'normal'. Those dates chosen for calculation broadly represent the major fluctuations of temperature and rainfall. From these dates, and by reference to the trends in Figures 11 and 12, smoothed 50-year trends of summer warmth and wetness were drawn for the period 1100–1950 for sites at the 1050 day-degree C isopleth (c. 320 m O.D.) in south-east Scotland.

Changes in exposure, particularly in the frequency of north-easterly winds, have been associated with fluctuations of temperature and rainfall,[7] but it has not been possible to quantify the changes as average windspeeds. Moreover, an assessment of the importance of changing exposure is complicated by the recent introduction of oat varieties less susceptible to wind damage, and by the recent planting of shelter belts in the uplands.

Figure 24 illustrates the changes that are produced in summer warmth and wetness by incorporating Lamb's estimates of secular changes in temperature and rainfall. It should be remembered that the early changes are based upon an uncertain climatic record and may only be used as general pointers to the fluctuation of potential for upland crop growth; with this reservation in mind, it is possible to identify four phases of change in north-west Europe:

(1) A secondary climatic 'optimum' (1150–1250)
(2) A cooling phase (1250–1450)

(3) A cold epoch (1530–1700)
(4) A warming phase (1700–1950).

The warm epoch, 1150–1250, was characterised by relatively frequent warm summers and dry autumns. The average levels of warmth and wetness at 320 m O.D. in the Lammermuirs in the thirteenth century were prevailing at elevations of only 200 m O.D. in the mid-nineteenth century; and the climatic limit to cultivation stood at over 450 m O.D. rather than at 320 m. Moreover, the high frequency of anticyclonic influence in summer is likely to have been characterised by sluggish westerly or south-westerly winds, associated with very low levels of exposure in upland and eastern Scotland. During the first phase of cooling, about 1250–1450, average summer warmth fell by 175 day-degrees C and end-of-summer PWS increased by about 70 mm. Both changes are equivalent to a rise in elevation in the Lammermuirs of 140 m. Moreover, the increased frequency of cyclonic north-easterlies is likely to have led to the greater exposure of the coastal moors, and

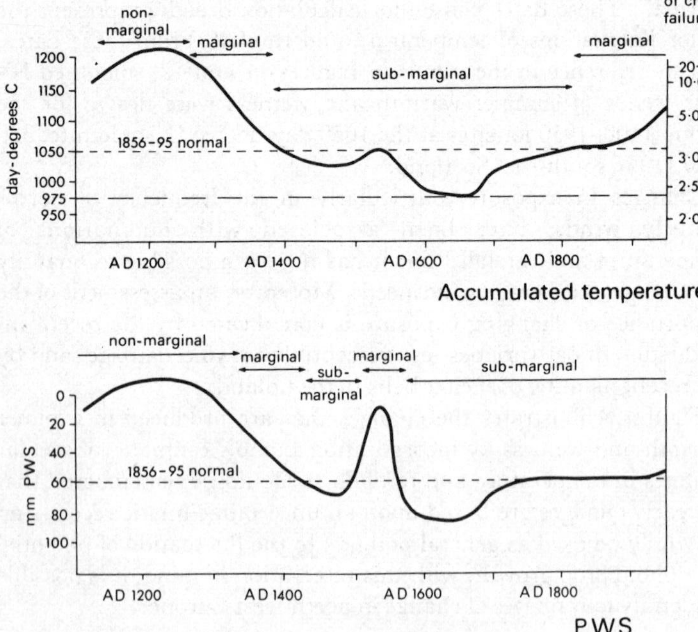

Fig. 24. Estimated trends of accumulated temperature and potential water surplus, A.D. 1000–1950, at sites on the climatic limit to cereal cultivation in 1856–95, based on 50-year averages of temperature and rainfall data. After Parry (1975).

summer wetness, exaggerated already by reduced evaporation, was probably compounded by the high incidence of especially damp autumns,[8] so that cloudiness and soil waterlogging would have severely delayed the later cereal harvest in upland areas. The increasing wetness, marked by recurrence surfaces in peat bogs throughout Europe, probably reached its short-term peak in the fourteenth century during the unbroken series of cold, wet summers from 1313 to 1317,[9] but the secular trend points to more consistently damp and cool summers in the early fifteenth and seventeenth centuries.

The cooling was temporarily checked by a short period of infrequently wet summers, which is reflected in a more marked warming of the growing season. After 1530, however, the deterioration continued with an increased incidence of wet summers, manifesting itself as a 10 per cent increase in mean 'high' summer rainfall and a 0·3°C fall in mean 'high' summer temperature over the period 1530–1600. The particularly high frequency of wet autumns between 1650 and 1700, the nadir of the cold epoch, seems to have resulted from a southward displacement of depression tracks in Europe.[10] It was clearly associated with lowered values of long-term mean temperatures and, indeed, with an increased variability of temperatures which, being already high in upland areas, would have significantly increased the frequency of crop failures. The run of severe winters and cool, damp summers in the 1690s, which brought famine to much of Scotland, is a part of this pattern of events. We shall look more closely at this run of 'the Seven Ill Years' in a later chapter, but it is interesting to note that an exceptional degree of cooling may have occurred in northern Europe owing to a southward shift of cold, polar water in the northern North Atlantic. This may have reduced temperatures in Scotland more than in England: Lamb has suggested that the coldest decade in Scotland may even have been more than 2°C cooler than the averages for 1931–60.[11] The same anomaly of sea temperature is likely to have affected southern Norway in a similar fashion,[12] and it seems that some regions which were already marginal were most severely affected by a regional trend towards excessive cooling.

But, even on the conservative basis of data for central England, it seems that over 50 years in the sixteenth century the intensity of average summer warmth at 320 m O.D. in southern Scotland fell by 6 per cent and the growing season was shortened by eight days, the equivalent of a 60-metre increase in altitude. Lamb has noted that the pessimum climate of A.D. 1550–1770 was probably a good deal colder than any previous cold phase since the major post-glacial warm epoch in 5000–3000 B.C.[13] From 1700 a trend towards warmer and slightly drier summers in Europe, interrupted only by minor and brief variations (e.g. the 1730s), placed growing conditions around 1950 at the same level as in the late thirteenth century – though well below those of the twelfth century. This was achieved through a phase of rapid warming over the period 1700–30, a longer period of little change up to about 1900, and renewed warming up to the 1940s.

Changes in Site Viability and in Probability of Harvest Failure

The implication in these trends is that, with the fluctuation of potential for upland plant growth, the theoretical climatic limit to cultivation has risen and fallen substantial distances over the last millenium. Some high-lying farmland, near the present cultivation limit, was therefore at one time climatically submarginal and at another supramarginal. It is possible to determine the dates at which the changes in the marginality of land occurred by reference to the trend line of summer warmth (Fig 24). This illustrates that land at the climatic margin of cereal cultivation in 1856–95 experienced a mean summer warmth in the 'optimum' period (1150–1250) of over 1200 day-degrees C. Even commercial cereal cultivation would thus have been possible at levels of over 300 m O.D. in Scotland in the early medieval period. The average frequency of crop failure was less than one year in twenty (Fig 24).

Deteriorating conditions in the late medieval period probably increased this frequency to 1 in 5 by the mid-fourteenth century and to more than 1 in 3 by the mid-fifteenth century. The high-lying lands in south-east Scotland probably became submarginal to commercial cereal cropping after about 1250. Indeed, at the nadir of the cold epoch the mean summer warmth was 975 day-degrees C, offering only an even chance to the full ripening of oats; and so at that time it was submarginal even to subsistence cultivation. The steady amelioration since 1700 had returned the moorland, at 300 m O.D., to the fringe of climatic marginality by the mid-nineteenth century.

The suggestion, therefore, is that, if Lamb's estimate of secular changes is correct, then the alteration to potential for crop growth in marginal, maritime uplands may have been sufficiently large to promote reclamation and subsequent abandonment. The areas in which these changes in land use may have been promoted can be identified by studying the movements of the isopleths of summer warmth and summer wetness.

Moving Climatic Limits to Cultivation

Figures 25 and 26 illustrate, at selected dates, the changing location over the last millenium of the absolute climatic limit to cultivation, the combined isopleths of 1050 day-degrees C and 60 mm PWS. The shift of these isopleths indicates the quantity and location of land whose marginal status may have been altered by secular changes in climate.

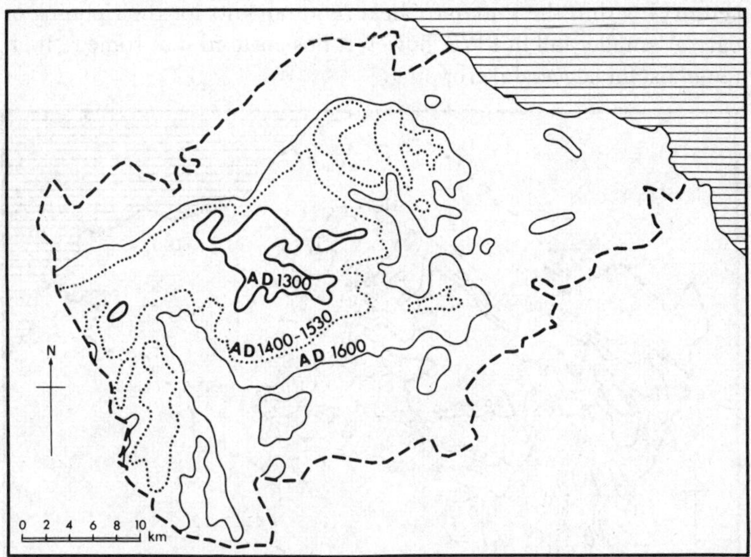

Fig. 25. Cooling A.D. 1300–1600: the 'fall' of combined isopleths of 1050 day-degrees C and 60 mm PWS in south-east Scotland. After Parry (1975).

During the warm epoch, 1150–1250, the limit to cultivation in the Lammermuirs stood at about 450 m O.D. By 1300, after the onset of the cooling phase, it had fallen by about 50 m, although all but the summits of the hills may still have been suited to cereal cropping (Fig 25).

The late medieval cooling promoted a fall, by 75 to 90 m, of the combined parameters with the result that the uncultivable upland core was more than doubled in area to 295 km². By 1600, which broadly represents average conditions existing in the cold epoch during the seventeenth century, the limits of excessive PWS had fallen to 210 m O.D., rendering much of the ill-drained moorland fringe almost certainly uncultivable. In this short, but swifter, climatic 'decline', which reached its nadir in the 1690s, at least 150 km² of foothill became submarginal to the cultivation of cereals owing to inadequate warmth and excessive spring and autumn wetness.

It is also possible to trace the spatial component of the modern warming phase by a study of the theoretical uphill advance of critical warmth and moisture levels (Fig 26). Since the late nineteenth century slowly rising mean temperatures have brought large areas of the Lammermuir Hills (about 150 km² in the last half century) within the minimum heat requirements for the ripening of oats. A smaller fall in PWS, however, has ensured that some remain too moist for successful cropping.

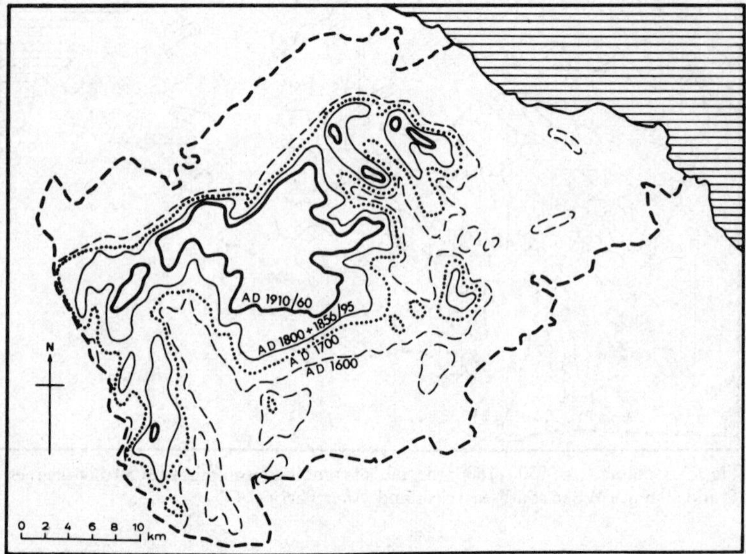

Fig. 26. Warming, A.D. 1700–1910/60: the 'rise' of combined isopleths of 1050 day-degrees C and 60 mm PWS in south-east Scotland.

It is thus possible to locate and measure those upland fringes whose status as potential agricultural land has depended upon changes in climate. We can now turn our attention to the specific environmental history of these areas.

Locating Marginal Land in Past Periods

The foothill fringe across which critical levels of warmth and wetness have shifted over the last millenium can be defined by the isopleths for A.D.1300 and 1600; these exhibit a total fall of 140 m and are mirrored by a ten-fold increase in the probability of crop failure on high-lying farmland. The land on this fringe, therefore, may be described as 'recurrently marginal', since it has at different times lain above and below theoretical climatic limits to successful cultivation. This area has been conservatively estimated because the full range of shift of climatic limits between A.D.1200 and about 1700 may have exceeded 160 m. Above it lies the zone of recurrently submarginal land which has consistently lain above average climatic limits to cultivation. Of course, the economic, rather than climatic, limits to cultivation tend also to shift with advances of technology and with changes in a whole range of other socio-economic variables; but the argument here is that changes of climate produce shifts of theoretical climatic limits to cultivation to create broad changes in marginality.

A comparison of this 'recurrently marginal land' with the climatically marginal zone illustrated in Fig 18 will indicate some locational resemblance between the two; and we have already noted a coincidence between the climatically marginal zone and fluctuations of the moorland edge. Perhaps fluctuations of the moorland edge are thus related to recurrently marginal land – the suggestion is that it is in the recurrently marginal areas that we should expect to find some ecological and economic response to changes of climate – if such responses did, indeed, occur.

Theoretical shifts in the location of climatic limits to cultivation can be mapped by adopting this methodology. For example, in the hills surrounding the Tweed Valley in southern Scotland and north-east England, about 60 per cent of the high-lying land that was sub-marginal in the seventeenth century was probably open to cereal cultivation in the early Middle Ages. Indeed, about 40 per cent was once again viable cereal land in the mid-twentieth century.

On a more extensive basis it is possible to map recurrently marginal land throughout the British Isles. In this instance it will be assumed that the general scale and direction of climatic change were roughly similar throughout the region – a point already established. Given the distribution of accumulated temperatures,[14] and recognising regional differences in temperature lapse rate, it is possible to map the general shift in climatic limits to cropping that would have resulted from the estimated changes in summer warmth which occurred in Britain between A.D.1300 and 1600. The foothill fringes over which such shifts have occurred are illustrated in Fig 27. This is based solely upon temperature accumulation, and does not account for variations in PWS – which may influence the regional pattern – and exposure – which would certainly affect land potential at the

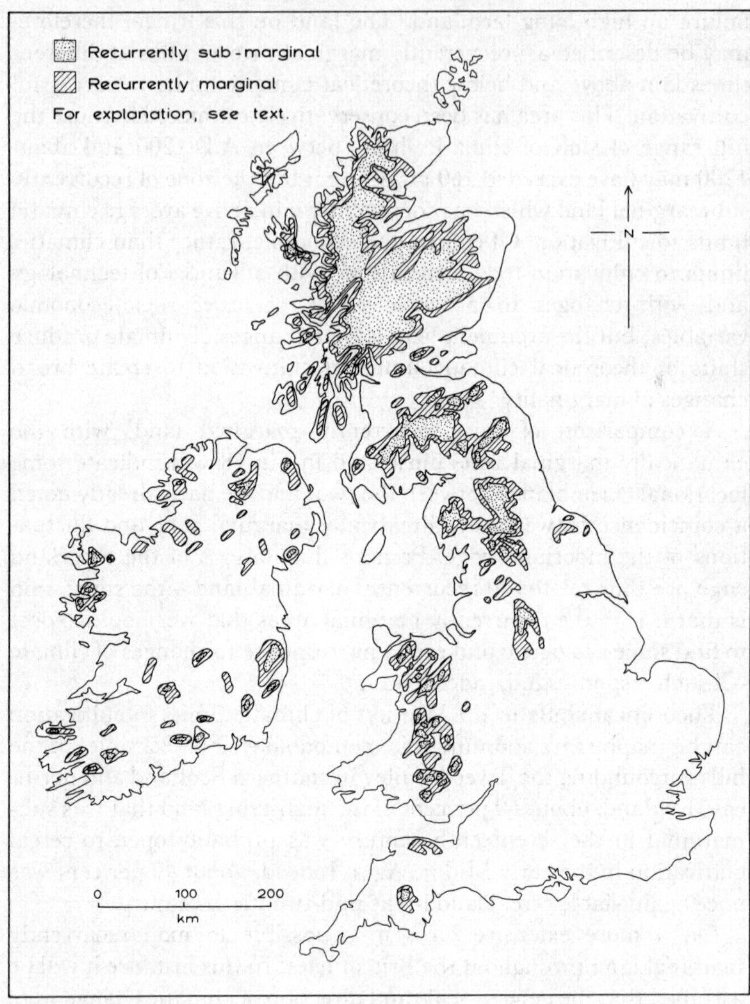

Fig. 27. Recurrently marginal land in the British Isles.

local level. Nevertheless, the synoptic distribution is instructive in pointing to the foothill zone as probably the area most strongly affected by recent changes of climate. Due to a latitudinal decline in summer warmth the zone tends to shelve northwards: on Dartmoor and Exmoor in south-west England it lies between 360 and 500 m; and the plateau nature of these uplands tends to create a quite wide belt of marginal land (Fig 27). It may be lower in north Wales, particularly where the land lies open to the west and where changes in exposure level due to anticyclonic backing of westerlies may have altered the agricultural potential of high-lying areas in Snowdonia. Indeed, there is quite extensive evidence of early settlement – both permanent and peripatetic – on the fringes of Dartmoor and Snowdonia.

In the centre and east of England the influence of easterly exposure on early summer temperatures tends to reduce accumulated warmth in the growing season. For example, in the southern Pennines and North Yorkshire Moors the recurrently marginal zone lies at 300–450 m and 290–430 m respectively. In the northern Pennines and in Scotland's Southern Uplands it lies at 260–400 m – and it is precisely in these areas that economic change has been most widespread.

However there is less certainty about the distribution of recurrently marginal land in the Scottish Highlands. Firstly, local differences in exposure are important and may have been significantly influenced by changes in the frequency of north-easterly gales, particularly in the seventeenth century. For example, in north-east Scotland the coastal estate of Culbin was covered in sand as a result of the storms in the 1690s.[15] On the other hand, more sheltered inland glens may have been little affected by increased exposure. Secondly, a westward shelving of the temperature gradient complicates the regional pattern, and of this there is no complete understanding.

In spite of these restrictions, however, it can be said that at least 2 million hectares (about one-third) of Britain's unimproved moorland were climatically viable for cereal cultivation in the early Middle Ages, and may have attracted settlement at this time. By 1600, however, this entire foothill zone was submarginal, and by 1700, which was more clearly the pessimum of the cold epoch, must have been profoundly submarginal. It is quite clear, then, that this is where the historian should look for the full economic consequences of climatic change.

The relevance of Fig 27 to the contemporary rural planner, should also be noted. The modern warm phase has returned much of Britain's uplands to a supramarginal state, potentially productive under improved, rather than moorland, uses of land. Therefore what was unattractive to pioneers in the early eighteenth century may deserve renewed interest now. Much depends, of course, upon the present trend of climate – if the very recent cooling continues unabated, then Britain's upland margins may once again become submarginal and prove the farmer right to be wary of responding hastily to environmental change.

In a similar fashion, areas that may have been especially affected by changes of climate may be identified in the climatically marginal regions of Scandinavia. Agro-meteorological studies in Norway have estimated that the minimum accumulated warmth required by the hardiest modern cereals is about 1170 day-degrees C.[16] But local modification of temperature by air movements, particularly in mountain valleys, can be great; of special importance is the effect that these can have upon the date of early autumn night frosts and, here, a more meaningful measure of growing potential may be accumulated temperature within the frost-free period. In southern Norway a heat accumulation of more than 1050°C between first and last frost is probably the minimum required for ripening, and it is interesting to speculate upon probable shifts of this theoretical limit.

In Tröndelag the lapse rate of temperature suggests that the shifts are likely to have been on about the same scale as those in Scotland – and we should remember that, as in Scotland, a southward extension of Arctic water in the seventeenth century may have brought a more severe reduction of temperature to this region than to Baltic Scandinavia. A study of data from the few meteorological stations in Tröndelag suggests that the minimum requirement of warmth may occur in the sheltered valleys (daler) and in the more exposed upland along Trondheims-fjord at greatly contrasting elevations – perhaps at 350 m and 200 m O.D. respectively. Given the scale of temperature changes that probably occurred between the Middle Ages and the 'Little Ice Age', we can suggest that the theoretical limits to cultivation fell from 450 m (in the daler) and 300 m (on the upland) in about 1300, to 300 m and 150 m in about 1600. In the particularly sheltered valleys in southern Tröndelag these limits may have been up to 50 m higher.

Figure 28 illustrates the area that is likely to have become profoundly submarginal for cereal growing in the sixteenth and seventeenth centuries.[17] We cannot be sure of its detailed pattern because changes in levels of exposure, of which we are uncertain, probably had important local consequences in the steep-sided inland valleys, but it is clear that the probable extent of this recurrently marginal land is quite remarkable. In Tröndelag, almost one-half of the land below 300 m may have become submarginal at the nadir of the 'Little Ice Age' owing to reduced summer warmth. Only the coastal plains around Trondheims-fjord and Namsos would not have been seriously affected; and in the upper valleys of Namdalen, Gauladalen and Orkdalen – some of the many deep valleys that penetrate the upland shield – submarginality would

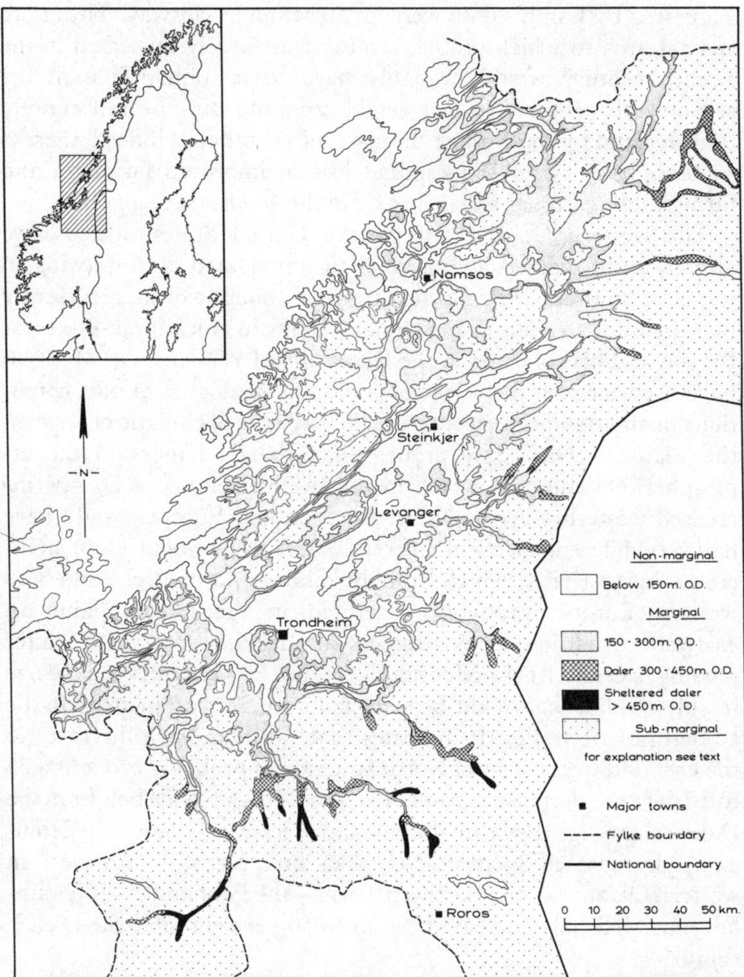

Fig. 28. Recurrently marginal land in southern Norway.

have arrived in the late Middle Ages and been maintained for several centuries. Farming communities which had been widely established in these valleys in the Middle Ages, would have faced a difficult time; and Tröndelag is not untypical of settled areas in Norway. In the region north and east of Oslo, recurrent marginality is likely to have occurred at similar levels – indeed, its effect in terms of the proportion of the settled area that was affected may have been substantially greater.

In Iceland the probable consequences of the scale of cooling suggested by Lamb's data were greater than in Norway. The entire coastal area to which arable farming was largely restricted in the twelfth century would probably have been submarginal in the seventeenth century. In fact cereal cropping disappeared entirely from Iceland by the close of the sixteenth century;[18] indeed, there is evidence of relatively widespread loss of improved farmland and farm buildings under advancing ice in the 1690s, (see page 128).

The western Great Plains of the United States, which have already been defined as marginal to unirrigated corn growing in terms of summer rainfall, also may be thought of as recurrently marginal due to shifts in the climatic limits to cultivation. Professor Bryson and his colleages in the University of Wisconsin at Madison have used modern meteorological data as analogues of past conditions in an attempt to reconstruct the patterns of climatic change on the Plains.[19] They have argued that global changes in the atmospheric circulation, which in the twelfth century A.D. saw increased westerlies across North America and Europe, would have had very different effects in different places. After about 1150, an increase in westerlies, which brought milder and moister winters to western Europe, probably generated in the Great Plains an eastward extension of a wedge of air dried by subsidence after passing over the Rocky Mountains. Figure 29 illustrates the change in July rainfall that might be expected from such an increase in the strength of westerlies. It indicates that, while causing increases to the east and west coasts of North America, it probably brought a 25 to 50 per cent decrease in rainfall across a 500-km wide belt from the Dakotas through Iowa to Illinois and a lesser, though still significant, decrease in western Nebraska and Kansas. However, in western Oklahoma and northern Texas – the Panhandle – July rainfall may well have increased by up to 50 per cent after the twelfth century.

If this modern analogue is correct, then it is apparent from a comparison of Figs 21 and 29 that the marginal status of part of the Great Plains would have been seriously affected by changes in the global circulation. For example, western Kansas and Nebraska, which were already marginal in terms of summer rainfall, may by the fourteenth century have become submarginal; and, by contrast, the once marginal Panhandle may have become more attractive to early Indian cultivators. The implication is that these areas, as well as parts of Iowa and the Dakotas, are *a priori* recurrently marginal and that ecological and cultural responses (if any) are likely to have been most marked here.

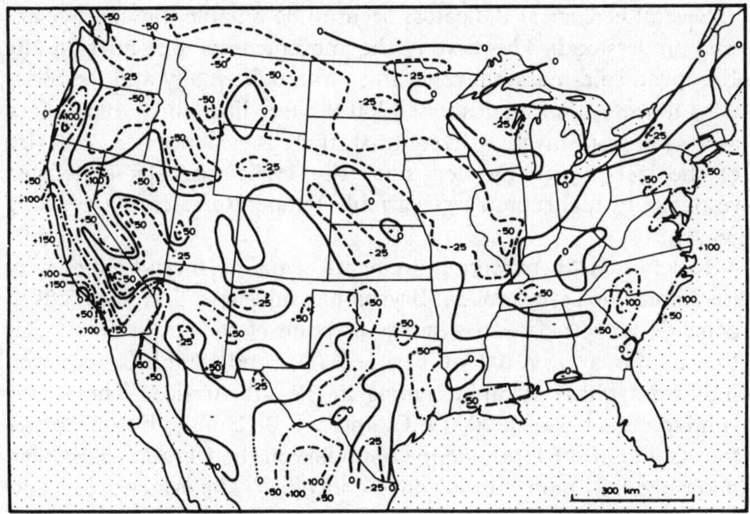

Fig. 29. July precipitation changes in North America to be expected with a change from weak westerlies to strong westerlies expressed as a percentage change of the weak westerly mean rainfall. Based on twenty years of modern data. After Baerreis and Bryson (1968).

Shifts in Ecological Boundaries – The *Prima Facie* Case

Interposed between environmental change and cultural response is a host of social, economic and political factors which operate in human communities; and it would be deterministic in the extreme to propose a direct link between the two. The socio-economic factors mediate – sometimes moderating, sometimes negating – between environmental change and cultural response. The relationship is indirect.

However, we can expect a more direct relationship between climatic change and certain ecological changes, particularly if we take a systems-type view of energy transfers within the natural environment. It is therefore likely that a survey of ecological changes would provide evidence of the biological significance of past fluctuations in climate, and furnish a *prima facie* case for the importance to the environment as a whole of climatic fluctuations in hypersensitive, marginal areas; though there is a risk of circular argument from the use of biological evidence to determine climatic fluctuations to pronouncements about probable biological changes that might have resulted from such fluctuations.

Several ecological indicators seem to be reliable, though few are well understood. The first is the movement of tree-lines in the European cold-marginal zone. In southern Germany and the Swiss Alps it seems that after about 1300 the tree-line fell by 100–200 m and 70 m respectively.[20] In contrast, there is evidence of a 20 m rise of the tree-line in Sweden since the 1930s, perhaps a delayed response to higher and less variable temperatures in the growing season.[21]

In addition, there were movements of the northern boundary of the boreal forest in Canada. Bryson has suggested that this tends to coincide with the mean summer position of the Arctic front, and that its retreat over 200 km between 1900 and 1800 B.C. may well indicate a phase of rapid cooling in the sub-Arctic.[22] These, and similar shifts between 2000 B.C. and 500 B.C. of the European oak forests and of the forest-steppe boundary in the Ukraine, have been described by Lamb, Lewis and Woodruffe.[23] The evidence is scant, and care must be taken to account for man-induced changes in vegetation. However, there is a clearer picture developing from recent pollen studies of coincident shifts in vegetation boundaries that apparently reflect an alteration of the climatic environment.

Such changes are also mirrored, of course, in shifts in the firn (or snow) line and of the limit of permafrost. In western Norway the firn line seems to have fallen about 150 m between the eleventh and seventeenth centuries[24] – a shift that is likely to have had a pronounced influence on the use of saeters (upland summer pastures) and improved 'inbye' land during the cold epoch (Fig 30).

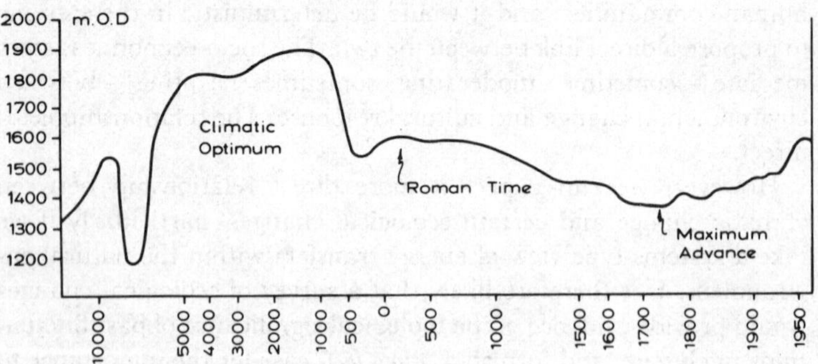

Fig. 30. The firn line in west Norway in post-glacial time. After Liestol (1960).

In the Scottish Highlands, for which we have suggested a similarly exaggerated range of cooling in the 'Little Ice Age', there are reports of perennial snow-lie on the Cairngorms almost throughout the eighteenth century.[25]

These ecological and hydrological responses, which exhibit a measurable shift of location, tend to support the notion that substantial movements of climatic 'boundaries' have occurred in the quite recent past. Moreover, there is now an appreciation of the speed of such responses: in addition to the exponential changes in the probability of achieving certain growth thresholds that occur with climatic fluctuations, there may be a quasi-exponential response by vegetation growth to climatic change. Moreover, there is an awareness of the remarkable pace of landform creation and destruction that can occur with fluctuations of rainfall. For example, in the south-west United States it seems that quite large arroyos (or gulches) and alluvial fans – indeed a whole landscape – were created in the late nineteenth century partly due to short-term increases in precipitation.[26]

Both the scale and pace of environmental change in recurrently marginal areas point to the particular significance here of past changes of climate. We can now investigate the scale of response by early agriculture and settlement.

5

The Shift of Cultivation Limits in North-West Europe

Along the sensitive margin of upland-maritime Europe the evidence for economic change is sometimes scant. Indeed, the very nature of these areas – at the edge of the sedentarily habitable world – would have discouraged the development of a comprehensive archaeological or documentary record. Consequently, we know little of their agricultural history.

However, there are signs that, in these areas, there has been a substantial movement of the cultivation limit. We shall now look at these long-term shifts of the cultivation limit in order to assess their timing and extent; thereafter, it will be possible to evaluate the relationship between these shifts and those changes of climate that we know to have been marked in the marginal areas of north-west Europe.

Attention will be given to those recurrently marginal regions in which we have hypothesised the occurrence of significant changes in the location of climatic limits to cultivation – changes which may have been sufficiently great to promote an agricultural response. The question now posed is: what was the scale and timing of agricultural change in these regions, and how coincident are these with the shifts of climatic limits to cultivation? The response to this question is made with reference, in turn, to upland Scotland, to the remainder of upland Britain, to Iceland, Norway and finally to other parts of Scandinavia.

Retreat of the Upland Margin in Scotland

The saying that when the Devil showed God all the countries of the world he kept his thumb over Scotland, has a genuine medieval ring to it. In the sixteenth century foreign visitors commented on the low level of Scottish husbandry – a product as much of the institutional structure of its agriculture as of its resource base. The people of Scotland could not make the best use of the relatively limited arable land; and over long periods they lived on such narrow margins that any disturbance, human or climatic, caused alarm.[1] Mass famine was frequently the product of uncertain weather towards the end of the sixteenth century; and this was compounded when rural life was dislocated, in the south by English invasion, and in the north by political anarchy and governmental weakness.

Over the short term a complex mix of these different factors affected the limits to which successful cultivation had been pushed; and over the long-term there was a substantial shift of cultivation limits. The problem now is that because long-term trends were seldom apparent to those who lived through them – the experience of a lifetime was too short to detect a major change – small changes were not communicated to later generations. There is, therefore, little contemporary documentation of any long-term shift of the cultivation limit. We must look instead to the landscape record.

The Distribution of Abandoned Farmland

In southern Scotland the quantity of once-improved farmland that now lies under moor is substantial. The high-water mark of cultivation, which was often reached in the twelfth century, now lies stranded in the heather high above the present limits of improved farmland. It is possible to map the distribution of this abandoned farmland from aerial photographs and by field survey. In the Lammermuir Hills the quantity of abandonment is surprising: more than 11,440 hectares, or about 21 per cent, of the existing moorland of these hills show signs of former cultivation in the shape of plough ridges, small enclosures and settlement sites.[2] Ordnance Survey maps dating from about 1860 show that 4890 hectares of this land reverted permanently to moorland before the mid-nineteenth century; and from a study of the typology of the ridges we can say that 2990 hectares were probably abandoned before 1800, since they exhibit the curved and high-backed characteristics of early plough ridges that were, in general, subject to improvement by straightening and levelling in the late eighteenth century.[3] Of this area, about 700 hectares (23 per cent) lie above the climatic limit to cultivation established for the period 1856–95 (Fig 31). Indeed, about 200 hectares stand at least 40 m above and some even more than 100 m above the nineteenth century limits. At this elevation, under nineteenth century conditions, average summer warmth would not have exceeded 915 day-degrees C and, on average, harvests would have 'failed' in two out of every three years.

Yet most of these traces of cultivation are the relics of longstanding, regular cropping and were associated with high-level settlement which had been established in the early Middle Ages. Fifteen of these settlements were probably abandoned before 1600, two of them lying well beyond the absolute climatic limits of 1856–95 (Fig 31). Of a further eighteen settlements deserted

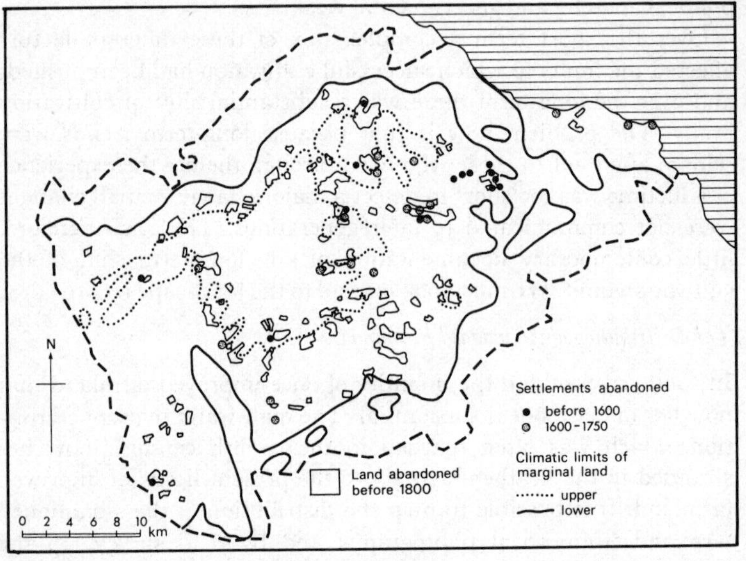

Fig. 31. Abandoned farmland and climatically marginal land in south-east Scotland. After Parry (1975).

between about 1600 and 1750, five lie on or above the limit.[4] Thus the *prima facie* evidence points to continuous, successful cultivation and settlement at elevations quite unsuited to cereal cropping in the nineteenth century.

Most of this abandonment seems to have been of land first reclaimed in the early medieval period. The reclamation is unlikely to have occurred any earlier because the mould-board plough, which was necessary for the construction of the high-backed ridges, did not appear in southern Scotland until the eleventh or twelfth centuries.[5] Here the advance of improved land was closely tied to the award of block grants of upland to abbeys in the Berwickshire lowlands; and a study of place-names, both in the charters of these

Plates 7 and 8. Cultivation ridges under light snow at 275 m O.D. on the Lammermuir Hills, south-east Scotland. This land attracted permanent settlement in the early Middle Ages, but was abandoned to moor in the late seventeenth century. Photos: M. L. Parry.

grants and in the rentals of abbey land, suggests that the maximum extent of cultivation in many parts of the Lammermuir Hills was probably achieved in the early thirteenth century, but never again exceeded – a pattern that is reflected throughout much of upland Britain.[6] The scale of this upland farming was substantial: for example, in 1300, one grange of Kelso Abbey, which stood at 300 m O.D. (the very limit of modern cultivation), contained two carucates (c. 108 hectares) of tillage, 1,400 sheep, and sixteen cottages for shepherds and their families;[7] and it is clear that, while the upland granges were largely devoted to livestock, cultivation was a permanent feature of the farming system.[8]

Evidence for the specific location of the cultivation limit in the twelfth and thirteenth centuries is limited by the lack of extant documents. However, the distribution of monastic granges, several of which lie above the 300 m contour, and the location of secular farming settlements give some indication of the limit. For example, the farm of Tollis Hill, sited at 365 m O.D. and active in 1252, was clearly associated with cultivation extending upwards to 425 m O.D.[9] This may be the highest level in northern Britain for which there is firm evidence of medieval cultivation.

The pace of advance may have been greatest in the late twelfth century. Near the summit of the Stow Uplands at elevations above 275 m O.D., the demand for ploughland seems to have been sufficiently strong in 1170 to invoke strictures against further reclamation.[10] It seems that cereal cultivation was practised at these high levels in the twelfth century under little restraint from cold, wetness or exposure.

Retreat in the Late Middle Ages

A substantial reversion of farmland to moor seems to have occurred before 1600. Most of this was later reclaimed, but some remained permanently as moor and is clearly linked with the sites of twelve deserted settlements which have been plotted from aerial photographs. Some of these sites can be confirmed and named by reference to monastic charters, but most remain unconfirmed by documentary evidence. A further twelve farms named in the charters cannot be located on relatively comprehensive surveys that date from about 1600.[11]

The distribution of late medieval abandonment is exhibited in Fig 32. It shows a remarkable coincidence with the upland zone which became submarginal, due to reduced temperatures and increased wetness, between about A.D.1300 and A.D.1530. At least 235 hectares stand above the climatic limit to cultivation in 1530, and most of the remainder lies in the zone which became climatically marginal. Moreover, of the fifteen settlements which were deserted over the same period, four were sited well above, and a further two close to the climatic limit to cultivation in the sixteenth century. Eight of the remainder lie on the coastal moors of Quixwood and Coldingham which were probably severely exposed to more frequent easterly gales in the sixteenth century.

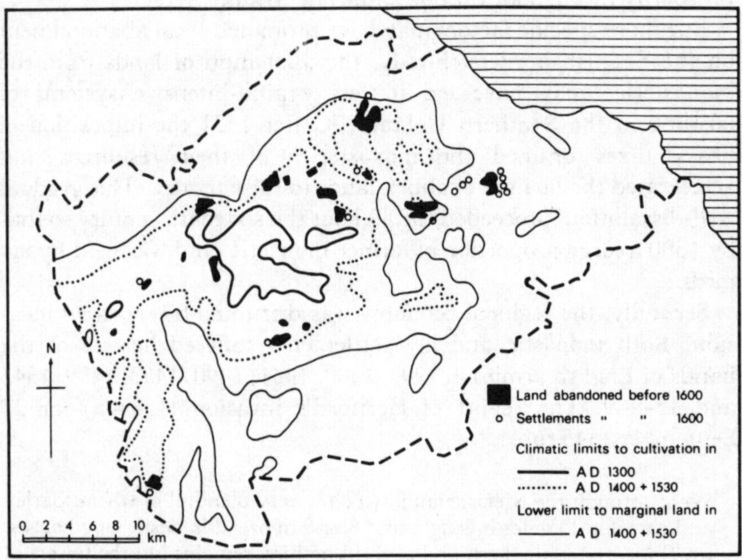

Fig. 32. Abandoned farmland and lowered climatic limits to cultivation in south-east Scotland, 1300–1600. After Parry (1975).

It is probable that much more farmland than that illustrated in Fig 32 reverted to moor in the late Middle Ages, but most was recovered before 1860. The balance, which was never reclaimed, may represent the response to a long-term increase in the disparity between potential for crop growth and the medieval limit of cultivation. Of course, a spatial correlation does not necessarily reflect an underlying causal one, and it is not suggested that climatic change was the most important factor in the abandonment of land. Indeed, it is likely that a whole range of social, economic and political factors provided the immediate stimulus for change – but it is evident that the long-term change of climate since the mid-thirteenth century had steadily reduced the potential for successful cereal cultivation in these marginal uplands. It increased both the sensitivity of agriculture to these stimuli and their long-term, rather than ephemeral, impact upon land use.

The immediate causes of a retreat from the uplands may have been numerous. A factor traditionally held to be important was the substantial decline of population, due to plague, in the fourteenth century. Also significant may have been the impoverishment of marginal farmland and a consequent decline in productivity. These two factors may account, in part, for the decline in agricultural prosperity throughout Europe in the late Middle Ages.

But more specific factors may have promoted local abandonment on the Scottish borders. Firstly, the alienation of lands from the monasteries may have led to less capital-intensive systems of farming in the Southern Uplands.[12] After 1531 the imposition of heavy taxes drained the monasteries of their resources and accelerated the 'feuing' of abbey lands to raise money. This gradual 'self-dissolution' proceeded throughout the sixteenth century so that by 1580 a large proportion of former monastic land was held by lay lords.[13]

Secondly, the regional economy was disrupted by repeated invasion. Both monastic and lay settlements suffered heavily at the hands of English armies in 1297–1300, 1461, 1490, 1497, 1499, 1542 and 1544–9. The report of Hertford's invasion (1544–5) for 27 September 1545 runs:

> Went through the Mersseland, which is very plentiful of wheat, barley and oats, for 20 miles in length and 8 or 9 in breadth, destroying houses, towers, corn, cattle, herb and peel till nothing remains but the towers of the lairds of Langton, Fermyhurst, and two or three others who are sworn English and protected by the lieutenant and council[14]

In some upland parishes it seems that more than half the farm-towns were burned in 1545,[15] whilst, following the earlier invasions of 1497 and 1499, it was reported in the Exchequer Rolls that the lands were so wasted that either they were not laboured or the crops were destroyed.[16] Persistent discouragement such as this, particularly to marginal upland farming, may have led to a decline in cultivation. It certainly accelerated the process of alienation of monastic lands for the loss of rents from pillaged granges and the debts incurred in reparations were often balanced by feuing large possessions. In 1549 the lands of Landshaw and Housebyres in the Stow Uplands were feued by the monks of Melrose to James Hopringle of Smailholm, 'on consideration of monies paid to them in their urgent necessity and for the use of the monastery now burnt by the English and to be applied in repairing the same . . .'[17]

It is not easy to distinguish the relative roles of the short-term socio-economic stimuli of change and the long-term changes occurring in the natural environment, but we can say that the Black Death, the decay of the monastic farming system, the fluctuation of demand or soil exhaustion may have 'triggered' the decision to retreat from less-favoured farming sites, but that long-term changes of climate may have tended to compound their influence. It made high-level agriculture and settlement particularly sensitive to any socio-economic or physical changes which touched upon their viability, and it may be argued that, had there not been this secular deterioration, then the immediate stimuli might have promoted a less widespread and a less permanent response.

This conclusion is given some support by the occurrence of blanket peat overlying medieval tillage. At Penshiel, a monastic grange at about 283 m O.D. in the central Lammermuirs, high-backed cultivation ridges of the type associated with early mouldboard ploughing disappear beneath the downward edge of a mass of hill peat that covers an adjacent hill. A study of aerial photographs of different dates has revealed that since at least the mid-1940s the peat edge has retreated uphill, exposing as it retreats the early plough ridges.

Burial by peat growth in this way is not uncommon, and there is abundant palynological evidence of bog development in cool, moist phases of climate, but in Europe this has been identified more with the prehistoric than the modern period. For example, peat burial of Bronze Age sites in Ireland and Scotland has frequently been commented upon; these are now being re-exposed, as the peat retreats, for the first time since their probable date of burial after about 2000 B.C.[18] However, 'peat burial' during the pessimum period of the seventeenth century, which must account for its superimposition on early tillage at Penshiel, is less widely recorded. At about 260 m O.D. on Bodmin Moor in Cornwall, medieval plough-ridges associated with a farmstead occupied probably from the thirteenth up to the fifteenth century, are reported to 'run into' a peat bog,[19] but the evidence for other upland areas is scant.

Retreat During the 'Little Ice Age'

Figure 33 illustrates the quantity and distribution of upland settlement in the Lammermuir Hills between 1583 and 1648. It has been reconstructed from the surveys of Timothy Pont and Robert and James Gordon which were published in Blaeu's *Atlas Novus* in 1654.[20] The settlement pattern is the most convenient indicator of the location of existing farmland that may have become marginal or submarginal in the cold epoch. Of 405 farmsteads in the Lammermuir Hills known to have been occupied at the onset of the cold epoch, twenty were sites that had probably already become submarginal by 1530. A further sixty-two became submarginal over the period 1530–1600 and about 120 became marginal. It is clear, then, that a sizeable proportion of the upland settlement is likely to have been affected by the climatic trend.

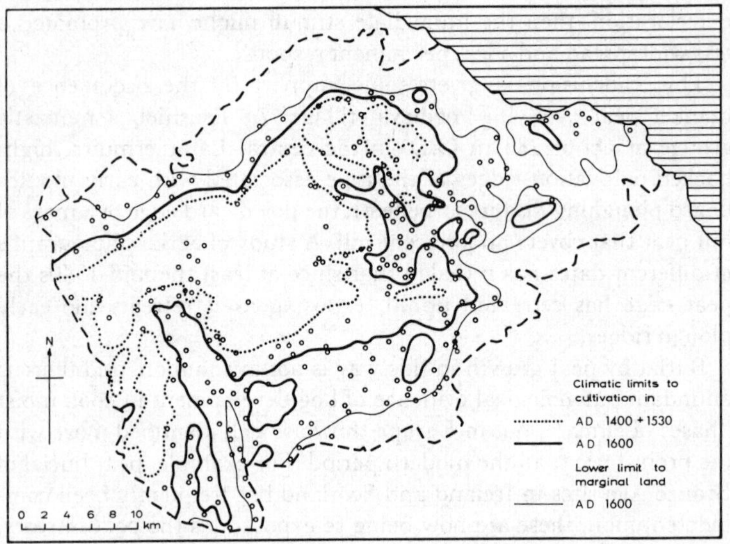

Fig. 33. The distribution of marginal settlement in about 1600 in south-east Scotland.

Indeed, the marginal nature of these farmsteads is reflected in the rate at which they were deserted (Fig 34). For example, three steadings which had become submarginal by 1530 were abandoned before 1750.[21] A further six disappeared from the fringe which became theoretically submarginal over the period 1530–1600, while only three marginal and no non-marginal steadings disappeared.

Figure 34 also illustrates the distribution of 2290 hectares of cultivated farmland which permanently reverted to moorland between 1600 and 1800. More than 80 per cent of this area lies between the isopleths for 1530 and 1600 of the climatic limit to cereal cultivation; in other words, probably became submarginal to cultivation in the sixteenth century.

There is, therefore, a coincidence between the retreat of cultivation and a trend to increasing climatic submarginality. Indeed, it would be remarkable if the highest cultivation had not been abandoned, as in the seventeenth century some farmland would have had to tolerate an average frequency of harvest failure as high as two years in five.

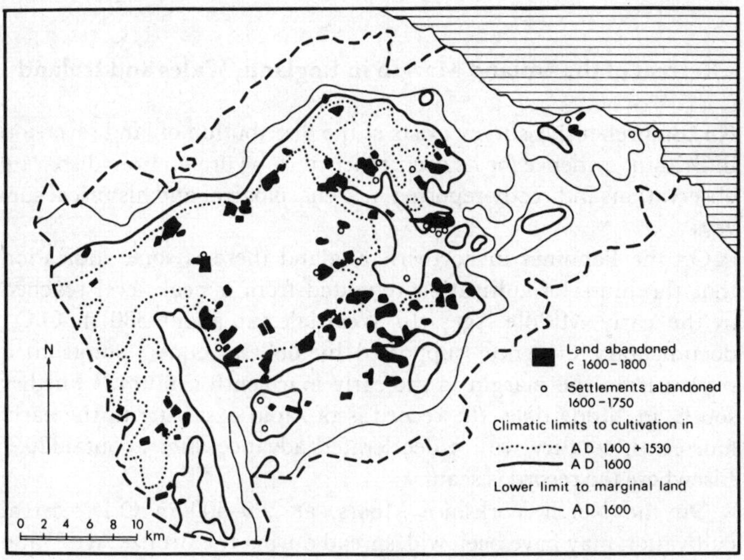

Fig. 34. Abandoned farmland and lowered climatic limits to cultivation in south-east Scotland, 1600–1750. After Parry (1975).

However, a firm and direct causal relationship cannot be established without detailed documentary evidence, and it is unlikely that this is available. The relationship might have been felt indirectly through changes in productivity and in the incidence of harvest failure, in other words through the influence of weather on crop growth. Short-term changes of climate, which may often have been the immediate stimuli to abandonment, were therefore a medium through which long-term shifts of climate may have affected the use of land, but we have implied that they are likely to have accounted for the permanent reversion of cultivation only in areas that had become submarginal to cereal growth through long-term changes of climate.

The incidence of poor harvest weather is thus reflected in the general trend that we have studied – and the influence of weather in the short-term is a matter to which we shall return in Chapter 7. At this point, however, we may only conclude that there is a spatial and temporal coincidence in south-east Scotland between a trend towards climatic submarginality on the upland fringe and a trend towards the permanent abandonment of cultivated farmland. Confirmation of these coincident trends may now be sought elsewhere in Britain and Scandinavia.

Retreat of the Upland Margin in England, Wales and Ireland

No comprehensive survey exists of the distribution of land reversion in Britain; evidence for its occurrence must be drawn from disparate observations indirectly reported in archaeological and historical surveys.

On the Pennines in northern England there is some indication that the limits of cultivation retreated from a peak level reached in the early Middle Ages. In Weardale, at about 380 m O.D., documentary evidence, supported by pollen counts, points to a retreat from the margin in the early fourteenth century.[22] Further south, in Nidderdale, the record is of rapid assarting in the early fourteenth century with a decelerated advance after about 1320.[23] Elsewhere the record is scant.

On the North Yorkshire Moors, at 200–300 m O.D., cereal cultivation may have been widespread during the Bronze Age,[24] and a second peak was probably achieved between A.D. 1100 and 1300, with subsequent reversion in the late fourteenth century.[25] By the 1320s some reversion had occurred; this has been ascribed to the lasting effects of poor harvests, during the period 1315–17, compounded by Scottish raids and by soil exhaustion.[26] In the Yorkshire Dales, and to a lesser extent on the North Yorkshire Moors, uncultivated land was widely reported in 1342.[27]

Dartmoor also exhibits evidence of widespread cultivation in the Bronze Age at elevations of around 500 m O.D., well beyond the present limit of cultivation.[28] These areas lie at about the present climatic limit to cultivation on Dartmoor, but well below those theoretical limits pertaining in the early Middle Ages and during the earlier Climatic Optimum, about 6000 to 3000 B.C., when the entire plateau would have, on average, experienced growing seasons as long as those now occurring at only 400 m O.D.

As on the North Yorkshire Moors, a second peak of advance, extending up to 350 m on both Dartmoor and Exmoor, seems to have occurred during the period A.D. 1100–1300.[29] Thereafter the record is of reverting cultivation and deserted settlements. Archaeological study of two farmsteads, both above 300 m O.D., has indicated desertion in the late medieval period.[30] One is clearly associated with medieval fields and cultivation ridges which run into blanket peat bog, an occurrence that has been interpreted as evidence of cooler and more moist conditions since the time of cultivation.[31]

In Snowdonia, North Wales, Jones has found signs of temporary outfield cultivation and settlement between 350 m and 450 m on the south side of Bwlch y Groes. These had been described as 'plough lands' in a record of 1352.[32] More generally, Snowdonia shared the experience of other northern lands in the medieval period, and Jones concluded that there occurred a period of high culture from about 1070 to around 1300, followed by a climatic deterioration with adverse effects on the economy.[33] Even the English army seems to have suffered, being thus described by the chronicler John Harding in the fifteenth century:

> The Kyng Henry thryce to Wales went,
> In the haye time and haruest dyuers yere,
> In euery time were mystes and tempestes sent,
> of wethers foule that he had neuer power
> Glendour to noye, but euer his caryage clere
> Owen had at certain straites and passage
> And to our host dyd full greate damage.
>
> (*Annales Henrici Quarti*)[34]

Little is known of medieval retreat in Ireland, although retreat has been detected;[35] there is more widespread evidence of Neolithic and Bronze Age field systems under blanket peat both in the north and west of the country.[36]

The disparate evidence of abandonment in England, Wales and Ireland seems, therefore, to confirm the patterns found in south-east Scotland – the extensive, often permanent, abandonment in the late Middle Ages of land that, sometimes, had been successfully cultivated since the eleventh century. In this history of abandonment there are two factors which correspond to those changes of climate that are believed to have occurred during this period. Firstly, limits of cultivation in the early Middle Ages appear frequently to have occurred at elevations well above present climatic limits to cultivation. Secondly, the timing and distribution of land reversion in the late Middle Ages shows a general coincidence with those 'recurrently marginal' upland fringes that probably became submarginal to cereal cultivation between about 1300 and 1600.

Arable Contraction on the English Lowlands

There is also much evidence of reduced cultivation in lowland and non-marginal areas in Britain in the fourteenth century; but it would probably be wrong to offer for this a climatic explanation. Its explanation has generally been sought in a confusing variety of socio-economic as well as environmental factors.

It seems that contraction first occurred on the least productive land – what Beresford termed 'half-wanted' land[37] – and it may have become more widespread with loss of manpower due to plague in the mid-fourteenth century. Beresford and St. Joseph suggest that it may have been common for mid-sixteenth century villages to have had arable land occupying no more ground than in the years before the Black Death; they refer to a passage by the Elizabethan surveyor, John Norden, to illustrate the contemporary picture:

> Because we saw not the earth's former deformities, we dreame as it was then, as now it is, faire and fruitfull, free from bryers bushes and thornes whereof they found it full . . . And this field wherein now we are may be an instance, for you see by the ancient ridges or lands though now overgrowne with bushes, it hath been arable land.[38]

The balance of evidence now suggests that contraction, both of arable land and of population, may have occurred before the Black Death. The *Nonarum Inquisitiones,* a valuation of agricultural production in 1341, points to large numbers of villages with uncultivated lands throughout England.[39] The most common reasons for abandonment, given by the contemporary jurors, were a shrinkage of village populations, a shortage of seed corn, soil exhaustion and a shortage of plough teams. The supply of seed corn and draught stock was, of course, closely related to the size of harvest. The loss of some lands in Cambridgeshire was directly ascribed to flooding.[40]

Most of this reversion was short-term. There was, for example, no re-establishment of woodland or scrub on the scale of that occurring in central Europe at this time.[41] It seems likely that any climatic element in the explanation of this occurrence was one of short-term rather than long-term trend; and there is some reason for believing that causes of the contraction of arable land were the serious decline in cereal yields over the period 1315–22, and the severe losses of sheep and cattle due to plague – possibly rinderpest and liver-fluke – the remarkable virulence of which would probably have been related to the weather. Kershaw has concluded from his study of the crisis years that, while a monocausal explanation would be simplistic, the wet, cool summers and disastrous harvests of 1314–16 and 1320–21 did produce a turning point in agricultural development in the Middle Ages.[42] From this arises the hypothesis that although the calamitous situation was shaped by the drying up of colonisable land together with falling yields on exhausted soils, the proliferation of smallholders on the verge of starvation, and other trends, it may have been the succession of bad seasons that triggered the crisis.[43]

It may be, in areas not climatically marginal to cereal cultivation, that the relative roles of socio-economic change, on the one hand, and environmental change, on the other, are reversed. Here, short-term variations of climate, which affect the yield of harvests in particular years or over short 'runs' of years, may act as the trigger of change in agriculture that was responsive because of more long-term changes in its economic, social or institutional base.

It is only at the climatic margin, however, that long-term changes in climate, are likely to have significantly altered the agricultural resource base. Apart from upland areas in Britain, the results of these changes may have been most marked in Iceland and Scandinavia.

Abandonment in Iceland

The cultivation of barley was once widespread in Iceland in the twelfth century. By 1350 it was limited to a few sites on the south of the island, had completely vanished by the end of the sixteenth century, and was only reintroduced, on an experimental basis, in the 1920s.[44] From landscape and place-name evidence, and from references in saga literature, ecclesiastical deeds and other documents, it is certain that grain cultivation occurred throughout the low-lying areas on the south and west coasts of Iceland, and may have been scattered along the north and east coasts. The tillage and the settlement associated with it was quite densely developed: at Faxaflói on the south-west coast Thorarinson has found evidence of more than sixty farmsteads likely to have been engaged in cereal cropping during the twelfth century; some of them are sited beyond the coastal plain at elevations exceeding 100 m O.D. (Fig 35).[45] Only twenty existed in about A.D. 1500, but these disappeared by 1600. Surviving farms moved over to stock-raising on shore-lyme grass (*Elymus arenarius*), but this seems to have provided inadequate forage to support the required number of cattle for, according to a farm register of 1703, occupied farmsteads in Iceland at that time

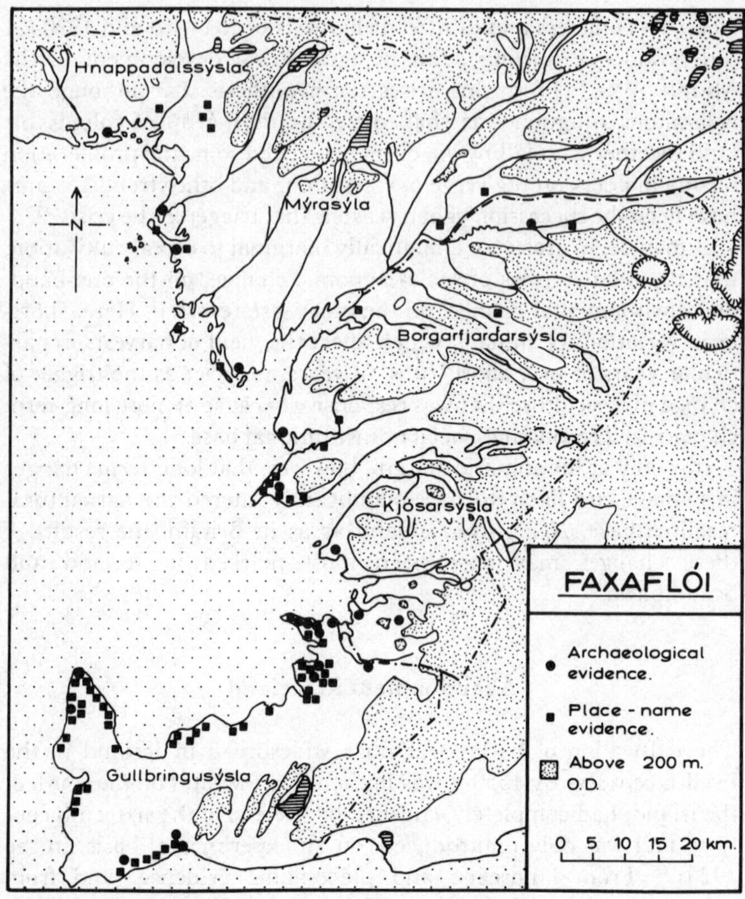

Fig. 35. Evidence of cereal cultivation in south-east Iceland before A.D. 1500. After Thorarinsson (1944).

numbered 4,059, while those lying deserted was given as approximately 3,200.[46] Destruction of the soil caused by overgrazing was probably an important element in this trend, however the overgrazing itself may have been the product of reduced grass-yield resulting from a shorter and less intense growing period. There is a positive and linear relationship between mean annual temperature and average hay yield in Iceland, and this is reflected in an apparent relationship between grass growth and the incidence of sea ice, for which data are available from the twelfth century onwards. Documentary evidence for this relationship in the past is also strong. Typical of the contemporary comment was an entry in the law officer's record for 1374: 'Winter and spring severest in memory, grass did not grow at all in the north. Sea ice was present until 24th August.'[47]

From our knowledge of the incidence of sea ice around Iceland, from the twelfth century onwards, we may hypothesise that significant changes have occurred in the productivity of forage grasses in Iceland. Fridriksson's studies of 'good', 'medium' and 'poor' years for grass growth seem to bear this out but, more significantly, he has illustrated the relationship between the livestock population of the island and the frequency of sea ice (Fig 36 and Table 3). Stocking

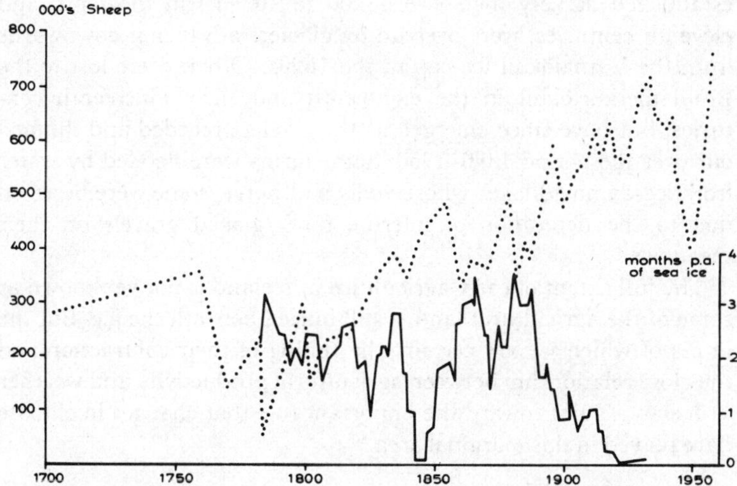

Fig. 36. Frequency of sea-ice and numbers of sheep in Iceland, 1700–1950. After Fridriksson (1969).

Table 3: SEA ICE AND STOCK FAMINE IN ICELAND

Century	Years of sea ice	Years of starvation		
		horses	cattle	sheep
Twelfth and before	2–3		1	5
Thirteenth	3–4	1	1	5
Fourteenth	6	3	3	9
Fifteenth	1	2	2	4
Sixteenth	8	8	6	12
Seventeenth	27	6	7	12
Eighteenth	23	12	3	15

(After Fridriksson, 1969)

rates were very closely related to grass growth because they depended upon the amount of winter grazing available to supplement hay from the preceding summer. An extreme example is that of 1750–1 when a short summer yielding little hay was followed by a very severe winter. Forty farms were abandoned in northern Iceland due to cattle losses. This was the beginning of a difficult period in the 1750s when over 50,000 sheep perished because of the cold and reduced grazing.[48]

Abandonment of land and farmsteads in Iceland was, in a few instances, more directly related to climatic change. In the south-east of the island several farms which, according to the sagas, had been established at very high levels (300 to 400 m) in the tenth and eleventh centuries, were overrun by glaciers advancing downwards from the Vatnajökull ice cap in the 1690s. Others were lost to the Breidamerkurjökull in the eighteenth and early nineteenth centuries, but have since emerged as the glaciers receded and thinned out over the period 1890–1950. Some farms were flooded by water from ice-dammed lakes whose walls had burst; some were deserted due to the deposition of infertile fluvio-glacial gravels on their meadows.[49]

The full extent of early agriculture in Iceland is not yet known as some of the agricultural land is still buried beneath the ice. But the limits of which we are certain, the timing of their contraction and the close relationship between agricultural productivity and weather in Iceland, point toward the important role that changes in climate have played in this marginal area.[50]

Retreat in Norway in the Late Middle Ages

The special sensitivity to climatic change of foothill areas in maritime Scandinavia is evidently the product of two factors. Firstly, we have seen that central and southern Norway and central Sweden are, in general terms, climatically marginal to cereal cropping. Secondly, it is probable that maritime Scandinavia, like Scotland, experienced a greater range of cooling in the 'Little Ice Age' than did regions either further south or otherwise removed from the influence of polar currents in the Atlantic and North Sea. It has been suggested that in Tröndelag the theoretical limits to cultivation fell at least 150 m between 1300 and 1600, with the result that almost one-half of the land below 300 m may have been submarginal in the seventeenth century. The quantity and timing of a

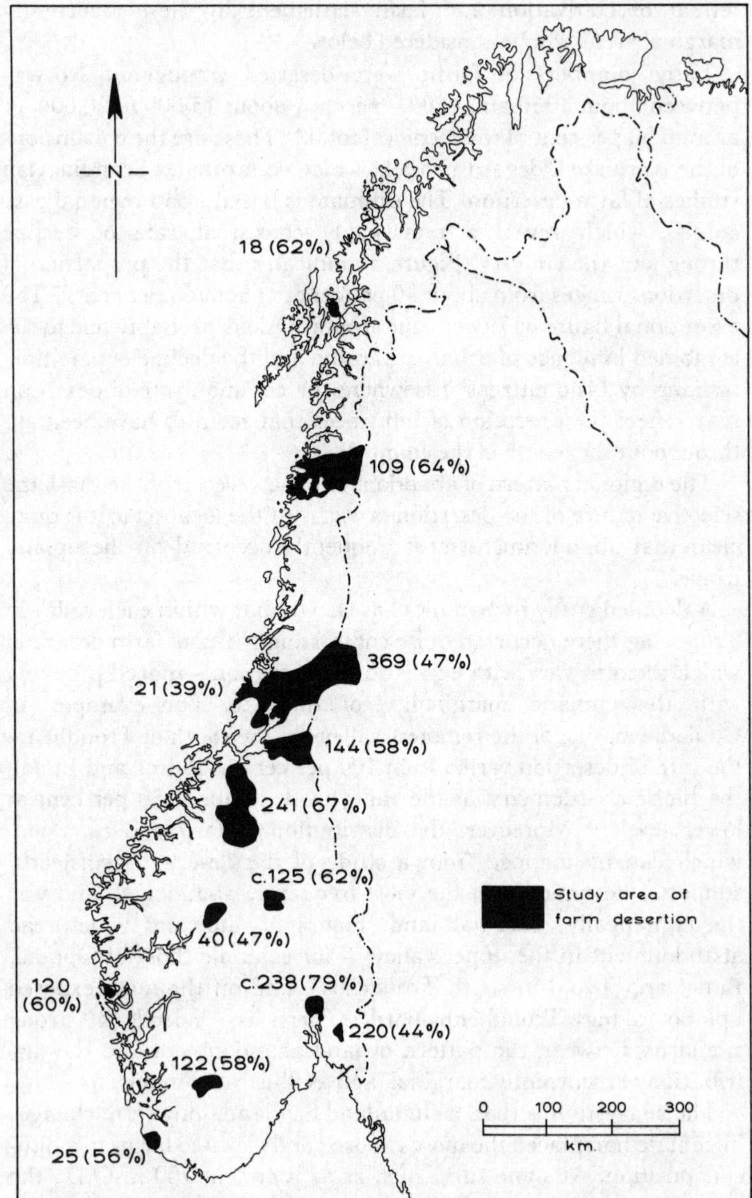

Fig. 37. Farm desertion in Norway in the late Middle Ages. Figures refer to the numbers of farms deserted and their proportion of the original total. After Salvesen (1976).

retreat of cultivation and farm settlement in these recurrently marginal areas will be considered below.

Large numbers of farms were deserted throughout Norway between about 1350 and 1500 – perhaps about 15,000 to 20,000, or around 50 per cent of the medieval total.[51] These are the conclusions of the Nordiske Ødegardsprosjekt which co-ordinates Scandinavian studies of farm desertion. The estimate is based upon regional case studies which reveal a remarkably consistent rate of decline throughout the country. Figure 37 indicates that the proportion of desertions ranges from about 40 per cent to about 65 per cent.[52] The exceptional figure of 79 per cent around Oslo is probably due to the combined influence of urban expansion and the decline of part-time farming by Oslo citizens. Elsewhere the common rate of desertion may reflect the operation of influences that seem to have been felt throughout the length of the country.

The regional pattern of abandonment, however, tends to mask the selective nature of the desertion process. At the local scale it is quite clear that abandonment most frequently occurred on the upland fringe.

A detailed study by Sandnes has shown that within each valley in Tröndelag there occurred quite contrasting scales of farm desertion which seem to vary with exposure and elevation – indeed probably with the climatic marginality of the site. For example, in Gauladalen, one of the remotest valleys to the south of Trondheim, the rate of desertion varied from 100 per cent in Røros and Budal, the highest settlements at the valleyhead, to about 50 per cent at lower levels.[53] Moreover, the distribution of farmland reversion, which can be mapped from a study of the deserted farmsteads, supports the notion that the most frequently abandoned land was the climatically marginal land. Figure 38 indicates widespread abandonment in the upper valleys – for example those of Oppdal, Budal and Tydal in south Tröndelag – and on the more exposed upland along Trondheims-fjord. There is, indeed, a strong similarity between the pattern of land abandonment and the distribution of recurrently marginal land as illustrated in Fig 28.

The suggestion is that, as in upland Scotland, long-term changes in climate had placed the more exposed and elevated farms in a difficult position. At some sites, such as at Røros at 700 m O.D., the cereal harvest in the late sixteenth century may have averaged a failure rate of 1 year in 2·5 years. Life here was, therefore, very delicately balanced: the Black Death, which cost Norway a substantial part of its population, in addition to other causes of abandon-

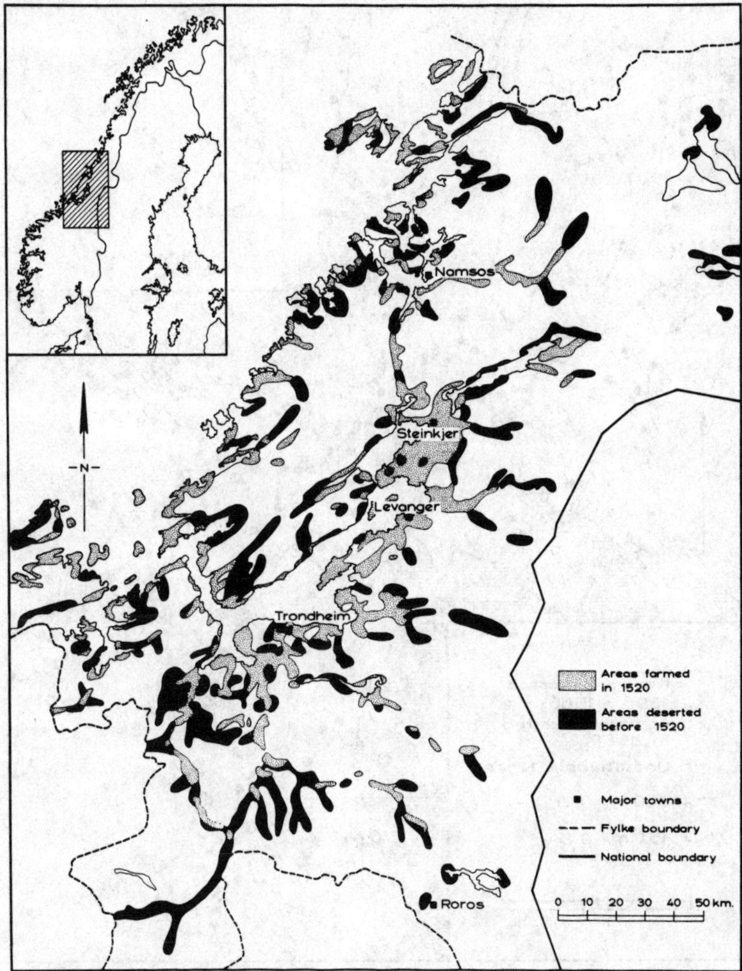

Fig. 38. Areas of desertion and of maintained settlement in Tröndelag, Norway in the late Middle Ages. After Sandnes (1971).

ment, such as civil unrest, high rates of tax and the occasional poor summer or severe winter, would have had a most lasting impact in these areas since long-term cooling of climate in the late Middle Ages seems to have greatly reduced the economic viability of very many elevated and exposed farms.

Some support for the theory of climatically-induced desertion is supported by the results of a detailed study of a single farm lying at almost 350 m O.D. at the head of the Leksadalen in north

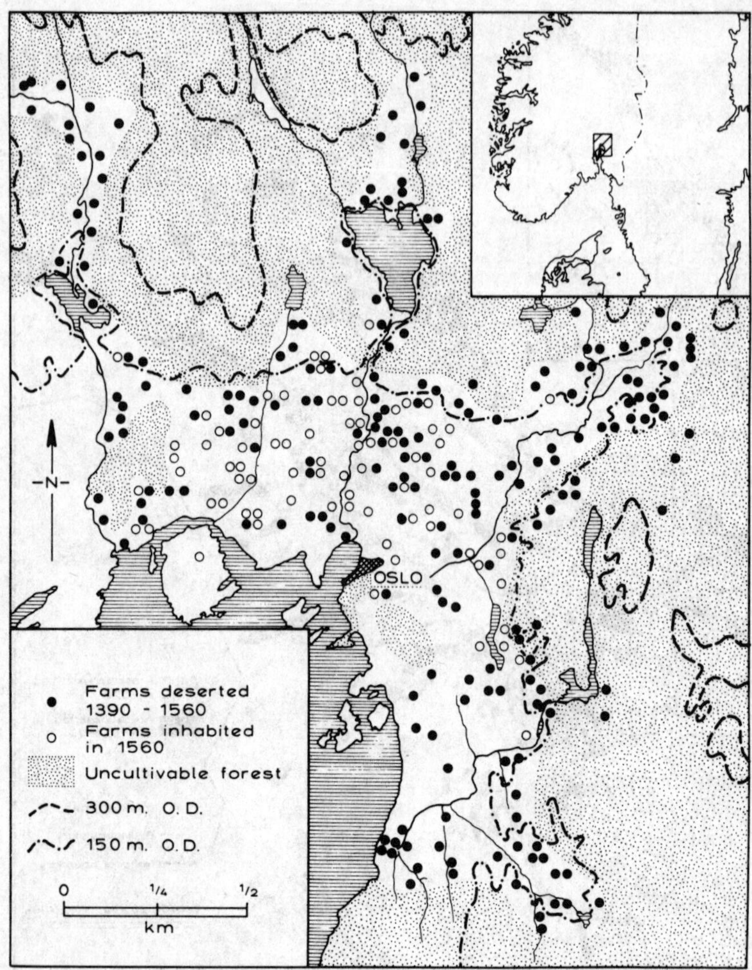

Fig. 39. Desertion of settlement in the region of Oslo, Norway in the late Middle Ages. After Holmsen (1962).

Tröndelag. This farm, which, like its neighbours, was deserted in 1520, was probably established in the early Middle Ages. Cereal cultivation at this elevation is hardly rewarding under present climatic conditions, even with the use of early-maturing varieties of cereals – and yet there is evidence of successful cropping of unimproved strains of cereals throughout the early Middle Ages.[54]

Elsewhere in Norway the pattern of desertion seems to have been the same, with the climatically marginal farms being those most frequently abandoned. In the area around Oslo, only one out of eighty-five farms located in the climatically marginal zone of 150–300 m O.D. was not deserted in the late Middle Ages (Fig 39). By contrast, only 55 per cent of farms below the 150-metre contour were deserted.[55]

We may, therefore, conclude that the evidence for late medieval abandonment in Norway shows some similarities to the pattern of land reversion in southern Scotland. There is a spatio-temporal coincidence between the distribution of abandonment and the location of land which became marginal and submarginal to cultivation owing to a secular trend toward cooler summers in the late Middle Ages.

Elsewhere in northern Europe the evidence for a long-term retreat of agriculture is less firmly based. In Sweden and Finland the peak of colonisation may have occurred as late as 1560,[56] but the subsequent decline has been attributed to famine, as a result of harvest failure, and aggravated by plague.[57]

In Denmark there occurred, some time after about 1340, a widespread decline in agriculture. Over the subsequent three or four hundred years hundreds of villages were abandoned, more than 50 per cent in some parts of Jutland; and the tithe records from seventy-nine Sealand parishes suggest a decline of about 70 per cent in their cultivated area.[58] In south-west Greenland, the Viking settlements, which had been established by Erik the Red during a warm phase in 982, died out between about 1350 and 1450 – the nadir of the cold epoch in Greenland where the climatic trend has preceded that of Iceland and north-west Europe by about 150 years.[59] The explanation for their loss is not likely to be simple. It may have been due to pirate raids, to plague which had already reached Iceland in 1402, or to a decline in the ivory trade as a result of increasing trade between Scandinavia and North Africa. However, there is archaeological evidence for the decline of cattle rearing in the early fifteenth century, and this has been linked – as in Iceland – with an increase in the incidence of sea ice. There are also signs of a rise in the permafrost layer during roughly the same period.[60] It would, therefore, be quite reasonable to think that the Norse communities struggled against increasing climatic adversity in the fourteenth and fifteenth centuries and finally succumbed to one or a number of the factors mentioned above. Their disappearance marks a singular failure in the long history of otherwise successful colonisation by European peoples.

It may be concluded that in the late Middle Ages a widespread retreat of cultivation occurred in northern Europe, particularly along the upland margins of Scotland, Iceland, Norway and perhaps also in Greenland. Clearly there is a need for more extensive investigation of the scale and location of this abandonment. However, the location and timing of that abandonment which has been mapped shows a strong coincidence with those areas of recurrently marginal land which would have become marginal to cereal cultivation under the conditions of secular climatic change which have been proposed in Chapters 2 and 3. This coincidence suggests a causal relationship – not a direct relationship, but one working either through the operation of harvest failure due to short-term fluctuations, or through the occurrence of socio-economic triggers of change. Indeed, it may even be that some apparently non-environmental factors, such as the occurrence of plague, may owe their lasting impact to a virility which was partly dependent upon prevailing weather conditions. The more complicated links between weather, disease, food supply, mortality and the shift of settlement are discussed in the following chapter.

6

Harvests, Mortality and the Shift of Rural Settlement

There is a link between certain types of climatic change and certain types of agricultural change; but it is not easy to distinguish between the relative roles of the many other factors that also may have been at work. It is even more difficult, however, to evaluate the role of climatic change in a shift of settlement, and yet most of the evidence for cultural and economic change – in both prehistory and documented history – is recorded in the archaeology and documentation of change in settlement, or dwelling-site, rather than in the cultivated area.

A change in the location and size of settlements generally reflects change in the number of inhabitants – the product of births, deaths and migration. In subsistence economies rates of fertility and mortality are influenced by the incidence of disease, which kills and debilitates, and by the quantity and quality of the food supply; and, where movement of food by trade is insignificant, local yields will have the major bearing upon the supply of food. Crop yields and meat supply (from hunting or grazing), which are themselves affected by the weather, may thus touch upon the viability of primitive settlements, but their influence is felt through a chain of effects, in each link of which there may also be felt the effect of non-climatic variables.

Settlement–climate relationships are therefore not only less strong but also more complicated than farming–climate relationships, and a good deal of caution is needed in their investigation. In general it can be said that archaeologists, in particular, have been too eager to adopt an environmental explanation for settlement changes without a clear understanding of the processes involved – of how environmental change may affect the viability of settlements.

This chapter first investigates the complex relationships that exist between climate and food supply, between food supply and mortality, and between climate and disease. Much of the discussion will focus upon medieval England since it is for this period and place that the relevant evidence is most abundant. The intention is that an improved appreciation of these relationships will enable, in the second part of the chapter, a more adequate assessment to be made of the role of climate in medieval settlement desertion. Finally there is some discussion of 'medieval' settlement desertion in the Midwest of the United States and of desertion in earlier periods.

Climate and Food Supply

In Chapter 3 it was shown that there is a direct but complex link between weather and crop yield and, in particular, that while farming technology has an important effect on the long-term trend, weather variability accounts for deviations in expected productivity and expected yields. Weather, thus, was the cause of unexpected fluctuations in levels of food supply, although other factors would have operated; and in periods of little advance in farming technology, together with less favourable climatic conditions for cropping, there would be expected a long-term decline in yields. Both long-term and short-term decline in food supply, due respectively to climatic change and the variability of weather, are two ways in which the viability of subsistence settlement may have been influenced by environmental change.

Declining yields against a background of static technology in England in the late Middle Ages provide a suitable example for study. Titow's work on the account rolls of the Winchester estates, for A.D. 1209–1349, has shown a correlation between outstandingly good or bad harvests (i.e., those at least 15 per cent above or below the average) and the weather of the summer, winter and previous autumn (Table 4).[1] The nature of the evidence does not enable variability of a lesser order to be similarly explained.

At the same time, however, the same data indicate a long-term decline of yields in the thirteenth and early fourteenth centuries.[2] The trends do, of course, vary from manor to manor, but the great majority of manors shows a decline in the early fourteenth century, and several of them seem to have suffered a continuous decline in yields during the whole of the period. The tendency has been to explain this by reference to the deteriorating quality of arable land

Table 4: CORRELATION BETWEEN WEATHER AND OUTSTANDING HARVESTS IN MEDIEVAL ENGLAND

Year	Yield deviation	Previous summer	Previous autumn	Winter	Summer
OUTSTANDINGLY GOOD HARVESTS					
1232	+19·58%	Very dry*	Very dry*	No reference	Very dry
1236	+33·42			Hard?	Very dry
1248	+23·50	Very dry	Dry?	Hard?	Very dry
1272	+20·89	Dry	No reference	Hard	Very dry
1287	+21·41	Dry	No reference	No reference	Very dry
1298	+27·94	Very dry	No reference	No reference	Very dry
1309	+17·49	No reference	Wet and long	No reference	Very dry
1311	+17·75	Dry	No reference	No reference	Dry
1313	+21·67	Dry?	No reference	Wet?	No reference
1318	+32·38	No reference**	No reference**	No reference	Very dry
1325	+28·98		Wet?	No reference	Very dry
1326	+34·46	Very dry	No reference	Hard and dry	Very dry
1332	+16·19	Very dry	Dry	No reference	Dry
1337	+27·42	Very dry	No reference	No reference	Dry
1338	+21·93	Dry	Very wet and long	Hard and long	Dry
1344	+27·68	Very dry	No reference	Wet?	Very dry
OUTSTANDINGLY BAD HARVESTS					
Wet pattern					
1224	–21·41%	Wet*	Wet*	No reference	No reference
1315	–35·77	Flooding	Very wet and long	Flooding	Very wet
1316	–44·91	Very wet	Very wet and long	Flooding	Flooding
1349	–41·25	No reference	Wet	Wet	Wet
1350	–29·24	Wet	Flooding	Flooding**	Flooding**
Dry pattern					
1226	–26·63	Very dry	Wet	Hard	Dry?
1283	–27·15			No reference	No reference
1290	–20·10	Very dry	Wet and long	Flooding	Dry
1310	–15·67	Very dry	Wet?	No reference	Dry?
1339	–40·73	Dry	Very wet	Hard and long	Dry
1343	–15·14	Dry	Wet and long	No reference	Very dry
1346	–18·54	Wet?	Wet and long	Wet	Dry

* No accounts exist but the chroniclers are explicit.
** Some fields still water-logged from the floods or rains of the preceding year.
(After Titow, 1960)

owing to over-cropping and mismanagement; this is partly borne out both by the higher rents that were occasionally being paid for newly reclaimed than for older arable land, and by frequent accounts of impoverished land – *terra debilis, frisca quia debilis*.[3]

However, Postan has explored two possible objections against the picture of long-term decline of average yields; and they may also raise some doubts about its explanation. Firstly, the contraction of arable on to the best land, which seems to have occurred at this time, should have tended to counter overall yield decline. However, yields on those late fourteenth century demesnes which had experienced some contraction do not seem to have risen appreciably.[4] Secondly, there is a tendency for yields not to fall inexorably but to level out, albeit at a low level, when there is continued cropping without manuring. The suggestion is that unfavourable weather conditions, particularly cool, damp summers and wet autumns, which certainly did occur more frequently in the early fourteenth century, may well have aggravated an already difficult situation. Some of the bailiffs' comments in the Winchester account rolls seem to bear this out, but it would be wrong to rely solely on these data as evidence of declining yields being a function of long-term climatic deterioration in the fourteenth century.

Medieval historians have taken a positive step in rejecting a simplistic climatic explanation. But the specific climatic conditions of the Middle Ages should be included among the many pieces in this puzzle. Indeed, it is interesting to note that several historians, while discounting climatic change, implicitly accept the notion of the variability of the environment from year to year. The concept of relative overpopulation in England in the early fourteenth century, which was later 'punished' by recurrent famines and rising mortality, implies a belief that the carrying capacity of the land varies through time, and that an agricultural population needs to leave a margin of safety below this threshold. The link between weather, yield and food supply was clearly an important one.

Food Supply and Mortality

Levels of food supply may, in turn, have influenced the mortality and fertility rates of agricultural populations, and thus have affected the size and distribution of farming villages. In England in the thirteenth century there is firm evidence of a link between death rate and harvest-size, the death rates being measured by the numbers of heriots or death duties levied on customary tenants and the size of harvest being reflected by grain prices. Figure 40 illustrates the related trends of grain prices and heriots found by Postan and Titow in the accounts for manors owned by the Bishop of Winchester. The form of collection of heriots tended to carry some entries over into one or two years following the actual years of death, so that the heriot figures might have been less liable to fluctuate from year to year than did actual deaths and thus be somewhat unresponsive to the immediate impact of bad harvests and famines. Postan and Titow emphasise that:

> It is therefore all the more remarkable to find how much our figures in fact fluctuate and how nearly the fluctuations coincide with harvests or other catastrophic mortality factors. In some years . . . the figures of heriots appear to reflect the deaths of preceding years while in others the high number of deaths follow not a dearth or famine in the year in which they occur, but a whole sequence of bad years. But in general the figures fluctuate sharply, and most of the sharper fluctuations appear to synchronise with the events which could be expected to cause deaths in thirteenth-century villages.[5]

The peaks of serious dearth and deaths seem to have occurred in 1271–2 (the chronicles attribute this to a wet spring in 1271 followed by a wet autumn and a summer drought in 1272 which brought famine throughout western Europe), in 1308–11, and in the disastrous years 1315–18 (in Chapter 7 some of these periods will be

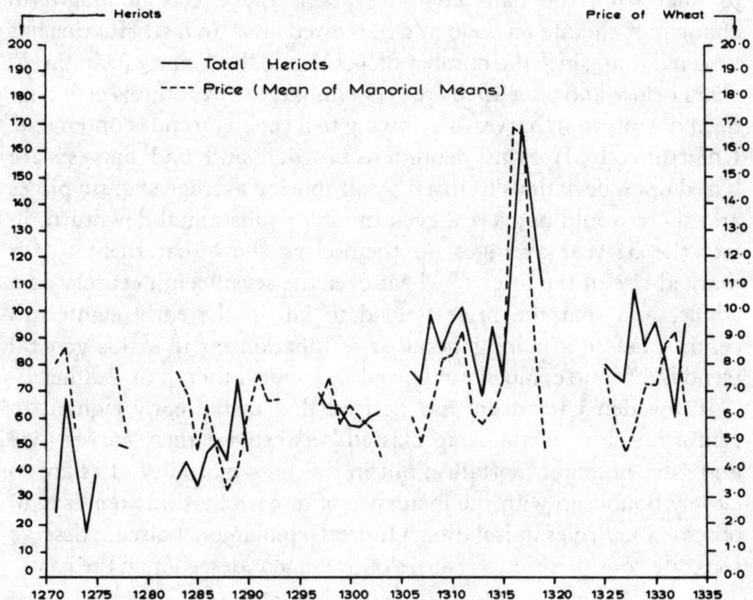

Fig. 40. Heriots and prices (shillings) on five Winchester estates. After Postan and Titow (1959).

examined in greater detail). Only in the years 1288–9, 1328–9, and possibly 1331–2, did summer epidemics occur outside a situation of severe food shortage. Postan and Titow conclude that: ‘All the other spectacular rises in mortality coincide with or follow bad harvests and conversely all the high peaks of prices (except that of 1332) are accompanied by corresponding peaks of mortality.'[6]

The correlation between these two forms of data is statistically significant and suggests that here was a society in which the population of small holders and labourers was immediately sensitive to harvest failures; it had expanded to a point at which it could be sustained only in years of favourable harvests which might be expected to occur in two out of three years. This, indeed, was the class of society that was balanced on the margins of subsistence, the class in which mortality moved closely with the supply of food from the year's harvest.

From short-term shifts of grain prices Hoskins has investigated the fluctuations of harvest size that occurred in England in the fifteenth and sixteenth centuries. The problems of relating harvest size (a function of yield and harvested area) to price (a function of supply and demand) are quite obvious; and it would be misleading to infer from the data anything about the effects of long-term changes of climate on yield and harvested area. In fact, Hoskins has asserted that, since the number of 'good' and 'bad' harvests in the 70 years before and after 1550 are very similar, the hypothesis of a long-term downturn in harvest-size owing to a cooling trend is untenable. Unfortunately, Hoskins' definitions of 'good' and 'bad' harvests are based upon deviations from a 31-year moving average of grain prices and these would not reveal even the most substantial downturn; in fact the 31-year averages do themselves show that there was a marked rise in the price of wheat over the seventeenth century as a whole, and that the price tended to fall in the early eighteenth century before a more general price inflation set in – this general trend is, of course, much influenced by factors other than weather.[7]

In Sweden Utterström has noticed that in the early eighteenth century a close relationship existed between weather, harvest-size and rates of infant mortality; but in this case mortality rates are so closely bound up with the incidence of disease that it is not easy to observe their roles in isolation.[8] Indeed, epidemics of disease deserve separate consideration as causes of settlement desertion in the past.

Weather, Disease and Mortality

The traditional interpretation of population changes in Sweden in the eighteenth century was a Malthusian one linking weather conditions, harvest-size, food supply and death rates.[9] For example, the death rate which peaked at 112 per thousand in Värmland in 1742 was put down to a succession of crop-failures and consequent starvation. Utterström, however, emphasises the disastrous effects of epidemics (probably of typhus and typhoid fever) on a population weakened by malnourishment.[10] At other times the supply of food may have influenced the small-pox cycle in such a way as to bring the peaks forward by a year or so. Utterström has also argued that harvest weather might, more directly, have influenced events by inducing mass migration among hungry rats thereby increasing the spread of plague.[11]

Moreover, there is some reason to suppose that the virulence of plague throughout Europe in the fourteenth century may have been encouraged by the prevailing weather conditions.[12] The Black Death, which probably cost England one-fifth of its population in 1348–9, was the second of three pandemics which have travelled Asia and Europe in the period of recorded history. The first was the plague which struck the Constantinople of Justinian; the most recent was that which began in the East in about 1894 and has so far had little impact on western Europe. The Black Death was the first of several plagues in the pandemic that continued to break out in isolated areas until the eighteenth century. Most of these plagues were bubonic, the plague bacillus being transferred by flea-bite from an infected rat and then affecting the lymphatic gland system, producing symptomatic 'buboes', or large swellings, in the groin or armpits. The ideal conditions for the spread of bacilli (*Xenopsylla cheopsis*) are a moderately moist climate with temperatures between 20°C and 25°C. Indeed, Bean has suggested that seasons of virulent plague in Britain, particularly the London plagues of the Elizabethan and Stuart periods, have coincided, in general, with warm summers. The bacillus multiplies less readily in cooler conditions, and deaths from bubonic plague tended to decline at the onset of a hard winter, though it might preserve its virulence in mild winter conditions; hence the saying that 'a mild winter leaves a full grave yard'.

Indeed, the highest mortality rates occurred where bubonic victims contracted pneumonia – and this tended to occur more in winter than in summer – both because an attack of pneumonic plague was nearly always fatal and because it was quickly spread by breathing in bacilli coughed out by an infected person. Mild winters in which the bacillus would multiply thus encouraged the virulence of plagues such as the Black Death which had a strong pneumonic element. Subsequent plagues in Britain probably lacked a strong pneumonic element but plagues with that element may have continued in Russia.

Of course, much is speculation. We have little knowledge of the relative importance of particular weather conditions for the bacillus, or of prevailing standards of domestic hygiene, or of the role of nourishment in relation to food supply; and these factors will surely have varied in importance from one phase of plague to another. But we cannot doubt the long-term effect of the high mortality on the economy of marginal areas.

There is also some evidence to suggest that particular weather conditions might upset the stability of village society. The infestation of the fungus ergot (*Claviceps purpura*), especially on rye but also on other cereals, is encouraged by damp springs and summers; its consumption in bread may lead to two types of ergotism – gangrenous and convulsive. Convulsive ergotism is characterised by symptoms such as disturbances of sensation, hallucination and epileptiform convulsions; these symptoms sometimes were mistaken for the work of Satan. In the seventeenth century, in Lorraine and Saxony, there were outbreaks of both ergotism and witchcraft persecution; and the crisis of 1692 in Salem, Massachusetts has been tentatively connected with ergotism.[13] This may lead to some speculation about a relationship between the Scottish witch-hunts of the 1590s and 1640s and the especially difficult weather of the periods 1591–98 and 1647–49.

Crop and Animal Diseases

The long-term abandonment of farmland in medieval England was sometimes the result of a shortage of draught power for the plough. According to the *Nonarum Inquisitiones* much land was lying idle in the 1340s 'for the lack of a plough team'.[14] The scarcity of both manure and draught stock may well have been a result of a sheep 'murrain' (possibly liver-fluke) which raged through England from 1313 to 1317 and a cattle 'murrain' (probably rinderpest) which was active from 1319 to 1321. It is not known how many animals died, but in some areas they may have exceeded one-half of the sheep and cattle population; as with human plague, the virulence of these diseases was probably increased by the exceptionally wet summers of 1314–16 and 1320–21.[15]

Some epidemic diseases in crops are triggered by particular weather conditions and have had a lasting effect upon early economies. The fungus attack on potatoes (*Phytophthora infestans*), generally known as blight, was the major cause of the failure of the potato crop in Ireland which led to the Great Famine of 1846. The famine was itself an important factor behind the widespread Irish emigration to America and consequent fall in population that 130 years later has still not been made good. Marginal land throughout Eire and Ulster – from the slopes of the Sperrin Mountains in Ulster to the Wicklows near Dublin – is characterised by relict 'lazy-beds', spaded ridges that were thrown up for the potato crop in the nineteenth century, and now abandoned to moor.[16]

Potato blight, which is carried over from year to year in infected potato tubers, is spread by means of spores which develop, germinate and re-infect in suitable conditions of temperature, humidity and moisture. Indeed it is possible to make accurate predictions of an outbreak of blight from a study of weather conditions alone, and throughout Europe and North America warnings of outbreak are now transmitted from observation stations when thresholds of high night temperatures and high humidity are surpassed during the growing season.[17] There is little doubt that the serious outbreak in 1846 was triggered by such conditions. In many other crops, including the cereals that were traditionally grown in northern Europe and North America, the relationship between disease and weather is also very strong.

The suggestion is that the relationship between climate and settlement is sometimes expressed in a complicated fashion through harvest-size, food supply, epidemic disease, mortality rates (including infant mortality rates) and population size. The final link between settlement shift and climate shift is no doubt a tenuous one, but it does exist and should be seen as one important factor among several that lie behind some (but only some) of the long-term abandonment of settlement in marginal Europe and North America. We can now proceed to investigate in greater detail the history of this abandonment.

The Shift of Settlement Limits in Medieval Britain

Lowland Britain

The most convincing argument against a major role of climatic change in medieval settlement desertion is that deserted and non-deserted villages are found side by side all over the English countryside and, as Beresford has said: 'local as the English climate is – it would be rather difficult to imagine the raindrops being so locally selective'.[18] Certainly the more marginal villages on the poorer soils would have been especially vulnerable in the fourteenth and fifteenth centuries, but even in these more difficult areas, such as the heavy Midland clays, village survival and village desertion occur in a very mixed pattern.

Less convincing is the historian's argument – quite frequently heard – that the direct relevance of climatic change to the history of deserted villages is bound to be minimal in view of the small proportion of depopulations that took place at the time of climatic 'deterioration', or even in the century following it.[19] This misconception seems to arise from adherence to an outdated climatic chronology, possibly that established by Brooks in 1925 which emphasised a phase of coldness and wetness in the twelfth century. But the bulk of desertions in England seems to have occurred over the period 1370–1500 (with a surge in about 1450–80)[20], and we now know that 1450 approximately marks the first of two nadirs in the Arctic Expansion when summer temperatures and summer wetness achieved their most extreme levels in north-west Europe. It is unfortunate, therefore, that the superseded chronology is still used by economic historians such as Van Bath and Beresford and that the more recent studies of climatic history are sometimes ignored.[21]

But the archaeological evidence for a climatic explanation is limited. On the Cotswolds and in Dorset, Rahtz has noted signs that in the thirteenth century improvements were made to domestic drainage systems and that floor levels were raised; he has interpreted these signs as possible responses to increasing wetness.[22] On Bodmin Moor, in Cornwall, the construction in the thirteenth century of platform houses on earth banks cut from the hillside has been regarded as a response to increased water-logging of the ground.[23] Hurst has concluded that these platforms were an attempt to cope with the deteriorating conditions and increasing wetness.[24] Increases in the incidence of other features, such as the cobbling of floors and the construction of corn-drying kilns, have also been remarked upon[25], but this type of archaeological evidence is not, in itself, convincing and seems to provide little substantive evidence to support the hypothesis of an important climatic agent promoting settlement change in lowland, non-marginal areas. Indeed, there have been some instances where the premise of 'desertion due to deteriorating weather' has, perhaps, coloured the interpretation of excavated material and not helped towards a reasoned conclusion. For example, at Goltho (15 m O.D., Lincolnshire) and Barton

Blount (90 m O.D., Derbyshire) the climatic explanation for abandonment, based on increasing intractability of the local clays, is not tested on *a priori* or empirical grounds – nor does it seem to relate closely to the excavated material and yet it is adopted in the conclusion of the excavation report.[26]

The case may be stronger for truly marginal sites such as that at West Stow in Suffolk where abandoned plough ridges of the fourteenth century were buried by wind-blown sand.[27] But, until more is known about the effect of climatic change on the medieval two- and three-field systems of cultivation, the more cautious explanation is the more reasonable. Enforced clearance for sheep stocking, encouraged by soil exhaustion and the reduced social cohesion of the farming village, was probably the main cause of depopulation in the lowlands; and the Black Death did much to accelerate what was already an established trend.[28]

Upland Britain

In the marginal uplands the balance of explanatory factors was different; moreover, rural settlement was mainly scattered, in the form of dispersed farmsteads or small farm-clusters, with only occasional hamlets and villages. Continued occupation of these farmsteads was entirely dependent upon successful operation of the farms, and their desertion was therefore more directly a function of local abandonment than was the desertion of nucleated settlement in the lowlands.

The quantity of deserted farmsteads in upland Scotland is remarkable. In south-east Scotland, in the Lammermuir Hills alone, at least fifteen steadings were deserted before 1600 and a further eighteen between 1600 and 1750. The concentration of these sites in remote locations, often adjacent to abandoned plough ridges, suggests that they represent a downhill retreat by agriculture and settlement. Desertions became more frequent in later years – twenty-one over the period 1750–70, seventy-one over the period 1770–1800 – but their distribution away from the moorland core suggests that these later desertions were more the result of the beginnings of farm amalgamation than of the abandonment *en bloc* of marginal farms.[29] But amalgamation might itself have been encouraged by difficult weather conditions: some contemporary writers noted that poor harvests frequently brought ruin to tenants with limited savings; often, the farms of those who went bankrupt would be amalgamated with adjacent tenancies and the land farmed at a lower level. Outlying cultivation on the amalgamated farm, now distant from the new centre of operations, was frequently allowed to revert to moorland. The result was an overall decrease in land value, a trend which was common in the Lammermuirs in the early seventeenth century, particularly on high land which was said to be 'subject to rotting in wet yeiris'.[30]

It is not known whether the pattern was similar in other parts of upland Scotland. There are signs of widespread settlement desertion throughout the Highlands, but they have not been adequately surveyed and dated. Most of this desertion dates from the sheep clearances in the nineteenth century, and it will require very close study to identify changes in settlement that occurred before the arrival of sheep. Some work which touches upon settlement desertion has been completed on Skye, in Kintyre and in Ayrshire[31]; the balance of the evidence from these areas points to peaks of settlement in the mid-eighteenth century with subsequent abandonment. Little has so far been noted of any earlier phase of retreat, although some work in Kintyre, Argyllshire, has revealed the devastating effects of both plague and starvation on rural settlement in the mid-seventeenth century.[32]

The evidence is also imperfect for upland Wales, although we know something of the distribution of rectangular platform houses. Most of these are probably medieval, though their desertion has not been precisely dated[33]. In Ireland we do not know enough about either the type of settlements or their desertion-date in order to form any hypothesis which would be likely to be confirmed.

The conclusion is that while the effects of climatic change can be quite adequately assessed in relation to agriculture itself, particularly to marginal agriculture, not enough is known to help elucidate the climatic component within the complex of factors behind the desertion of medieval villages. Because of the close functional relationship between farmland and dispersed settlement in upland Britain, it is likely that the desertion of settlement was linked to the abandonment of marginal farmland – and some of this, it has been argued, was related to changes in the climatic potential for crop growth. The role of climatic change in the desertion of nucleated settlement – villages and hamlets – in lowland, non-marginal areas is, however, likely to have been much less important.

The question will not be fully resolved without the further study of the local distribution of settlement desertion and farmland abandonment in the marginal uplands of north-west Europe. However, it is instructive to investigate the shifts of settlement that occurred in

North America at the same time, and which also coincided with changes in local climate; although radically different, these changes of climate were certainly linked to those occurring at the same time in Europe.

Indian Settlement on the American Great Plains

Because of unreliable summer rainfall the western Great Plains are marginal to unirrigated corn cultivation. As an example of the effects of climatic marginality upon subsistence cultivation they thus provide a vivid contrast to northern Europe.

In 1937, at the worst of the great drought on the Plains, Waldo Wedel, an archaeologist from the Smithsonian Institution, after a summer of excavation in Kansas, formed the idea that the Dust Bowl of the 1930s reflected an earlier dust bowl, in the thirteenth century, which was partly responsible for the abandonment of settlement by corn-growing Indians in Nebraska and Kansas.[34] The idea was later adopted to explain concurrent cultural changes in the south-west and also in the eastern United States;[35] it now represents a partial explanation of cultural change that is quite widely held amongst American anthropologists and historians.

Modern Analogue and Historical Parallel: Great Plains Droughts

Two major causes of the soil erosion which created the Dust Bowl in the Texas Panhandle, Oklahoma and south-west Kansas in the 1930s were mismanagement by over-grazing and over-ploughing, and drought brought on by abnormally low summer rainfall and abnormally high summer temperatures over the periods 1929–34 and 1936–9.[36] This sequence of hot, dry years is illustrated in Fig 41.

It is important to establish this point, not only to correct the overemphasis on mismanagement given by the United States government agencies, but to establish the environmental conditions of the Great Plains in the 1930s as an analogue of what could have occurred at an earlier date – though with reduced effect owing to less disturbance of vegetation and soil by grazing and by the plough – and indeed what has since occurred, on a lesser scale, in the 1950s. In fact eight periods of drought, each of more than two years' duration, have occurred on the Great Plains between 1800 and 1960. The drought of the 1930s was exceptional only in its severity.

The drought started in the winter wheat area in Texas in 1930 and increased in intensity as it spread into the western part of the Corn Belt in Kansas and Iowa. It reached a peak in 1936 when the entire Corn Belt received less than half its normal rainfall and temperatures averaged 5°C above normal. As crop failures became widespread, spring wheat and corn yields were greatly reduced – the

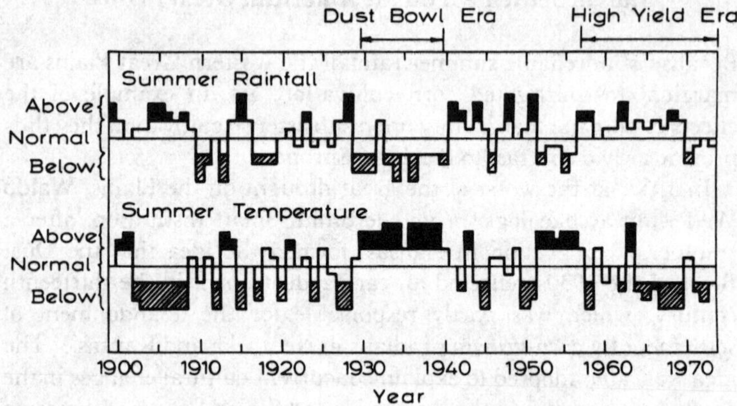

Fig. 41. Summer temperature and summer rainfall on the Great Plains. Averages for Oklahoma, Kansas, Nebraska, S. Dakota and N. Dakota. After Beltzner (1976).

average spring wheat yield for Saskatchewan for 1933–7 was less than one-half the 1920s average. Many people left the Great Plains for the west coast and the cities of the east: about $\frac{1}{3}$ million from the American plains and $\frac{1}{4}$ million from the Canadian plains.[37] The grass was also lost: on some parts of the short-grass prairie up to 30 per cent of the vegetation cover was lost by 1937, and was lost again by over-grazing during the drought of 1952–6.[38]

It is useful to hypothesise the occurrence of similar environmental changes in the past during the pre-European period of subsistence corn-cultivation. In the twelfth century A.D. increased westerlies across North America and Europe would probably have generated a peninsula of dry air extending eastwards from the Prairies into Illinois – a dryness caused by subsidence after passing over the Rocky Mountains. Figure 29 indicates that a change from weak to strong westerlies would tend to have been reflected in substantially reduced July rainfall in Iowa, western Kansas and Nebraska, and increased rainfall in Oklahoma and north Texas. The drought caused in Iowa by this change in weather pattern would probably have been severe – as severe as that which occurred in the 1930s, and in this case occurring over perhaps a century. Baerreis and Bryson have thus argued that, since summer rainfall is critical to corn farming, then the corn-growing Indian communities – part of the Mill Creek culture – occupying western Iowa in the twelfth and thirteenth centuries would have experienced deteriorating environmental conditions in the thirteenth century.[39]

Subsistence Indian cultivators settled in three separate areas on the Great Plains where the evidence for cultural change is remarkably consistent with a hypothesis of environmental change – in western Iowa (the Mill Creek culture), in western Kansas and Nebraska (the Upper Republican peoples), and in the Dakotas (the Middle Missouri culture).

Climatic Change and the Mill Creek Culture

The Mill Creek culture, named after the initial excavations along Mill Creek in Cherokee County (Iowa), refers to one of a number of Indian groups which were the first peoples to establish fixed villages on the central plains before A.D. 1000. These groups have been given the general name of Village Indians.[40]

In Iowa and Wisconsin it seems that an immigration of village peoples may have occurred as early as A.D. 700–800, part of a northward and westward movement of cultivators which reached its limits in the Great Lakes area and on the western Great Plains around A.D. 1200. Thereafter, the archaeologists have found signs of cultural decline – a move away from agriculture to hunting and a retreat from earlier agricultural limits – and this has been taken as a possible response to the drought in the west and the shorter growing season in the north which may have occurred in the mid-thirteenth century.[41]

In the north, in Wisconsin, there is as yet little evidence from excavations to confirm this hypothesis.[42] But in Iowa, from large middens that characterise the sites of the Mill Creek culture, studies of bone, pollen and gastropods tell a story that is still not clear. Earlier excavations had revealed a trend, around A.D. 1200, towards more bison bone, more arrow-heads and fewer bison-scapula hoes, an indication of increased reliance on hunting rather than farming for subsistence. But excavations in 1963 suggested the reverse; that hunting decreased in relative importance to agriculture.[43] Thus, the hypothesis that an increase in the strength of the westerlies brought less summer rainfall, and perhaps reduced corn yields, is not confirmed. The new hypothesis offered by Baerreis and Bryson is that the changed climatic conditions reduced the grazing for deer and bison, that hunting was therefore less productive and that people became more dependent upon agriculture even though productivity had declined.[44] This reversal in argument is not entirely convincing. What can be said is that the pollen evidence suggests a shift from tall-grass prairie to a less lush steppe-like vegetation, and that this occurred probably around A.D. 1150–1200. There is some resemblance between the curves of grass pollen and the trend of Lamb's winter severity index for Europe which is itself a fair indicator of the strength of the westerlies, since the winter mildness in western Europe is influenced by the frequency of westerly winds. But it seems unwise, without further archaeological evidence, to propose a further relationship between this environmental change and any economic change in the Mill Creek villages.

Upper Republican Cultivators of the West Central Plains

Evidence from excavations in western Nebraska and western Kansas during the 1930s suggested to Wedel the possibility that Indian cultivators in the thirteenth century A.D. may have had to cope with adverse conditions similar to those faced in the great drought of the 1930s; Wedel was convinced that the climatic fluctuations to which the region was subject could have been of sufficient magnitude to render Indian settlement precarious.[45] Drought like this would have an awesome effect on the village communities which had pushed westward in the Upper Republican period, and had adapted from a woodland culture with a creek valley hunting and gathering economy to a sedentary life subsistent upon successful corn cultivation.

For communities largely dependent on unirrigated cereal crops, summer rainfall would have been of prime significance. It was suggested in Chapter 3 that the 40 cm April–September isohyet represents an approximate minimum required for dependable but unirrigated agriculture; and that periodic fluctuations of rainfall may cause a shift of the isohyet over quite a wide area of the western Great Plains. Wedel, studying the effect of the drought of 1860 upon Indian cultivators in eastern Nebraska and eastern Kansas, concluded that 'if the 1860 conditions had continued for a few years, the Indians would have had to move out altogether or perish'.[46] Conditions would probably have been worse for the earlier Indian communities, which lived on land up to 300 km to the west of the nineteenth century limit.

Yet Wedel has noted that there is indubitable evidence of successful cultivation of corn, beans, squash and sunflowers:

> far beyond the western margins of successful native horticulture in historic times, and about as far west as maize can be grown through highly specialised methods. From the abundance of these remains along almost every arable stream valley with dependable water west to, or beyond, the Colorado line, I doubt that they were merely 'strays' from better watered lands to the east. On the contrary I suspect that they were people with horticultural traditions of long standing who spread westward through a climatically favourable environment that represented something quite different from a one- or two-year westward swing of the rainfall zones.[47]

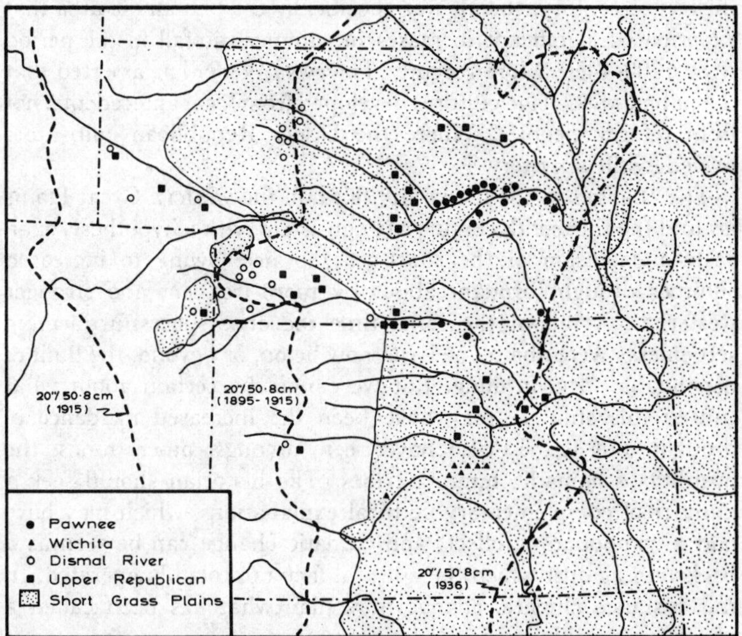

Fig. 42. Distribution of principal known semi-horticultural complexes in the central Great Plains west of the Missouri River. Symbols indicate localities of occurrence rather than specific sites. After Wedel (1953).

The location of these sites, in relation to the 50 cm annual isohyet which follows a very similar line to the 40 cm April–September isohyet, is shown in Fig 42. At some of the sites the occupation levels lie beneath sterile layers of wind-blown sand. Wedel concluded:

> It can be assumed that these peoples farmed intensively and that they were far-sighted enough to lay by seed corn and food against a year or two of crop shortage . . . (But) . . . If drought conditions recurred for

> several successive years, or if there was a drop of several inches in the average annual precipitation over a period of 10 or 20 years or more, perhaps with springs and watercourses drying up, there would have been no choice for the natives other than that of abandoning their villages and removing eastward to better-watered and more dependable regions . . . the outstanding physiographic aftermath of which is seen in the dust which today covers many of their ancient living sites.[48]

From further evidence Wedel concluded that, after abandoning western Kansas, the Indian cultivators moved not east but south towards the Oklahoma and Texas panhandles[49] – and it should be remembered that, if Baerreis and Bryson are correct in their postulation of changes in the pattern of summer rainfall in the thirteenth century, then it was specifically the panhandle area that experienced significant increases in summer rainfall in the period A.D. 1200–1450. More recently, however, Wedel has asserted that the panhandle village cultures developed from local antecedents, not from refugee peoples. Where the Upper Republican cultivators moved is still a mystery.[50]

The changes in the fauna and flora on the western Great Plains around the thirteenth century are consistent with a hypothesis of an eastern extension of the short-grass prairie owing to increased summer drought brought about by more frequent and stronger westerlies. At about the same time the once successful farming settlements were abandoned and now lie on, or beyond, the limit of dependable 'dry' farming. But we cannot be certain about what caused this shift. It may have been the increased incidence of drought, but it may also have been, amongst other things, the hostility of nomadic hunting tribes. The historian should seek a number of complementary cultural explanations, which may have had a compounding effect; and climatic change can be seen as a backcloth against which the cultural factors probably operated. In this instance climatic change may play what has been called a 'deviation-amplifying' role.[51]

Climate and Cultural History in the Middle Missouri Valley

The third area for which there is evidence of a culture–climate link on the Great Plains lies along the Middle Missouri on the borders of North and South Dakota. Immigration of sedentary horticulturalists to the area seems to have taken place at about the beginning of the moist period 800–1250, and by A.D. 1250 settlement had spread northwards to a point more than 300 km west of the present 40 cm isohyet (Fig 43). The temptation has been to attribute this move to

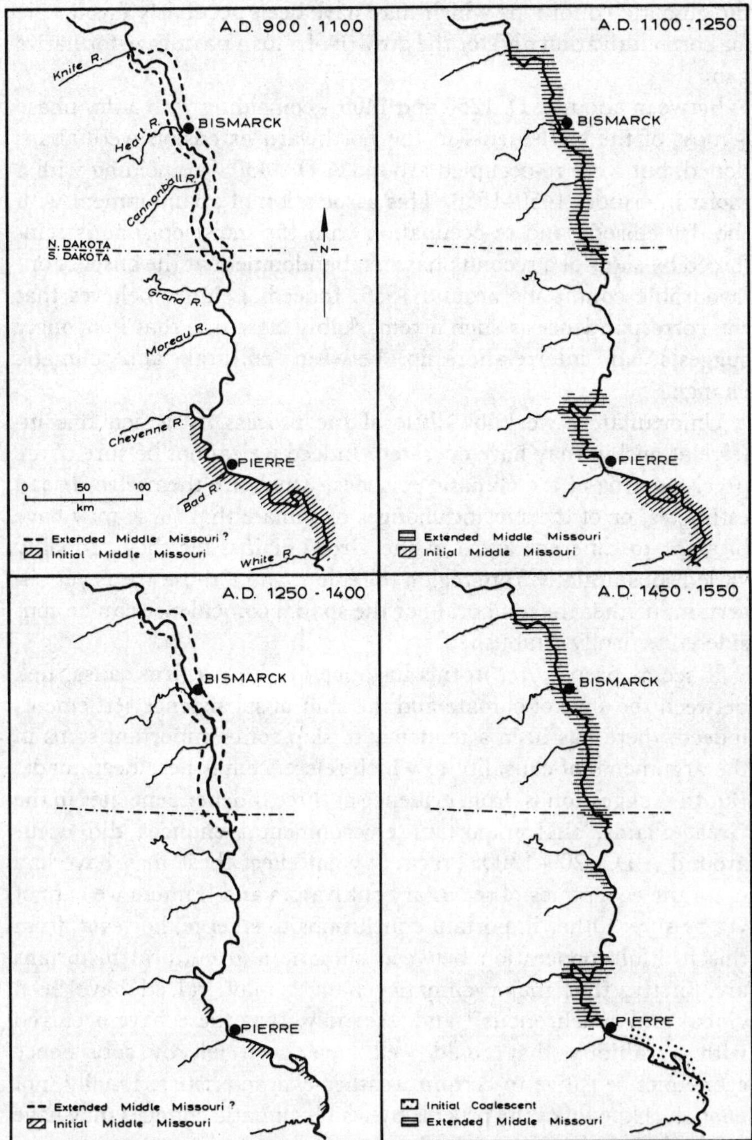

Fig. 43. Distribution of Indian villages on upper Missouri, A.D. 900–1550. After Lehmer (1970).

the climatic conditions which may have been peculiarly favourable for corn cultivation and for the growth of a lush pasturage for native game.[52]

Between about A.D. 1250 and 1400 – coinciding with a dry phase – most of the settlements in the northward extension were abandoned, but were re-occupied around A.D. 1450 – coinciding with a moist interlude, 1450–1550. This association of abandonment with the dry episode and re-occupation with the moist episode is reinforced by signs of a second phase of abandonment at the onset of unfavourable conditions around 1550. Indeed, Lehmer believes that the correspondence is such a remarkably close one that it strongly suggests an interrelationship between cultural and climatic change.[53]

Unfortunately we know little of the process by which this interrelationship may have operated. Indeed we cannot be sure of the precise dating of the climatic episodes, which are themselves broad estimates, or of the specific changes of climate that these may have brought to different areas of the Great Plains, for they probably varied substantially from region to region; and if these are as yet uncertain, neither the temporal nor the spatial coincidence can be considered as firmly established.

It seems premature, in this instance, to draw a firm causal link between the shift of climate and the shift of subsistence settlement; indeed, there has been a tendency to skip some important steps in the arguments of causality to which reference has here been made. But the suggestion is, from evidence at three independent sites in the Great Plains, that important environmental changes did occur around A.D. 1200–1300. Precisely what effect these may have had upon the economies of sedentary cultivators and hunters we cannot yet be sure. Other important conclusions to emerge, however, from this fruitful cooperation between climatic and cultural historians are, firstly, that major climatic changes may indeed have been global and synchronous[54] and, secondly, that these have occurred with a rapidity that could well have been felt by subsistence economies sensitive to certain weather characteristics. Finally, not enough is known of the process by which climatic changes may have affected the viability of Indian settlements – indeed, without a detailed investigation of plant–climate relationships of the kind pursued in Chapters 3 and 4, the process will not be fully comprehended. It seems that while archaeologists are increasingly prepared to accept the notion of environmental change as an agent of cultural change, they do not always accept it in a critical fashion.

Climatic Change, Agriculture and Settlement

A distinction should be made between those archaeological studies that adopt the environmental argument when considering cultural elements, such as hunting and farming, which are highly dependent upon environmental resources, and those that adopt the environmental argument in a discussion of cultural elements, such as settlement location, that are less closely related to the natural environment. Two brief examples illustrate this point: the first concerns the domestication of cereals and the diffusion of sedentary agriculture – activities immediately dependent upon climate; the second concerns settlement change in classical Greece – an occurrence not immediately related to climate.

One of the many studies of domestication which embraces the notion of environmental change comes from an investigation of the pollen record in the Zagros Mountains in Iran. This indicates that, around 9000 B.C., there was an increase in both temperature and rainfall, these being reflected at certain elevations in a change from steppe to the oak-pistachio woodland which still survives today. Wright has argued that this probably occurred at approximately the same time as the first domestication of plants and animals in this area.[55] The change of climate might have encouraged the spread of wild emmer and barley, as a component of the oak woodland, into the Zagros area thus enabling either their domestication independently of earlier domestication in Palestine, or the ready import of domestic strains. This was accompanied by a shift from cave-dwelling in the mountains to settlement in open sites on the foothills where ground was more suitable for cultivation.

Wright concludes that:

> Although I have always felt that cultural evolution – gradual refinement of tools and techniques for coping with the environment – is a stronger force than climatic determinism in the development of early cultures, the chronological coincidence of important environmental and cultural change in the area during initial phases of domestication is now well enough documented that it cannot be ignored.[56]

To test this hypothesis much more data are required than presently available. However, a similar notion of climatically-encouraged cultural change has been proposed as occurring in Europe during the Boreal and Atlantic phases, 8000 to 3000 B.C. Waterbolk has argued that the spread of village-farming settlements from the Aegean in about 7000 B.C. to the Hungarian Plain by about 5000 B.C., and throughout all western Europe by 3000 B.C., may have been encouraged by increasing wetness and warmth during the Boreal-Atlantic transition (c. 5500 B.C.).[57] The replacement of open pine woodland by dense oak forest would have decreased the grazing land for large animals, thus reducing the game upon which the traditional hunting economy depended; and throughout north-western Europe there seems to have been a move toward the coast in order to supplement the hunting of big game with the more reliable supply of food from fishing, seal-hunting and the collection of shellfish. The consequences of this adaptation may have been far-reaching because the coastal resources allowed a higher degree of sedentary occupation, and thus fulfilled an important precondition for the subsequent development of a farming economy.

A less convincing hypothesis of climatically-induced settlement change is offered by Rhys Carpenter as an explanation of decline of the Mycenaean civilisation between about 1200 and 900 B.C.[58] The abandonment of Mycenaean palaces and evacuation of settlement in the south Peloponnese has generally been attributed to invasion by the Dorians from the north-east. A few palaces which have been excavated show signs of destruction by fire, suggesting a violent end, but there is also much evidence of abandonment with no accompanying destruction. Carpenter has proposed that the Dorians were moving into an area that had already been depopulated by an outward migration – an evacuation induced by famine caused by recurring drought; and this may have been true not only of the south Peloponnese but also of the string of islands in the south Aegean, which archaeologically show little sign of a continuity between the Mycenaean and Doric settlements and yet show no sign of a violent end. The signs are that Mycenaean settlement shifted toward Achaia on the north-west Peloponnese and to Attica on the mainland to the north-east, particularly on the west-facing slopes of Panakhaiken Mountain.

Carpenter suggests that a weakening of the polar high pressure at this time would have caused a more northerly track of the Atlantic depressions which, generally, bring spring and autumn rain to the Aegean. If this had occurred, then the only rainfall that would have continued to be reliable would have fallen on the western flanks of the mainland and of the Peloponnese. The original Mycenaean settlements could have suffered persistent drought, bringing famine and perhaps the pillaging of the palaces of the rich – which, Carpenter believes, may explain the signs of destruction.

In archaeological and documentary terms, there is little evidence to support Carpenter's hypothesis; and the alternative hypothesis of military overthrow is not entirely discredited.[59] Moreover, the initial response from physical scientists to Carpenter's thesis was not promising. Lamb thought it seriously over-simplified the nature of climatic changes and has emphasised that an intensification of summer droughts in Greece would be more likely to have occurred as a result of a southward displacement than a northward displacement of north-westerlies.[60] Moreover, Wright has emphasised that no evidence exists either for the climatic changes *per se*, or for their possible effects in terms of changes of vegetation in the region.[61] But, more recently, an analysis of the patterns of winter climate in the south Aegean has revealed the occurrence of a type of hemispheric circulation which was characterised by patterns consistent with the proposed pattern of the Mycenaean drought.[62] This pattern was dominant during the period November 1954 to March 1955 and can be used as an analogue of the dry weather postulated for the late Mycenaean period. The drought pattern suggested by Carpenter could, therefore, have occurred – but did it occur at that time and over several consecutive years? The scattered evidence of floods, droughts and storms that occurred at the same time, but in different places, seems *prima facie* to fit the 1955 analogue, but the argument remains inconclusive. What is needed is a more thorough investigation of the agricultural implications of this hypothesised drought in terms of Mycenaean food supplies; Carpenter's arguments connecting settlement desertion with drought exclude an important link in the proposed causal chain.

The foregoing examples illustrate briefly the contrasting issues in archaeology for which a climatic explanation is sometimes offered. In each case the credence of the explanation is, at present, limited. But in each case it would be rewarding to pursue a detailed study of the process by which changes of climate may have induced concurrent changes of an economic or social nature.

7

Short-Term Fluctuations of Climate

Attention has focused upon long-term changes in climate on the assumption that long-term changes have long-term effects, and that short-term fluctuations – the differences in weather from year to year – have an impact that is generally ephemeral. The hypothesis has been that where short-term change has a lasting effect it is only as an immediate stimulus or 'trigger' of an economic response in areas already made sensitive by the long-term climatic trend.

As a 'trigger' of change its role is fortuitous as it could have been performed by a variety of occurrences – for example, epidemics of disease or political instability. However, it may be the agent of socio-economic change where extreme marginality has been established by the long-term trend of social and economic conditions. Indeed, economic historians have on the whole been more prepared to accept the impact of short-term climatic change on economically marginal areas than of short-term economic changes on areas made marginal by the long-term climatic trend. Postan, for example, has noted the extreme vulnerability to environmental changes of subsistence farmers with no reclaimable waste.[1]

Moreover, year-to-year fluctuations of climate are the medium through which long-term shifts of climate are ultimately felt; and they are closely related to the long-term trend in Britain because the variability from year to year of warmth and wetness generally moves inversely with fluctuations in average warmth and average rainfall – when average temperatures fall as part of a long-term cooling trend the probability of 'runs' of cool summers increases. In maritime Europe the probability of occurrence of summers with accumulated temperatures failing to reach the threshold required for cereal ripening tends to increase almost exponentially with long-term cooling –

the effect is very similar to that of increasing elevation in maritime hill areas.[2]

Sequences of adverse summers occur infrequently but their effect upon the lives of early cultivators was profound as consecutive failure of the harvest led to the consumption of seed-corn and thus to the continuation of famine beyond the immediate period of adverse weather. Thus economic historians have, for some time, been aware of the tendency for good and bad harvests to run in sequences of three or four.[3] The importance of these runs can be examined by reference to a few examples of brief phases of particularly adverse weather and to the way in which these triggered socio-economic events – events which had perhaps been preconditioned by long-term agents and which were latent at the time of adverse weather. Among these examples we shall refer to the crisis of 1315–16, the famines of the 1590s and 1690s, the spectacularly poor summers of 1782 and 1816, and the difficult seasons which coincided with depressed prices during the Great Depression of the late nineteenth century.

In these examples the interest is on the rural economy in Scotland whose marginality made it so sensitive to fluctuation of the seasons. Before the eighteenth century famine in Scotland was always near at hand. One of the reasons for this is that, throughout northern Europe, shortage of food grains was, more commonly than not, the result of a short summer produced by a preceding cold, wet spring and followed by an early cold autumn. Whereas in central and southern England cold autumns are normally dry, in Scotland they are generally wet.[4] Climatic cooling in Scotland, therefore, is often linked with the onset of coldness and wetness at both ends of the growing season, leading to a compounded decline in potential for crop growth. Wetness in the early autumn is particularly adverse to the Scottish cereal farmer because even today he can expect to often harvest oats into October and, on high land, into November; moreover, prior to the introduction of improved strains, autumn harvesting would have been even more frequent an occurrence. Wet, cloudy autumns not only discourage ripening but encourage sprouting in the ear, and frequently the grain would have to be harvested green and wet and thus, before the days of efficient corn drying, easily became mildewed. This might partly explain the closer correlation between climatic marginality, crop failure and population trends that has been noticed in upland Scotland and Sweden more than in lowland England.[5]

The Crisis of 1315–16

The spell of adverse weather that seems most profoundly to have affected the agricultural economy of medieval Europe was that which occurred over the period 1315–16. In passing it has been suggested that the effects of this were still being felt when the Black Death occurred in 1348. The impact of extreme adversity in 1316 was greater as a result of the preceding run of below average, though not dramatically poor, harvests. During the period 1308–10 these were sufficiently poor to produce heavy price increases and a situation approaching dearth in some parts of England. In Scotland there was already famine.[6]

The spring of 1314 was wet and cold. The *Croniques de London* recorded that: 'In this year were so great the rains that corn and all other things were lost in August and the rain lasted from Pentecost to Easter.'[7] The harvest was deficient and grain prices rose sharply in the summer of 1315. The summer of 1315 was also particularly wet, and several chroniclers agree that widespread flooding was the main reason for very low levels of production:

> Now in this past year there was such abundance of rain that men hardly gathered any crops for sale or stored it safely in the barn. For the inundation of rain consumed nearly all the seed, so that now was seen the fulfilment of the prophecy of Isaiah, and in several places hay was so hidden under water that it could neither be cut nor garnered. Sheep also perished in flocks and the animals died of a sudden murrain.
>
> *Annales Paulini* (from Latin)[8]

The winter of 1315–16 seems to have been mild and wet, and there was again flooding in the following summer. Changes in incomes for two manors on the estate of the Bishop of Winchester in 1316 were explained by the bailiffs as follows:

> *De Pastura in . . . in estate nichil hoc anno propter nimiam habundanciam aque existentem in aliis pasturis*
> (From the pasture in . . . in the summer, nothing this year because of the abundance of water lying in the other pastures)
> *De lana angnorum nichil hoc anno quia non tondebantur propter magnam incongruitatem temporis in estate*
> (From lamb's wool, nothing this year because they were not shorn on account of the great inconsistency of the weather in the summer)[9]

Titow has calculated that on this estate wheat yields in 1315 and 1316 were respectively 36 and 45 per cent below the average for the period 1209–1350, in which there was only a 3·83 return per unit of seed. In other words the mean gross yield of wheat from the manors was only 2·4 in 1315 and 2·1 in 1316.[10] In the north of England average yields were consistently lower, and on some demesnes in the West Riding of Yorkshire gross yields of wheat in 1315 and 1316 fell by as much as 19 per cent below their average.[11]

It was suggested earlier that the wet weather at this time was also an important factor in the spread of disease among sheep and cattle – probably liver-fluke and rinderpest. Outbreaks of these diseases would not have been unusual in the fourteenth century, and they did not always completely destroy flocks and herds. What seems to have been unusual was that they occurred over a remarkably large area. While the cattle plague of 1319–21 was more localised the sheep murrain of 1315–17 was on a national scale; Kershaw has suggested that the combination of crop and livestock losses generated the worst agrarian crisis faced by England as a whole since the aftermath of the Norman invasion.

Certainly the consequences were both widespread and long-lasting. By the summer of 1316 wheat prices were more than four times the average of the first decade of the century. Starvation was widespread and rates of mortality increased substantially in the years immediately after 1315 (Fig 40). A consequence of this, as well as of the shortage of seed and of draught animals, was the abandonment of marginal farmland. There is quite widespread evidence of uncultivated arable land on the Winchester estates, and on some demesnes in Leicestershire and West Yorkshire for which there is a surviving documentary record. There is similar evidence from Derbyshire, Devon and Cornwall.[12] The indications are of a substantial desertion of the poorer land on particular demesnes and a widespread vacancy of the poorer holdings.

It is not yet known whether the contraction of tillage was a direct effect of adverse weather on crops and livestock; if it was, then the occurrence was not short-lived. Kershaw has evidence of vacant and uncultivated holdings in Yorkshire in the 1320s; even in 1341 the returns of the *Nonarum Inquisitiones* recorded land that had not been sown for thirty years.[13]

Kershaw believes that this succession of difficult years exposed for the first time the precarious position of the agrarian economy in fourteenth-century England. It marked the turning point from an era of population growth, rising prices, rising land values and extensive reclamation to an economic contraction that was needed to correct an imbalance between the agrarian population and its rural resources.[14]

Farmers in the 'Little Ice Age'

The 1590s No instrumental record is available for the 1590s, but the wine-harvest records point to a run of particularly cool summers from 1591 to 1598. The ensuing famine that extended across Europe over the period 1594–7 was, like the crisis of 1315–16, partly the product of a slow decline of food reserves due to a preceding three decades of generally poor summers. A cruelly hard winter in 1555 was followed by cool, cloudy summers in the years 1563–5, 1568–70 and 1576–7, and in 1579, 1581 and finally 1585–7.[15]

In 1596 there were food riots in many counties in England,[16] and in Scotland serious famine on a national scale. Indeed, as early as 1550–2 there was alarm in Scotland about the food supply which had been reduced by two poor seasons and by recent English invasions. In 1550 the Privy Council issued sumptuary regulations prescribing the maximum number of courses per meal. Prices had returned to normal by 1553, but the winter of 1554–5 was exceptionally hard and snowy; 'The great snow began on Yowl da and ilk da fra that furth mayr and mayr without ony thryfft quhyl the xvii day of Januar.'[17]

After a short break it snowed and froze again until the end of February, with heavy losses of livestock. Severe winters in 1560 and 1562 brought further losses; and high meal prices and substantial grain imports over the period 1560–3 suggest below average harvests. After this the record is silent, but severe winters in 1571 and 1572 ushered in another phase of shortage up until 1575. From 1585 to 1587 food shortage is once again indicated by the promulgation of new restrictions on meat-eating in Lent and on grain hoarding and grain exports. The catch of herring off the west coast was much below average – quite possibly the result of a southward shift of stocks that occurred as a result of reduced sea temperatures. There was some recovery in 1589, but the true dearth came in 1594 and was critical until 1598. There were food riots in Edinburgh in 1596 and starvation was widespread throughout Scotland.

The 1590s were also disastrous years in Scandinavia. In Norway the summer of 1591 has been described as 'the black year in which the grass did not turn green at all north of the Dovre'[18]; and over the period 1596–8 there is evidence of severe famine around Stavanger in south-west Norway.[19]

Conditions appear to have been similar in Sweden. A contemporary account which survives for the parish of Ålem on Kalmar Sound noted widespread flooding, with heavy losses of stock and grain, in August 1596 and June 1597.[20] The summer of 1599 seems to have been unexceptional, but that of 1600 was evidently very short and in 1601 very heavy snows in February were followed by spring flooding, by persistent drought in July and by early autumn rains. The cereal crop was cut unripe and, therefore, heated or rotted in the barns.

The year of 1601 was certainly one of extremes. Its main effect, coming as it did on a sequence of poor harvests, was to create a severe local food shortage. The mortality rate increased markedly due to the incidence of starvation and the spread of plague. About one-quarter of the population of Småland was lost in 1601 alone.

Throughout Europe the years of extremes continued into the seventeenth century. Spells of very harsh dry winters and wet, tempestuous summers seem to have alternated with periods of moist, mild winters and quite warm summers. The Thames was frozen in 1607–8, 1649 and 1662–3. Over these years there was an occasional summer that was exceptionally adverse which, coming as it did in the midst of a long-term trend of cold and of wetness, sometimes caused dearth to Scotland in a single season. It was fortunate, however, that these occurred more generally in isolation than in consecutive runs. One such summer was 1649.

The Summer of 1649 The years 1643–7 seem to have been prosperous enough, but they were followed by a very wet summer in 1648, a

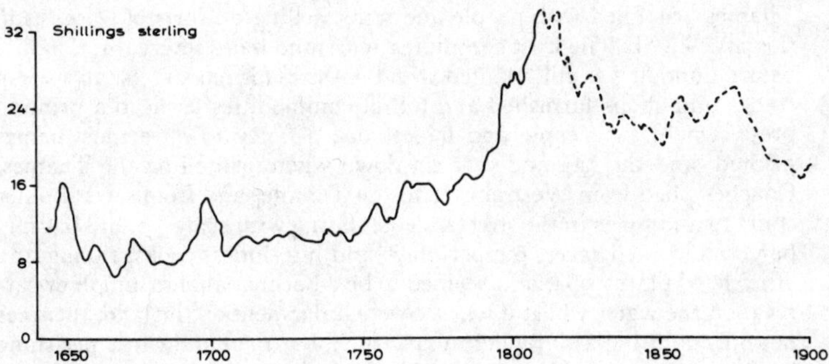

Fig. 44. Price of oats at Haddington, south-east Scotland, 1643–1900. Adapted from Mitchison (1965).

mild, wet winter which delayed the autumn sowing, a cattle murrain and a spectacularly late harvest in 1649.[21] The wine harvest in northern France was the latest for twenty-eight years. In Scotland the difficulty was aggravated by bubonic plague which had been brought back by the Covenanting army after the storming of Newcastle in 1644. In England the epidemic reached its peak in 1645, but in the more remote upland 'touns' in Scotland it was still active up to 1648. In 1651 in a rental for two parishes in Kintyre in south-west Argyllshire, 29 out of 55 holdings were entered as wholly waste and 13 as partially waste. McKerral believes that this was the combined result of poor harvests, plague and military hostilities but that it is difficult to separate the three.[22]

In the south-east of Scotland it is likewise difficult to distinguish the relative influences of the weather and of the Cromwellian occupation. But the sharpness of the rise and fall in the price of oats at Haddington, in East Lothian, in 1650 and 1651 certainly suggests a short-term effect consistent with the occurrence of good seasons both preceding and following this adverse spell (Fig 44).[23]

The Seven Ill Years The fairly stable phase of 1650–80 was followed by a long run of severe winters and cool summers. The winter of 1684–5 was one of the severest in memory. The Thames was frozen at London and the diarist Evelyn noted:

> January 1. The weather continuing intolerably severe, streets of booths were set upon the Thames. The air was so very cold and thick as of many years there had not been the like. – 6th. The river quite frozen. – 9th. I went across the Thames on the ice, now become so thick as to bear not only streets of booths, in which they roasted meat, and had divers shops of wares quite across as in a town, but coaches, carts and horses passed over. So I went from Westminster Stairs to Lambeth. – 16th. The Thames was filled with people and tents, selling all sorts of wares as in the city. – 24th. The frost continuing more and more severe, the Thames before London was still planted with booths in formal streets, all sorts of trades and shops furnished and full of commodities, even to a printing press, where the people and ladies took a fancy to have their names printed, and the day and year set down when printed on the Thames. Coaches plied from Westminster to the Temple, and from several other stairs to and fro as in the streets, sleds, sliding with skates, a bull baiting, horse and coach races, puppet plays and interludes, cooks, tipling and other lewd places, so that it seemed to be a bacchanalian triumph or carnival on the water whilst it was a severe judgement on the land, the trees not only splitting as if by lightning struck, but men and cattle perishing in divers places, and the very seas so locked up with ice that no vessels could stir out or come in. The fowls, fish and birds, and all our exotic plants and greens universally perishing. Many parks of deer were destroyed, and all sorts of fuel so dear that there were great contributions to preserve the poor alive. Nor was this severe weather much less intense in most parts of Europe as far as Spain.[24]

In December the following year the Thames was again frozen over – both these extreme winters were followed by excessively hot and dry springs. Evelyn noted 'such two winters and summers I have never known'.[25] The Thames was frozen again in 1688 and almost frozen in 1689, but while there had been substantial losses of stock in these conditions, the cereal harvests – except for that of 1687 which in Aberdeenshire was remembered for the 'great deluges of rain and constant mists and fog . . . whereby the corn in the fields and stackyards was in danger of heating and rotting and so being destroyed'[26] – had not suffered greatly. The price of oats, which had risen slightly over the period 1689–90, was by 1691 at about the average level for the period 1650–1700.

From 1692 there began a series of extraordinarily poor summers characterised by short growing seasons, due to damp, cool springs, and by high rainfall. The summers of 1692 and 1695 – following a harsh January during which the Thames was frozen for the eighth time in the century – were cool and wet, and were followed by early autumns which delayed the harvests even longer. By 1696 oats were selling at Haddington for more than twice the price than five years previously. There were mildly deficient harvests in 1696 and 1697 prior to the disastrous summer of 1698 when the onset of the growing season was effectively delayed until early May. Manley's calculations for central England yielded a mean monthly temperature for May 1698 of only 8·6°C – the lowest on the 300-year record. The subsequent months of high summer were not exceptionally cool, but were followed by an early, damp autumn.[27]

In England the harvest was poor; in Scotland it was disastrous for it concluded a sequence of seven deficient harvests. In the south-west of Scotland it was reported that:

> these manifold unheard-of judgements continued seven years, not always alike, but the seasons, summer and winter (were) so cold and barren, and the wonted heat of the sun so much withholden that it was discernible upon the cattle, flying fowl and insects decaying, seldom a fly or a cleg was to be seen; our harvests (were) not in the ordinary months; many were shearing in November and December, some in January and February; many contracted their deaths and lost the use of feet and hands working in frost and snow; and after all, some of it was still standing and rotting upon the ground; much of it was of little use to man or beast and it had no taste or colour of meal.[28]

In the short term there was famine. In the Old Statistical Account, written ninety-seven years after the event, it was recalled that in the parish of Monquitter, in Buchan in north-east Scotland:

> one Thompson, wadsetter of Hairmoss, driven from his home by want, was found dead, near the shore, with a piece of raw flesh in his mouth. Of

sixteen families that resided on the farm of Littertie, thirteen were extinguished. On the estate of Greens which (in 1793) accommodates 169 individuals, three families, the proprietor's included, only survived. The extensive farms of Touchar, Greeness, Overhill and Burnside of Idoch, being entirely desolated, were converted into a sheep-walk by the Errol family to whom they then belonged. The inhabitants of the parish in general were diminished by death to one half, or as some affirm, to one fourth of the preceding number.[29]

Over the long term, however, there was desertion of the higher farms and abandonment of the more marginal land. This was particularly the case where famine had extinguished the farming population, such as in western Aberdeenshire, in the glens of the Foudland Hills[30] and in the parish of Insch where the Old Statistical Account attributed the reversion of high arable land to depopulation by famine.[31] In the parish of Monquitter many farms lay waste until 1709 and even at that time the landlord had difficulty getting in tenants.[32] Indeed it became fashionable to blame the 'Seven Ill Years' for much of the problems of Scottish agriculture. In 1811 a well-known farming journal commented:

Those who are acquainted with the state of Scotland at the end of the seventeenth century, need not be informed that the distressed situation of the husbandmen at that time, from a series of bad crops and adverse seasons, was the sole cause why farms frittered down to a small size, the tenantry being quite unable to stock or cultivate a farm of any considerable extent[33]

Written long after the event, and often with political aims in mind, comments like these, and those of the Old Statistical Account, should be treated with scepticism. But there are contemporary accounts that reveal something about the significance of poor harvests. One of the earliest Scottish essays on agricultural practice first published in 1699 declared:

First I have observed ordinarily, the thing that breaks the Tenant is bad Years, that is to say, Bad Crops, when the Ground brings not forth according to its usual Fertility. When the Crop proves bad the Price of Victual ariseth often to the Double, and Pease to the triple of what they are sold at in Years of Plenty.

In these years, the poor Tenant not having wherewith to pay his whole Rent, whatever he falls short in a Year of Scarcity, he is not able to make it up in two or three Years of Plenty, because then the Corns fell at a very low Rate, and so being once intangled with Debt, he is discouraged to prosecute his Labour with Diligence, Expense and Heartiness, and so dwindles away to Nothing.[34]

We have seen that farm amalgamation was encouraged by tenant bankruptcy and that amalgamation led, in turn, to the abandonment of outlying arable land. Of course, amalgamation was also inspired – particularly from 1750 onwards – by the increasing commercialisation of Scottish farming, and it would be quite wrong to attribute most of it to bankruptcies. But we do know that some of the amalgamation which occurred in the early seventeenth century and a small proportion of that which occurred after 1750 – perhaps after the difficult seasons in 1756 and 1782 – was indirectly the product of runs of adverse weather.

From a variety of documentary sources it is evident that in the Lammermuir Hills about 60 farms (7 per cent of the total) disappeared between 1600 and 1750, about 200 (22 per cent) over the period 1750–1800. During 1770–1850, the period of most amalgamation, the average size of farms increased by 21 per cent. Over the same period, 4500 hectares (about 8·6 per cent of the entire moorland area) was allowed to revert to rough pasture.[35]

In the 1690s there was dearth in most parts of Europe. In France the substandard harvests of 1690, 1691, and 1692 brought the real prospect of widespread famine. In October 1692 the *intendant* of Auvergne wrote to the controller general in Paris:

> What is to be feared is a great dearth of wheat not only next year, 1693, but also in 1694. I do not mean they are left fallow or that there is not enough seed to sow; but the bad weather has held back the harvest and sowing so much that most of the men have not dared to sow and those who have dared are convinced there will be nothing to reap.[36]

In Finland at least a quarter, and possibly a third, of the population died in the Great Famine of 1696–7, largely as a result of epidemic diseases spreading through a very weak population.[37] Scant harvests in 1693 and 1695 had left food supplies precariously low. The spring was late in 1696 and there was a severe frost on 17–18 August. On average it seems that the crop was about a third of that of a good year, but this figure conceals the remarkably variable yields: in some regions about a fifth of the villages may have had almost no crop at all. An uncompromising government attitude to the import and distribution of grain led to the first deaths by starvation in April 1697; and although the summer of 1697 was favourable, the grain ships from Riga arrived too late for the spring sowing and therefore the planting was deficient. In addition, consignments of seed from Stockholm arrived too late for the autumn sowing. In Lower-Sääksmaki only 12 per cent of the villages had a complete autumn sowing and 30 per cent either sowed none at all or the poor seed had not germinated. The combined effect of adverse weather and lack of concern by the government was appalling – Jutikkala believes that the distribution of small amounts of oats from Riga in late 1697 would have been sufficient to prevent another famine simply because of the decline in population that had already occurred.[38]

In Finland the desertion of farms that accompanied depopulation was more than recovered with the widespread advance of farm settlement in the nineteenth century. In Iceland, however, farm abandonment in the 1690s was more permanent. For example, two farms which once lay below the southern edge of the Breidamerkurjökull in southern Iceland were buried by advancing ice in the seventeenth century. At the time of their establishment in the eleventh century the edge of the ice cap must have been many kilometres further north for, although the probable sites of the farms have been recently re-exposed, they are still flooded by annual discharges from an ice-dammed lake. Thorarinsson's studies of the documentary record point to burial of the first farm, Fjall, (at 180 m O.D.) between 1695 and 1709; the second farm, Breida, (at 100 m O.D.) was abandoned before 1698 but its ruins were still visible in 1712.[39]

Isolated Incidents: the Summers of 1782 and 1816

There were, as a result of poor harvests, minor food shortages in Scotland in 1741, 1767 and 1772, but none seem to have had a lasting effect. The year 1782 was, however, an exception. April and May were windy and cold; the average temperatures calculated by Manley were 5·2°C and 9·0°C – nearly the lowest on record.[40] The already foreshortened summer was also below the average in intensity of warmth and was abruptly ended by heavy frost on 3–4 October. On the high land the oats crop was not gathered in until after Christmas, and was further hampered by quite heavy falls of snow in October in the north-east of Scotland. By late November in Aberdeenshire there was still much corn uncut and by 8 December some hill parishes had hardly begun their cutting.[41]

In the Cabrach in upland Banffshire the Old Statistical Account reported that the population had decreased by about 200 during the decade following 1782 'at which time the house-holders and crofters were driven in quest of subsistence to other countries and towns where manufactures are carried on'.[42] In the Lammermuir Hills local commentators thought there was some reversion of high arable as a result of the adverse weather:

> The quantity of ground that has at different times been under the plough is so great, that it is hard to say, unless it was to extirpate the heath, what could be the inducement. In wet seasons the corn crops seldom arrive at maturity. In 1782 heavy losses were sustained from a total failure of the crop, which, in many places, was not thought worthy of being thrashed.[43]

There is some confirmation that reversion occurred through the bankruptcy of tenants and the amalgamation of tenancies. The Old Statistical Account reported for the parish of Lauder:

> In 1782 and 1783, the situation of the inhabitants was truly deplorable. It was the end of December before the harvest was finished, after a great part of the crop was destroyed by frost and snow. None of the farmers could pay their rent; some of them lost from £200 to £500 sterling . . .[44]

About 25 km away, on the estate of Marchmont, the total rent paid by tenants fell in 1783 and 1785 and it was not until 1789 that it recovered to its former level. This fall was due largely to tenant bankruptcies and subsequent farm amalgamations. Between 1764 and 1819 the number of farms on this estate was reduced by a third, and its arable area was probably reduced by 4 per cent. On two other estates, those of Innerwick and Dunglass, respectively, 38 and 54 per cent of the farms were amalgamated over the period 1750–1820.[45] Even after this reorganisation several of the hill tenants could not, in poor seasons, pay the heavy rent that they had agreed to pay in the prosperous period of inflated wartime prices. A report on the estate of Marchmont noted that 'the imposition of (a high rent) is calculated, on the occurrence of adverse times, to deprive him of all the funds necessary for the cultivation of his land'.[46]

Indeed, the suggestion is that the occurrence of poor harvests contributed substantially to the difficulties of British farmers after the Napoleonic wars – difficulties traditionally attributed largely to the post-war depression of prices; for, both in terms of length of growing season and intensity of warmth, the summer of 1782 was not as poor as that of 1816. In this year summer temperatures seem to have been markedly reduced in many parts of the northern hemisphere, possibly as a result of a dust veil from the eruption of the volcano Tambora on Sumbawa Island, east of Java, in April 1815 – an eruption which probably ejected into the stratosphere more than four times the quantity of fine ash ejected by Krakatao in 1883.[47] In central and western Europe the summer was characterised by very low pressure which allowed the penetration of polar air from the north; and in the north-east United States a northerly air stream seems to have been maintained well into high summer. The result, on both continents, was a late and long spring, cool summer and relatively wet autumn.

In northern England the effect of the cool summer in 1816 was compounded by the legacy of preceding seasons. The year 1814 had not been easy: the early summer did not warm up as usual – although it was generally dry the nights were cold and even frosty. The third week of July saw a turn to warmth and rain, but this was followed by coldness and rain in early August and this interrupted the ripening of the crops. It was a disappointing harvest.

The high summer of 1815 was generally fine and dry and much of the lowland cereals were cut before heavy rain came toward the end of September. But, as often happened, the upland crops suffered heavily – and prices remained low (66 per cent of the decadal average) because of the generally copious harvests. There was already some sign of distress among upland farmers.[48]

The monthly temperature for July 1816 was the coldest on Manley's record; and those for April, May and June were, respectively, 21 per cent, 14 per cent and 12 per cent below the average for 1931–60. The summer temperatures in August and September were 13 and 14 per cent below the present 'normal'.[49] The cool, humid conditions nurtured disease in the wheat and prevented oats from ripening properly. By the autumn of 1816 oats prices were almost double that of the preceding year; and the turnip crop, which had been left in the fields during the winter, was destroyed by rot. By the beginning of 1817, ten of the thirty-eight parishes in Dumfriesshire were operating a soup kitchen or distributing oatmeal to the poor.[50]

In France the wine harvests were the latest ever known. Ladurie records the correspondence of a Brie peasant: 'In the month of May (1817) wheat had got so dear everyone thought to die of hunger. In June came revolutions in all the markets and towns, for bread was no longer to be had at the bakers.'[51] The pattern was much the same over the whole of north-west Europe.

In New England there was a similarly slow warm-up in summer. A correspondent from Montpelier, Vermont, reported to the *Connecticut Gazette* that:

> The oldest inhabitants do not recollect ever to have experienced so extraordinary cold weather at this season, as on the sixth, seventh and eighth of June. We are informed that on the morning of the eighth, the snow drifts of many adjacent hills were more than a foot deep. Many sheep have perished with the cold.[52]

Throughout the north-east United States the corn and vegetable crop failed.

The Complicity of Climate in the Great Depression

An explanation frequently given by contemporaries for the depressed state of British agriculture at the end of the nineteenth century was the run of poor harvests in the 1870s and 1880s. Today, agricultural historians find it curious that farmers would not accept that crushing imports of wheat were here to stay and that farming systems would, in future, have to accommodate this.[53] The fall in prices, as a result of these imports, is generally regarded as the most conspicuous cause of the Great Depression in British agriculture.[54] Yet, the evidence given to the Royal Commission on the Depressed Condition of Agricultural Interests, 1880–82 (the 'Richmond Commission'), although often exaggerated by individual farmers, is quite consistent – and is supported by evidence given by the assistant commissioners who toured the regions. The difficult weather of the late 1870s and late 1880s was clearly an important – albeit secondary – factor behind the agricultural distress. W. C. Little, the Assistant Commissioner for the southern counties, had in 1879

> seen corn crops which would barely pay the cost of harvesting and marketing; hop gardens which the pickers have never entered; meadows from which the whole crop had been carried away by flood, and others from which the hay was being carted in the month of October, to be used for manure; fallows upon which the labour and expenses of months had been absolutely thrown away; root crops upon which no expense had been spared, and yet the crop was worthless. These things I have seen not merely in single and isolated instances but frequently and in many different parts of the country; and, perhaps most serious loss of all, I learn from many quarters that whole flocks of sheep have been removed by the fatal disease, sheep-rot.[55]

Given this contemporary emphasis on adverse weather, it is instructive to evaluate its role in the Great Depression by observing, firstly, the meteorological data available for the period, and secondly, the relationship between these data and the agricultural conditions pertaining at the time.

The general trend of temperatures, which had exhibited a steady rise since about 1700, shows a pronounced dip throughout western Europe in the last quarter of the nineteenth century (Figs 2 and 9). In the Alps the major glaciers enjoyed a brief phase of re-advance (Fig 4) and in Iceland more farms were buried by ice at the front of the Breidamerkurjökull.[56] More specifically we can say that summer

Table 5: WARMTH OF THE GROWING SEASON AT EDINBURGH, 1875–95

	Accumulated temperature in day–degrees C	% deviation from 1856–95 'normal' (1525 day–degrees C)
1875	1571	+ 3·0
1876	1522	– 0·2
1877	1371	–10·1
1878	1716	+12·5
1879	1150	–24·6
1880	1584	+ 3·9
1881	1477	– 3·1
1882	1640	+ 7·5
1883	1486	– 2·6
1884	1575	+ 3·3
1885	1326	–13·0
1886	1540	+ 1·0
1887	1487	– 2·5
1888	1371	–10·1
1889	1565	+ 2·6
1890	1591	+ 4·3
1891	1402	– 8·0
1892	1374	– 9·9
1893	1852	+21·4
1894	1616	+ 6·0
1895	1686	+10·6

Note: Temperature data from Mossman (1896–7), 117–18.

warmth over this period was particularly limited in certain groups of years: 1877–81, 1885–8 and 1891–2 (Table 5). In some years it was spectacularly low – like the summer of 1879 which at Edinburgh had an accumulated warmth that was 24 per cent below the 'normal' for the second half of the nineteenth century.

Annual rainfall was generally in excess of the 30-year average in the early 1870s; in 1879 it was close to the average and in the 1880s was frequently below it. But for the months May to September it was frequently above average: in 1879, over Britain as a whole, June rainfall was almost twice the average for 1881–1915 and July–August rainfall was almost 50 per cent above average. The summers of 1877, 1878 and 1882 were also a good deal wetter than average, as were the late summers and autumns of 1885 and 1891–2.[57] In terms of both summer warmth and summer rainfall the periods 1877–81 and 1891–2 were, therefore, difficult periods for the farmer – and it is not a coincidence that these correspond with the periods of greatest difficulty named by the Royal Commission as being 1879–82, 1885–7 and 1893–5.[58]

The consequences of adverse weather were three-fold. Firstly, yields were well down and harvesting costs increased. The wheat yield for the United Kingdom as a whole was 9·7 bushels per acre (0.69 tonnes/ha) below the 10-year average; and this had occurred at a time when many upland farms were beginning to show a regular loss. In his evidence to the Richmond Commission in 1880 one Berwickshire farmer reckoned that 'if we have another bad season the whole farming district will collapse'.[59] Less likely to have overstated the case was the assistant commissioner reporting on southern Scotland. He estimated that the average tenant had lost capital equivalent to one year's rent.[60]

Secondly, the runs of cold, wet summers favoured the spread of livestock disease. Over the period 1879–81 outbreaks of liver-fluke occurred on almost a national scale, killing about 10 per cent of the sheep in Britain. Pleuro-pneumonia and rinder-pest also presented an acute problem – perhaps 100,000 cattle died of pleuro-pneumonia alone during 1869–94.[61]

Finally, at least on the more marginal land, the combined effect of adverse weather and depressed prices was felt in long-term changes in the use of agricultural land. Across the entire country there was both a move to longer leys and a tendency for old grass to revert to rough pasture. Annual acreage returns for south-east Scotland reveal a 5 per cent reduction in the area under crops and grass between 1880 and 1885 and reductions of about 1 per cent every five years from 1885 to 1900. Over the period 1880–1900 the proportion of agricultural land under crops and grass fell by more than 8 per cent. Similar trends were evident throughout upland Britain.[62]

Indeed the general picture is of a nationwide retreat of improved farmland at the moorland edge – and an advance of rough pasture that in some places was not checked until the plough-up campaign of 1917. Moreover, in contrast to the reversion of farmland that was widespread in the 1930s, reversion in the 1880s was frequently permanent – it remains moorland today, lying in large tracts along the slopes of hills throughout Britain. In the Lammermuir Hills it amounts to 450 hectares, or 6·9 per cent of the area that is now moorland but which once was cultivated.[63] In the Peak District it approximates 21·5 per cent.[64]

The story of British agriculture in the Great Depression is a complicated one and it would be quite wrong to suggest that changes in land use or in the structure of farming at this time were primarily a response to short-term changes in climate. They were not; but it is clear that the incidence of difficult weather – part of a decadal lowering of mean temperatures and increase in rainfall – tended to compound the adversity of depressed prices. While placing in true perspective the exaggerated attributions to weather claimed by contemporary farmers we should not lose sight of the 'triggering' effect in 1879 that livestock disease and poor harvests had upon an already-depressed farming economy – an economy that was poorly adjusted to its economic environment.

The period of the Great Depression in Britain illustrates clearly the way in which short-term fluctuations of climate, which are part of a longer trend, may have a small, but certainly significant, impact upon agriculture which has been already weakened either by the long-term climatic trend itself or, more likely, by a change in socio-economic circumstances. While the contention of this book has been that, in special circumstances, long-term changes of climate can have a long-term socio-economic effect, it must be recognised that short-term fluctuations, which comprise the secular trend, may on occasion act as the ultimate 'trigger' of change. More often, however, it seems that the 'trigger' is socio-economic or political in nature.

Notes and References

Chapter 1: *New evidence, old attitudes*

1 Kutzbach, J. E., 'Fluctuations of climate – monitoring and modelling', *WMO Bulletin,* 155–63 (July 1974).

2 Lamb, H. H., 'Climatology 1: The need to make up for lost time', *Times Higher Educational Supplement,* IV (21 January, 1977).

3 Bryson, R. A., Ross, J. E., Hougas, R. W. and Engelbert, L. E., *Climatic change and agricultural responses,* Institute of Environmental Studies, University of Wisconsin, IES Report No. 20, 21 (Madison 1974).

4 McQuigg, J. D., *et al., The influence of weather and climate on United States grain yields,* National Oceanic and Atmospheric Administration, United States Department of Commerce, (1973); Bryson, R. A. *et al., op. cit.,* 24 (1974).

5 Beltzner, K. (ed.), *Living with climatic change,* Science Council of Canada, 10 (1976); McQuigg, J. D., *et. al., op. cit.,* 21–3 (1973).

6 Attempts to measure the costs of weather changes are in their infancy. Work in this field is summarised by Maunder, W. J., *The value of the weather* (1970).

7 Lamb, H. H., 'Climatic change and foresight in agriculture: the possibilities of long-term weather advice', *Outlook in Agriculture* **7,** 203–10 (1973).

8 Bryson, R. A., Baerreis, D. A. and Wendland, W. M., 'The character of late- and post-glacial climatic changes' in Dort, W. and Jones, J. K. (eds.), *Pleistocene and recent environments of the central Great Plains,* 53–75 (1970).

9 Pittock, A. B., 'How important are climatic changes?', *Weather* **27,** 262–71 (1972).

10 Bryson, R. A. *et. al., op. cit.* (1974); Bryson, R. A. and Murray, T. J., *Climates of hunger,* xi–xiv (1977).

11 Le Roy Ladurie, E., *Times of feast, times of famine,* 119 (1972).

12 Huntington, E., *The pulse of Asia,* 365–67 (1907); Huntington's theory was an extension of that developed by Brückner, E., *Klimaschwankungen seit 1700,* (Vienna 1890).

13 Huntington, E. and Visher, S. S., *Climatic changes – their nature and causes,* 61–63 (1922). The argument was developed more fully in Huntington, E., *Earth and sun: an hypothesis of weather and sunspots* (1923).
14 See page 28.
15 Huntington, E., *Civilization and climate,* 3rd edn., 332, 344–5 (1925).
16 See for example, Sears, P. B., 'Climate and civilization' in Shapley, H., *Climatic change: evidence, causes and effects,* 35–50 (1953).
17 The philosophical reaction to environmental determinism is summarised by Tatham, G., 'Environmentalism and possibilism' in Taylor, G. (ed.), *Geography in the twentieth century,* 3rd edn., 128–62 (1957).
18 Beveridge, W. H., 'British exports and the barometer – I', *The Economic Journal* **30,** 13–25 (1920); Beveridge, W. H., 'British exports and the barometer – II', *The Economic Journal* **30,** 209–13 (1920); Beveridge, W. H., 'Weather and harvest cycles', *The Economic Journal,* **31,** 429–52 (1921).
19 Britton, C. E., *A meteorological chronology to A.D. 1450,* Meteorological Office, Geophysical Memoirs, No. 70 (1937).
20 Russell, J. C., *British medieval population,* 232–4 (1948); Van Bath, B. H. S., *The agrarian history of western Europe A.D. 500–1850,* 160–1 (1963).
21 Brooks, C. E. P. and Glasspoole, J., *British floods and droughts,* 83, 155, 186 (1928).
22 Brooks, C. E. P., *Climate through the ages,* 2nd edn., 310 (1949).
23 Postan, M. M., *The medieval economy and society,* 2nd edn., 19, (1975).
24 Beresford, M. and Hurst, J. G. (eds.), *Deserted medieval villages,* 21 (1971).
25 Russell, J. C., *op. cit.,* 232–4 (1948).
26 Hoskins, W. G., 'Harvest fluctuations and economic history, 1480–1619', *Agricultural History Review,* **2,** 28–46 (1964).
27 Utterström, G., 'Climatic fluctuations and population problems', *Scandinavian Economic History Review,* **2,** 103–65 (1955); Le Roy Ladurie, E., 'Histoire et climat,' *Annales,* 3–34 (1959); Utterström, G., 'Population and agriculture in Sweden', *Scandinavian Economic History Review,* **9,** 176–94 (1961).
28 Postan, M. M., 'Die wirtschaftlichen Grundlagen der mittelalterlichen Gesellschaft', *Jahrbücher für Nationolökonomie und Statistik,* **166,** 180–205 (1954); Postan, M. M., *op. cit.,* 42 (1975).
29 Le Roy Ladurie, E., *op. cit.,* 244 (1972).
30 *Proceedings of the Conference on the Climate of the Eleventh and Sixteenth Centuries,* Aspen, Colorado, 1962, National Centre for Atmospheric Research, NCAR Technical Notes 63–1 (1963).

Chapter 2: *The process and chronology of climatic change*

1 Further details may be found in Lamb, H. H., *Climate: past, present and future,* Vol. 1, 254–306 (1972).
2 Mitchell, J. M., 'Causes of climatic change', *Meteorological Monograph,* **8,** 155–59 (1968); Mason, B. J., 'Towards the understanding and prediction of climatic variations', *Quarterly Journal of The Royal Meteorological Society,* **102,** 476–98 (1976).

3 Kutzbach, J. E., 'Fluctuations of climate–monitoring and modelling', *WMO Bulletin,* 155–63 (1974).
4 Bryson, R. A., Ross, J. E., Hougas, R. W., Engelbert, L. E., *Climatic change and agricultural responses,* Institute of Environmental Studies, University of Wisconsin, IES Report No. 20 (Madison 1974).
5 Bryson, R. A., 'A perspective on climatic change', *Science,* **184,** 753–60 (1974).
6 Schneider, S. H. and Mass, C., 'Volcanic dust, sunspots and temperature trends', *Science,* **190,** 741–46 (1975).
7 King, J. W., Hurst, E., Slater, A. J., Smith, P. A. and Tamkin, B., 'Agriculture and sunspots', *Nature,* **252,** 2–3 (1974).
8 Mason, B. J., *op. cit.,* 476–98 (1976).
9 See for example Wood, C. A. and Lovett, R. R., 'Rainfall, drought and the solar cycle', *Nature,* **251,** 594–96 (1974).
10 Hines, C. O. and Haley, I., 'On the reality and nature of a certain sun-weather correlation', *Journal of Atmospheric Science,* **34,** 382–404 (1977).
11 Wood, K. D., 'Sunspots and planets', *Nature,* **240,** 91–3 (1971).
12 For a further discussion of these theories see Gribbin, J., *Our changing climate,* 74–83 (1975).
13 Lamb, H. H., *op. cit.,* 421 (1972).
14 Bryson, R. A., *op. cit.,* 758 (1974).
15 Bryson, R. A., *op. cit.,* 759 (1974).
16 Bryson, R. A., *op. cit.,* 759 (1974).
17 Further detail may be found in Lamb, H. H., *op. cit.,* 385–410 (1972).
18 Lamb, H. H., *op. cit.,* 393 (1972).
19 Bryson, R. A.; Baerreis, D. A. and Wendland, W. M., 'The character of late- and post-glacial climatic changes' in Dort, W. and Jones, J. K. (eds.), *Pleistocene and recent environments of the central Great Plains,* 53–75 (1970).
20 Labrijn, A., 'Het Klimaat van Nederland gedurende de laatste twee en een halve eeuw' (with English summary), *Meded en Verhandelingen,* Koninklijk Nederlandsch Meteorological Institute, **49,** No. 102 (1945); Lysgaard, L., 'Recent climatic fluctuations', *Folia geographica danica,* **5,** supplement (1949); Liljequist, G. H., 'The severity of winters at Stockholm, 1757–1942', *Geographical Annaler,* **25,** 81–97 (1943).
21 Lysgaard, L., *ibid.* (1949).
22 Manley, G., 'The mean temperature of central England, 1698–1952', *Quarterly Journal of the Royal Meteorological Society,* **79,** 242–61 (1953); Manley, G., 'Central England temperatures: monthly means 1659–1973', *Quarterly Journal of the Royal Meteorological Society,* **100,** 389–405 (1974).
23 Vanderlinden, E., *Chronique des evénements météorologiques en Belgique jusqu'en 1834,* (Brussels 1924) quoted by Brooks, C. E. P., *Climate through the ages,* 2nd edn., 287 (1949).
24 For further discussion see Brooks, C. E. P., *ibid,* 281–94 (1949).
25 Britton, C. E., *A meteorological chronology to A.D. 1450,* Meteorological Office, Geophysical Memoirs No. 70 (1937).
26 Britton, C. E., *ibid,* 76 (1937).
27 Britton, C. E., *ibid,* 129 (1937).
28 Britton, C. E., *ibid,* 130 (1937).

29 Britton, C. E., *ibid,* 132 (1937).

30 Van Bath, B. H. S., *The agrarian history of western Europe, A.D. 500–1800,* 161 (1963).

31 Titow, J. Z., 'Evidence of weather in the account rolls of the Bishopric of Winchester, 1209–1350', *Economic History Review,* **12,** 360–407 (1960).

32 Titow, J. Z., *ibid,* 385 (1960).

33 Britton, C. E., *op. cit.,* 133 (1937).

34 Utterström, G., 'Climatic fluctuations and population problems in early modern history', *Scandinavian Economic History Review,* **3,** 3–47 (1955).

35 Lamb, H. H., *The changing climate,* 94 (1966).

36 Pearson, M. G., 'The winter of 1739–40 in Scotland', *Weather,* **28,** 20–24 (1973); Pearson, M. G. 'Snowstorms in Scotland, 1782–1786', *Weather,* **28,** 195–201 (1973); Pearson, M. G., 'Never had it so bad', *Weather,* **30,** 14–21 (1975).

37 Buchinsky, I. E., *The past climate of the Russian Plain,* 2nd edn (in Russian, Leningrad 1957) – A translation is held by the Royal Meteorological Society at Bracknell, Berkshire.

38 Hennig, R., 'Katalog bemerkenswerter Witterungsereignisse von den ältesten Zeiten bis zum Jahre 1800', *Abhundlungen Preussichen der Meteorlogische Institut,* 2 (4) (Berlin 1904).

39 Lamb, H. H., *op. cit.,* 94–101 (1966). The subsequent discussion is based closely upon this source.

40 Cooke, R. U. and Reeves, R. W., *Arroyos and environmental change,* 187–89 (1976).

41 *Proceedings of the Conference on the Climate of the Eleventh and Sixteenth Centuries,* Aspen, Colorado, 1962, National Centre for Atmospheric Research NCAR Technical Notes 63–1, 34 (1963).

42 See selected chapters in Wright, A. E. and Moseley, F. (eds.), *Ice ages: ancient and modern* (1974).

43 Hoinkes, H., 'Glacier variation and weather', *Journal of Glaciology,* 3–21 (1968).

44 Manley, G., 'Problems of the climatic optimum: the contribution of glaciology' in *World climate from 8000 to 0 B.C.,* Royal Meteorological Society, 34–9 (1966).

45 Le Roy Ladurie, E., *Times of feast, times of famine* (1972). A comprehensive study of glacier change is given on pp. 99–226.

46 Le Roy Ladurie, E., *ibid,* 163–4 (1972).

47 Le Roy Ladurie, E., *ibid,* 170 (1972).

48 Manley, G., *op. cit.,* 34–9 (1966).

49 Utterström, G., 'Some population problems in pre-industrial Sweden', *Scandinavian Economic History Review,* **2,** 103–65 (1954).

50 Arakawa, H., 'Fujiwhara on five centuries of freezing dates of Lake Suwa in central Japan', *Archiv. für Meteorologie, Geophysik und Bioklimatologie,* series B6, 152–66 (1955).

51 Sokolov, A., 'Reduction in duration of river ice with climatic warming' (in Russian) *Priroda,* 96–8 (1955).

52 Kassner, C., 'Das zufrieren des Lake Champlain von 1816 bis 1935', *Met. Zeitschr.,* 333 (1935), cited by Le Roy Ladurie, E., *op. cit.,* 228 (1972).

53 Moodie, D. W. and Catchpole, A. J. W., *Environmental data from historical documents by content analysis,* Manitoba Geographical Studies No. 5, University of Manitoba (Winnipeg 1975).

54 Thorarinsson, S., *The thousand years' struggle against ice and fire,* 8 (Reykjavik 1956).

55 Bergthórsson, P., 'An estimate of drift ice and temperature in Iceland in 1000 years', *Jökull,* **19,** 94–101 (1969).

56 Dansgaarde, W., Johnsen, S. J., Reek, N., Gundestrup, N., Clansen, H. B. and Hammer, E. U., 'Climatic changes, Norsemen and modern man', *Nature,* **255,** 24–8 (1975); Dansgaarde, W., Johnsen, S. J., Möller, J. and Langway, C., 'One thousand centuries of climatic record from Camp Century on the Greenland ice sheet', *Science,* **166,** 377–81 (1969).

57 Libby, L. M., *Final technical report on historical climatology,* Defense Advanced Research Projects Agency, ARPA No. 1964–1, 10 (Santa Monica 1974).

58 See for example: Douglass, A. E., *Climate cycles and tree growth,* Carnegie Institute, Pubn. No. 289 (Washington 1919); Schulman, E., 'Tree-rings and history in the western United States', *Smithsonian Report for 1955,* 459–73 (1956); Fritts, H. C., 'Tree rings and climate', *Scientific American,* **226,** 93–100 (1972).

59 Matthews, J. A., 'Little Ice Age palaeotemperatures from high altitude tree growth in S. Norway', *Nature,* **264,** 243–45 (1976).

60 See for example Godwin, H., *The history of the British flora* (1956); Pennington, W., *The history of British vegetation* (1969).

61 *Proceedings of the Conference on the Climate of the Eleventh and Sixteenth Centuries, op. cit.,* 34 (1963).

62 Angot, A., 'Etude sur les vendages en France', *Annales du Bureau central météorologique de France* (1883); Duchaussoy, H. B., 'Les bans de vendages de la région Parisienne', *La météorologique,* 111–18 (1934); Le Roy Ladurie, E. *op. cit.,* 50–79 (1972).

63 Le Roy Ladurie, E., *op. cit.,* 347–65 (1972).

64 Manley, G., 'Possible climatic agencies in the development of post-glacial habitats', *Proceedings of the Royal Society,* B 161, 363–75 (1965).

65 Henderson, J. A., *Annals of Lower Deeside,* 96 (Aberdeen 1892), quoted by Walton, K., 'Climate and famines in north-east Scotland', *Scottish Geographical Magazine,* **68,** 13–22 (1952).

66 Arakawa, H., 'Climatic change as revealed by the blooming dates of the cherry blossom at Kyoto', *J. Met.,* **13,** 599–600 (1956); Arakawa, H., 'Twelve centuries of blooming dates of the cherry blossoms at the city of Kyoto and its own vicinity', *Geofisica pura e applicata,* **30,** 147–50 (1955).

67 Titow, J. Z., *Winchester yields: a study in medieval agricultural productivity* (1972).

68 Utterström, G., *op. cit.,* 103–65 (1954).

69 Quoted by Utterström, G., *op. cit.,* 27 (1955).

70 Baker, T. H., *Records of the seasons and prices of agricultural produce and phenomena observed in the British Isles,* 170 (1884).

71 Hovgaard, W., 'The Norsemen in Greenland, recent discoveries at Herfoljness', *Geographical Review,* **15,** 615–16 (1925).

72 Lysgaard, L., 'Recent climatic fluctuations', *Folia Geographica Danica,* **5**, supplement (1949).
73 Manley, G., *op. cit.,* 252 (1953); Manley, G., 'The range of variation of the British climate', *Geographical Journal,* **117**, 43–68 (1951).
74 La Marche, V. C., 'Palaeoclimatic inferences from long tree-ring records', *Science,* **183**, 1043–48 (1974).
75 *Proceedings of the Conference on the Climate of the Eleventh and Sixteenth Centuries, op. cit.,* 88 (1963).
76 Lamb, H. H., *op. cit.,* 186–87 (1966). The following discussion is based upon this source.
77 Lamb, H. H., Lewis, R. P. W. and Woodruffe, A., 'Atmospheric circulation and the main climatic variables between 8000 and 0 B.C.: meteorological evidence', in *World climate from 8000 to 0 B.C.,* Royal Meteorological Society, Proceedings of the International Symposium April 18–19, 174–217 (London 1966).
78 Lamb, H. H., Lewis, R. P. W. and Woodruffe, A., *ibid,* 194 (1966).
79 Lamb, H. H., Lewis, R. P. W. and Woodruffe, A., *ibid,* 178 (1966).
80 Bryson, R. A., *World climate and world food systems III: The lessons of climatic history,* Institute of Environmental Studies, University of Wisconsin, IES Report 27 (Madison 1974).
81 See for example Turner, J. 'A contribution to the history of forest clearance', *Proceedings of the Royal Society,* B 161, 343–54. (1965).
82 Brooks, C. E. P., *British floods and droughts,* 186 (1925); Britton, C. E., *op. cit.,* 177 (1937); Van Bath, B. H. S., *The agarian history of western Europe, A.D. 500 to 1850,* 161 (1963).
83 Thomas, M. K., 'Recent climatic fluctuations in Canada', *Climatological Studies No. 28,* Environment Canada (Ottawa 1975).
84 Bryson, R. A., *op. cit.,* 12 (1974).
85 Bryson, R. A., Ross, J. E., Hougas, R. W., and Engelbert, I. E., *op. cit.,* 18 (1974).
86 Bryson, R. A., Ross, J. E., Hougas, R. W. and Engelbert, I. E., *ibid,* 21 (1974).

Chapter 3: *The significance of climatic change: harvest yield and harvest failure.*

1 Postan, M. M. and Titow, J. Z., 'Heriots and prices on Winchester manors', *Economic History Review,* **11**, 392–411 (1959).
2 Beaver, S. H., comment in Lamb, H. H., 'Climatic variation and our environment today and in the coming years', *Weather,* **15**, 447–55 (1970).
3 Brandon, R. F., 'Late medieval weather in Sussex and its agricultural significance', *Transactions of the Institute of British Geographers,* **54**, 1–17 (1971).
4 Hudson, J. P., 'Agronomic implications of long-term weather forecasting' in Johnson, C. G. and Smith, L. P. (eds.), *The biological significance of climatic changes in Britain,* 129–34 (1965).
5 Hudson, J. P., *ibid,* 129 (1965).
6 See for example Fleming, A. 'Bronze age agriculture on the marginal lands of north-east Yorkshire', *Agricultural History Review,* **19**, 1–24

(1971); Soulsby, J. A., 'Palaeoenvironmental interpretation of a buried soil at Achnacree, Argyll', *Transactions of the Institute of British Geographers,* New Series 1, 279–283 (1975); Atherden, M. A. 'The impact of late prehistoric cultures on the vegetation of the North York Moors', *Transactions of the Institute of British Geographers,* New Series 1, 284–300 (1975).

7 Bessell, J. E., 'The measurement of managerial efficiency in agriculture', *Journal of Agricultural Economics,* **21,** 391–401 (1970); comment by Stansfield, J. M., in Taylor, J. A., *Weather economics,* 93–4 (1968); both quoted by Milner, J. S., *An assessment of the influence of weather on the productivity of cereal farming,* unpublished M. Phil. thesis, University of Nottingham (1974).

8 Guise, J. W. B., 'Factors associated with variation in aggregate average yield of New Zealand wheat, 1918–67', *American Journal of Agricultural Economics,* **51,** 866–81 (1969).

9 Britton, D. K., *Cereals in the United Kingdom – production, marketing and utilisation,* 95 (1969).

10 Britton, D. K., *ibid.,* 99 (1969).

11 Milner, J. B., *op. cit.,* 92 (1974).

12 See Britton, D. K., *op. cit.* (1969), Figure 3.2 p. 98 for correlation between rainfall and cereal yields in the United Kingdom.

13 McQuigg, J. D. and others, *The influence of weather and climate on United States grain yields,* National Oceanic and Atmospheric Administration, United States Department of Commerce (1973).

14 McQuigg, J. D. and others, *ibid.,* 23 (1973).

15 Bryson, R. A., 'Heyuppskera: An heuristic model for hay yield in Iceland', *Research Institute Netri Ås,* Bulletin No. 18 (Hveragerti, Iceland 1974).

16 Fridriksson, S. 'The effects of sea ice on flora, fauna and agriculture', *Jökull,* **19,** 146–57 (1969).

17 See for example, Mitchell, V. C., 'A theoretical tree-line in Central Canada', *Annals of the Association of American Geographers,* **63,** 296–301 (1973).

18 Harrison, S. J., 'Problems in the measurement and evaluation of the climatic resources of upland Britain' in: Taylor, J. A. (ed.), *Climatic resources and economic activity,* 47–63 (1974); Taylor, J. A., 'Upland climates' in: Chandler, T. and Gregory, S. (eds.), *The climate of the British Isles,* 267–87 (1976).

19 Taylor, J. A., *ibid,* 267–87 (1976).

20 Smith, L. P., 'The changing climate', *Agricultural Meteorology,* **7,** 361–2 (1970).

21 Hunter, H., *Oats: their varieties and characteristics,* 13 (1924).

22 Manley, G., 'The effective rate of altitudinal change in temperate Atlantic climates', *Geographical Review,* **35,** 408–17 (1945).

23 Eyre, S. R., 'A consideration of the factors limiting land improvement and settlement on the upland east of the Derbyshire Derwent', Chapter 10, unpublished Ph.D. thesis, University of Sheffield (1954); Taylor, J. A., 'Climatic change as related to altitudinal thresholds and soil variables', in Johnson, C. G. and Smith, L. P. (eds.), *The biological significance of climatic change in Britain,* 37–49 (1965).

24 Taylor, J. A. (ed.), *Hill climates and land usage with special reference to the highland zone of Britain,* Memo. No. 3, 3 University College of Wales (Aberystwyth 1960).

25 Smith, L. P., 'Variations of mean air temperature and hours of sunshine on the weather slope of a hill', *Meteorological Magazine,* **79,** 231 (1950).

26 Gloyne, R. W., 'Wind as a factor in hill climates', in Taylor, J. A. (ed.), *op. cit.,* 23–30 (1960).

27 Parry, M. L., 'Secular climatic change and marginal agriculture', *Transactions of the Institute of British Geographers,* **64,** 1–13 (1975).

28 McVean, D. N. and Ratcliffe, D. A., *Plant communities in the Scottish Highlands,* Monographs of the Nature Conservancy, No. 1 (1962); Birse, E. L. and Robertson, L., *Assessment of climatic conditions in Scotland, 2: based on exposure and accumulated frost,* Macaulay Institute for Soil Research (Aberdeen 1970).

29 Ventskevich, G. Z., *Agrometeorology,* Israel Program for Scientific Translations, 97 (Jerusalem 1961).

30 *Statistical Account of Scotland,* Sir John Sinclair (ed.), VII, 112 (1791–99).

31 Scola, P. M., 'The Lothians', in Stamp, L. D. (ed.), *The land of Britain,* Pts. 16–18, 151 (1944).

32 Parry, M. L., *op. cit.,* 1–13 (1975).

33 Taylor, J. A., *op. cit.,* 267–87 (1976).

34 Manley, G., *op. cit.,* 408–17 (1945).

35 Manley, G., *Climate and the British scene,* 182 (1952).

36 Manley, G., *op. cit.,* 408–17 (1945).

37 Bryson, R. A., 'A perspective on climatic change', *Science,* **184,** 753–60 (1974).

38 Manley, G., *op. cit.,* 408–17 (1945).

39 Taylor, J. A., *op. cit.,* 267–87 (1976).

40 Manley, G., 'The range of variation of the British climate', *Geographical Journal,* **117,** 43–68 (1951).

41 Taylor, J. A., *op. cit.,* 1–3 (1960).

42 Manley, G., *op. cit.,* 408–17 (1945).

43 The measure is described by Gregory, S., 'Accumulated temperature maps of the British Isles', *Transactions of the Institute of British Geographers,* **20,** 59–73 (1954). It has been criticised by Shellard, H. C., *Averages of accumulated temperature and standard deviation of monthly mean temperature over Britain, 1921–50,* Professional Notes No. 125, Meteorological Office, 1 (1959).

44 Nuttonson, M. Y., *Wheat-climate relationships and the use of phenology in ascertaining the thermal and photo-thermal requirements of wheat,* American Institute of Crop Ecology, 380 (Washington D.C. 1955).

45 The temperature data were corrected for elevation by a lapse rate of 1 °C per 148 m which has been calculated as appropriate for south-east Scotland.

46 Nuttonson, M. Y., *op. cit.,* 329 (1955).

47 Ragg, J. M., *The soils of the country around Kelso and Lauder,* 24 (1960).

48 Gregory, S., 'Accumulated temperature maps of the British Isles', *Transactions of the Institute of British Geographers,* **20,** 59–73 (1954).

49 Thran, P. and Broekhuizen, S., *Agro-ecological atlas of cereal growing in*

Europe: volume I, agro-climatic atlas of Europe, Maps 374, 506 (Amsterdam 1965).

50 Hoskins, W. G., 'Harvest fluctuations and economic history, 1480–1619', *Agricultural History Review,* **12,** 28–46 (1964).

51 Mossman, R. C., 'The meteorology of Edinburgh', *Transactions of the Royal Society of Edinburgh,* **1,** 63–207 (1896–7).

52 For 1762 see *The Statistical Account of Scotland, op. cit.,* I, 76 and II, 387; for 1816, see Low, D., *Report relative to the Lordship and Estate of Marchmont,* Scottish Record Office, GD 158/20, 46 (1819).

53 Mossman, R. C., *op. cit.,* 117 (1896–7).

54 Shellard, H. C., *op. cit.,* 1 (1959).

55 Further discussion of this point may be found in Parry, M. L., 'The significance of the variability of summer warmth in upland Britain', *Weather,* **31,** 212–17 (1976).

56 Manley, G., *op. cit.,* 43–68 (1951); Manley, G., 'Central England temperatures: monthly means 1659 to 1973, *Quarterly Journal of the Royal Meteorological Society,* **100,** 389–405 (1974).

57 McQuigg, J. M. and others, *op. cit.,* 23 (1973); appreciation by farmers of the drought risk is discussed by Saarinen, T. F., 'Perception of the drought hazard on the Great Plains', Chicago University Geography Department, Research Paper No. 106 (1966).

58 Bryson, R. A., *op. cit.,* 755 (1974).

59 Gould, P. R., 'Man against the environment: a game theoretic framework', *Annals of the Association of American Geographers,* **53,** 290–7 (1963).

Chapter 4: *Climatic change and changes in the limit to cultivation*

1 Lamb, H. H., 'Trees and climatic history in Scotland; a radiocarbon dating test and other evidence', *Quarterly Journal of the Royal Meteorological Society,* **90,** 382–94 (1964); Lamb, H. H., *Climate: Present, past and future,* Vol. 2, 476–7 (1977), where it is claimed that temperature changes in England, averaged over the whole year and taking 10 or 20 years together have probably been a fair approximation for the whole Earth.

2 Manley, G., 'The mean temperature of central England 1698–1952', *Quarterly Journal of the Royal Meteorological Society,* **79,** 242–61 (1953).

3 Goldie, A. H. R. and Carter, H. E., 'The trend of annual rainfall in Scotland', *Transactions of the Institute of Water Engineers,* **44,** 93–7 (1940).

4 Such doubts have been expressed by Oliver, J., 'Problems in agro-climatic relationships in Wales in the eighteenth century', in Taylor, J. A., (ed.), *Climatic change with special reference to the Highland zone of Britain,* Memorandum No. 3, 6–14 University College of Wales (Aberystwyth 1965); and in Taylor, J. A. (ed.), *ibid.,* 94–5.

5 Professor G. Manley has indicated his agreement on this point (personal communication, 1972).

6 Smith, L. P., 'Possible changes in seasonal weather', in Johnson, C. G. and Smith, L. P. (eds.), *The biological significance of climatic changes in Britain,* 187–191 (1965).

7 Lamb, H. H., 'What can we find out about the trend of our climate?', *Weather,* **18,** 194–216 (1963).
8 Lamb, H. H., *op. cit.,* 448 (1977).
9 Lamb, H. H., *op. cit.,* 451 (1977).
10 Lamb, H. H., *op. cit.,* 466 (1977).
11 Lamb, H. H., *op. cit.,* 526 (1977).
12 Lamb, H. H., personal communication (1977); some support for this proposition is lent by Matthews, J. A., 'Glacier and climatic fluctuations inferred from tree-growth variations over the last 250 years, central southern Norway', *Boreas,* **6,** 1–24 (1977).
13 Lamb, H. H., *op. cit.,* 212 (1966).
14 Gregory, S., 'Accumulated temperature maps of the British Isles', *Transactions of the Institute of British Geographers,* **20,** 59–73 (1954).
15 Lamb, H. H., *op. cit.,* 460 (1977).
16 Fjellbygdenes Økonomiske Problemer (Economic problems of the mountainous areas), *Innstilling fra komiteen til undersnþkelse av,* argitt 1 Mars 1958, Landbruksdepartement, 8.
17 Submarginal areas have been mapped by Sandnes, J., *Ødetid og Gjenreisning,* 15 (Oslo 1971); marginal areas were mapped by the present author at 1 : 100,000.
18 Thorarinsson, S., *The thousand years' struggle against ice and fire,* 16 (Reykjavik 1956).
19 Baerreis, D. A. and Bryson, R. A. (eds.), 'Climatic change and the Mill Creek Culture of Iowa', *Archives of Archaeology,* **29,** 1–673 (1967).
20 See Lamb, *op. cit.,* Table 17.1 (1977).
21 Barry, R. G. and Chorley, R. J., *Atmosphere, weather and climate,* 2nd edn., 322 (1971).
22 Bryson, R. A., 'Airmasses, streamlines and the Boreal Forest', *Geographical Bulletin,* **8,** 228–69 (1966); Mitchell, V. L., 'A theoretical tree-line in Central Canada', *Annals of the Association of American Geographers,* **63,** 296–301 (1973).
23 Lamb, H. H., Lewis, R. P. W. and Woodruffe, A., 'Atmospheric circulation and the main climatic variables between 8000 and 0 B.C.– meteorological evidence' in *World Climate from 8000 to 0 B.C.,* Royal Meteorological Society, 174–217 (1966).
24 Liestol, G., 'Glaciers of the present day' in Holtedahl, O. (ed.), *Geology of Norway,* 482–90 (Oslo 1960).
25 Lamb, H. H., *op. cit.,* 524–5 (1977).
26 Cooke, R. U. and Reeves, R. W., *Arroyos and environmental change,* 187–93 (1976).

Chapter 5: *The shift of cultivation limits in North-West Europe*

1 Lythe, S. G. E., *The economy of Scotland, 1550–1625,* 9 (1960).
2 Parry, M. L., 'Abandoned farmland in upland Britain', *Geographical Journal,* **142,** 101–10 (1976).
3 A full description of this dating procedure is given in Parry, M. L., 'A typology of cultivation ridges in southern Scotland', *Tools and Tillage,* **3,** 3–19 (1976).

4 Parry, M. L., 'Secular climatic change and marginal land', *Transactions of the Institute of British Geographers,* **64,** 1–13 (1975).

5 Fenton, A., 'Early and traditional cultivation implements in Scotland', *Proceedings of the Society of Antiquaries of Scotland,* **96,** 264–317 (1962–3).

6 Romanes, C. S., (ed.), *Selections from the records of the regality of Melrose, Vol. 3: 1547–1706,* Scottish History Society Volume 8 (the rentale of the Abacie of Melrose pertenying presentlie to the Abbott . . . 1576), 140–6 (1917); Bannatyne Club, *Liber Sancte Marie de Dryburgh,* Bannatyne Club, Vol. 83 (Rentale of Dryburgh c. 1535), 330–38, Appx. 28 (1847); Bannatyne Club, *Liber Sancte Marie de Calchou 1113–1567,* Bannatyne Club, Vol. 82 (Rotulus antiquus redituum monasterii de Kelso, 1300), 455–70 (1846); Bannatyne Club, *Registrum Sancte Marie de Neubotle, 1140–1528* (the rental of Neubotle [no date]), 325–35, Appx. 3 (1849).

7 Bannatyne Club, *op. cit.,* 465 (1846).

8 Bannatyne Club, *ibid.,* xxxii–xxxiii (1846).

9 Bannatyne Club, *op. cit.,* 62 and 225 (1847).

10 Bannatyne Club, *op. cit.,* Nos. 110, 111 (1847).

11 Parry, M. L., *op. cit.,* 1–13 (1975).

12 Before dissolution, monastic farming in southern Scotland seems to have been quite efficiently organised. Here, in contrast to England, the transference of lands to lay ownership did not, over the short-term, bring greater investment of capital.

13 Romanes, C. S., *op. cit.,* 237–45 (1917).

14 *Letters and Papers,* Henry VIII, xx, ii, 200 quoted in Royal Commission for Ancient and Historical Monuments (Scotland), *Inventory of monuments and constructions in the county of Berwickshire,* xxiv (Edinburgh 1915).

15 Gibson, R., *An old Berwickshire town: history of the town and parish of Greenlaw, from earliest times to the present day,* 24, (Edinburgh 1905).

16 Royal Commission for Ancient and Historical Monuments (Scotland), *op. cit.,* xxv (1915).

17 Scottish Record Office, Elibank MSS, GB 32/22/2 Charter of the lands of Langshaw, 1549.

18 Cass, H. J. and ApSimon, A., *The neolithic and early bronze ages in the north of Ireland,* 51 (1970).
It should be noted that a phase of peat growth can be initiated by changes in drainage as a result of grazing and cultivation. It is not always a function of changes in the physical environment.

19 Dudley, D. and Minter, E. M., 'The medieval village at Garrow Tor, Bodmin Moor, Cornwall', *Medieval Archaeology,* **8,** 272–94 (1963).

20 For a discussion of the comprehensiveness of these surveys, see Parry, M. L., 'County maps as historical sources: A sequence of surveys in south-east Scotland', *Scottish Studies,* **19,** 15–26 (1976).

21 Parry, M. L., 'The abandonment of upland settlement in southern Scotland', *Scottish Geographical Magazine,* **92,** 50–60 (1976).

22 Roberts, B. K., Turner, J. and Ward, P. F., 'Recent forest history and land use in Weardale, Northern England', in Birks, H. J. B. and West, R. G., *Quaternary Plant Ecology,* 207–21 (1973).

23 Jennings, B. (ed.), *A history of Nidderdale,* 50–1 (1967).

24 Fleming, A., 'Bronze Age agriculture on the marginal lands of N.E.

Yorkshire', *Agricultural History Review,* **19,** 1–24 (1971). Fleming's conclusions have not yet been confirmed by other studies.

25 Beresford, M. W., 'Medieval settlement' in Raistrick, A., *North York Moors,* 55 (1969).

26 Kershaw, I., 'The great famine and agrarian crisis in England, 1315–1322', *Past and Present,* **59,** 1–50 (1973).

27 Baker, A. R. H., 'Evidence in the "Nonarum Inquisitiones" of contracting arable lands in England during the early fourteenth century', *Economic History Review,* **19,** 518–32 (1966).

28 Hoskins, W. G., 'The making of the agrarian landscape' in Hoskins, W. G. and Finberg, W. P. R., *Devonshire Studies,* 294 (1952); for example on Challacombe Common.

29 Hoskins, W. G., *ibid,* 318 (1952); Linehan, C. D., 'Deserted sites and rabbit-warrens on Dartmoor, Devon', *Medieval Archaeology,* **10,** 113–44 (1966).

30 Fox, A., 'A monastic homestead on Dean Moor, South Devon', *Medieval Archaeology,* **2,** 141–57 (1958); Dudley, D. and Minter, E. M., *op. cit.,* **8,** 272–94 (1963).

31 Dudley, D. and Minter, E. M., *ibid,* 272–94 (1963).

32 Jones, G. R. J., 'Agriculture in north-west Wales during the later Middle Ages' in Taylor, J. A. (ed.), *Climatic change with special reference to Wales and its agriculture,* Memo. No. 8, 47–53, University College of Wales (Aberystwyth 1965).

33 Jones, G. R. J., *ibid,* 47 (1965).

34 Quoted by Britton, C. E., *A meteorological chronology to A.D. 1450,* Meteorological Office, Geophysical Memoirs No. 70, 153 (1937).

35 Orme, A. R., *Ireland,* 113 (1970).

36 Cass, H. J. and ApSimon, A., *op. cit.,* 51 (1970).

37 Beresford, M. W., *The lost villages of England,* 201–5 (1954).

38 Beresford, M. W. and St. Joseph, J. K., *Medieval England: An aerial survey,* 92 (1958).

39 Baker, A. R. H., *op. cit.,* 518–32 (1966).

40 Baker, A. R. H., *op. cit.,* 518–32 (1966).

41 Jager, H., 'Die Ausdehnung der Wälder in Metteleuropa über offenes Siedlungsland', *Geogr. Hist. Agraires,* 300–11 (Nancy 1959).

42 Kershaw, I., *op. cit.,* 1–50 (1973).

43 Kershaw, I., *op. cit.,* 48–50 (1973).

44 Thorarinsson, S., *The thousand years' struggle against ice and fire,* 16 (Reykjavik 1956).

45 Thorarinsson, S., 'Tefrokronologiska studier på Island', *Geografiska Annaler,* **26,** 1–217 (1944).

46 Thorarinsson, S., *op. cit.,* 17 (1956).

47 Quoted by Fridriksson, S., 'The effects of sea ice on flora, fauna and agriculture', *Jökull,* **19,** 146–57 (1969).

48 Fridriksson, S., *ibid,* 146–57 (1969); obvious difficulties arise in comparing the incidence of recorded famine between different centuries, and Table 3 should be treated with caution.

49 Thorarinsson, S., *op. cit.,* 37–40 (1956).

50 For a full discussion of the distribution of deserted farms in Iceland, see Teitsson, V. B. and Stefánsson, M., 'Islandsk ödegardsforskning' in

Nasjonale Forskningsoverikter, *Det. nordiske þdergårdsprojekt,* Pubn. No. 1, 111–48 (1972).
51 Sandnes, J., personal communication (1975).
52 Salvesen, H., 'The agrarian crisis in Norway in the late Middle Ages' in Dyer, C. C. (ed.), *Medieval Village Research Group Report,* No. 23, 58–60 (1976).
53 Sandnes, J., *Ødetid og gjenreisning,* 156–67 (Oslo 1971).
54 Salvesen, H., *Fra Landnåm til matrikelgård; studier framveksten av utkantgården Hoset,* (Trondheim 1974).
55 Holmsen, A., 'Desertion of farms around Oslo in the late Middle Ages', *Scandinavian Economic History Review,* **10,** 165–202 (1962).
56 Larrson, L-O, 'Settlement in Finland. A review of Suomen asutus 1560-luvulla', *Scandinavian Economic History Review,* **23,** 171–5 (1975).
57 Utterström, G., 'Climatic fluctuations and population problems in early modern history', *Scandinavian Economic History Review,* **3,** 3–47 (1955).
58 Steensberg, A., 'The archaeological dating of the climatic change about A.D. 1300', *Advancement of Science,* **9,** 31-3 (1952).
59 Dansgaarde, W., Johnsen, S. J., Reeh, N., Gundestrup, N., Clausen, H. B., and Hammer, C. U., 'Climate changes, Norsemen and modern man', *Nature,* **255,** 24–8 (1975).
60 Report by C. L. Vebaek in *Proceedings of the Conference on the Climate of the Eleventh and Sixteenth Centuries,* Aspen, Colorado 1962, National Centre for Atmospheric Research, NCAR Technical Notes, 63–1, 17–18 (1963).

Chapter 6: *Harvests, mortality and the shift of rural settlement*

1 Titow, J. Z., 'Evidence of weather in the account rolls of the Bishopric of Winchester, 1209–1350', *Economic History Review,* **12,** 360–407 (1960).
2 Titow, J. Z., *Winchester yields: A study in medieval agricultural productivity,* Appx. N. (1972).
3 Postan, M. M., *The medieval economy and society, 71* (1975).
4 Postan, M. M., *ibid.,* 75 (1975).
5 Postan, M. M. and Titow, J. Z., 'Heriots and prices on Winchester manors', *Economic History Review,* **11,** 392–411 (1959); this paper has been criticised by Ohlin, G., 'No safety in numbers' in Floud, R. (ed.) *Essays in quantitative economic history,* 59–78 (1974).
6 Postan, M. M. and Titow, J. Z., *ibid.,* 408–9 (1959).
7 Hoskins, W. G., 'Harvest fluctuations and economic history, 1480–1619', *Agricultural History Review,* **12,** 28–47 (1964); Hoskins, W. G., 'Harvest fluctuations and economic history, 1620–1759', *Agricultural History Review,* **16,** 15–31 (1968).
8 Utterström, G., 'Population and agriculture in Sweden', *Scandinavian Economic History Review,* **9,** 176–94 (1961).
9 Heckscher, E. F., 'Sveriges befolkning från det stora nordiska krigets slut till Tabellverkets början (Sweden's population from the end of the Great Northern War to the beginning of the Board of Statistics), 1720–50', *Ekonomisk-historiska studier,* 255–85 (1936).

10 Utterström, G., 'Some population problems in pre-Industrial Sweden', *Scandinavian Economic History Review,* **2,** 103–65 (1954).
11 Utterström, G., 'Climatic fluctuations and population problems in early modern history', *Scandinavian Economic History Review,* **3,** 3–47 (1955).
12 This discussion is based upon Bean, J. M. W., 'Plague, population and economic decline in England in the later Middle Ages', *Economic History Review,* **15,** 424–37 (1963).
13 Bove, F. J., *The story of ergot* (1970); Barger, G., *Ergot and ergotism* (1931); Caporael, L. R., 'Ergotism: The Satan loosed in Salem', *Science,* **192,** 21–6 (1976).
14 Baker, A. R. H., 'Evidence in the "Nonarum Inquisitiones" of contracting arable lands in England during the early fourteenth century', *Economic History Review,* **19,** 518–32 (1966).
15 Bean, J. M. W., *op. cit.,* 424–37 (1963); Ollerenshaw, C. B. 'Climate factors and liverfluke disease' in Taylor, J. A. (ed.) *Climatic factors and diseases in plants and animals,* Memo. No. 5, 37–42, University College of Wales (Aberystwyth 1962).
16 The literature on this is extensive; see references in Finch, T. F., 'Cultivation limits in the Dublin Mountains', *Irish Geographer,* **2,** 206–10 (1953); and in Connell, K. H., 'The colonisation of waste land in Ireland, 1700–1845', *Economic History Review,* 2nd series, **3,** 44–71 (1950).
17 Bourke, P. M. A., *The forecasting from weather data of potato blight and other plant diseases and pests,* World Meteorological Organisation, Technical Note No. 10 (1955).
18 Beresford, M. W., 'A review of historical research (to 1968)' in: Beresford, M. W. and Hurst, J. G. (eds.), *deserted medieval villages,* 21 (1971).
19 See for example Beresford, M. W., *ibid.,* 21 (1971).
20 The broader period is favoured by many economic historians; Beresford emphasises the shorter period, 1450–80.
21 Van Bath, B. H. S., *The agrarian history of western Europe A.D., 500–1850,* 160–1 (1963).
22 Rahtz, P., 'Upton, Gloucestershire, 1959–1964', *Transactions of Bristol and Gloucestershire Archaeological Society,* **85,** 70–140 (1966); Rahtz, P., 'Upton, Gloucestershire, 1964–68', *Transactions of Bristol and Gloucestershire Archaeological Society,* **88,** 74–124 (1969); Rahtz, P., 'Holworth, medieval village excavation, 1958', *Proceedings of Dorset Natural History and Archaeological Society,* **81,** 127–147 (1959).
23 Dudley, D. and Minter, E. M., 'The medieval village of Garrow Tor, Bodmin Moor, Cornwall', *Medieval Archaeology,* 8, 272–94 (1963).
24 Hurst, J. G., 'A review of archaeological research (to 1968)' in Beresford, M. W. and Hurst, J. G., (eds.), *op. cit.,* 121 (1971).
25 Hurst, J. G., *ibid.,* 115, 122 (1971).
26 Beresford, G., 'The medieval clay-land village: excavations at Goltho and Barton Blount', Society for Medieval Archaeology, Monograph Series No. 6 (1975); the climatic explanation offered here has been criticised by Wright, S., 'Barton Blount: climatic or economic change?' *Medieval Archaeology,* **20,** 148–52 (1976).

27 Hurst, J. G., *op. cit.,* 136 (1971).
28 For a full discussion of this issue, see Beresford, M. W., 'The lost villages of medieval England', *Geographical Journal,* **117,** 129–49 (1951); Beresford, M. W., *The lost villages of England* (1954); Beresford, M. W., *op. cit.,* 3–75 (1971).
29 Parry, M. L. 'The abandonment of upland settlement in southern Scotland', *Scottish Geographical Magazine,* **72,** 50–60 (1976).
30 MacGrigror, A., *Reports on the state of certain parishes in Scotland (1627),* Maitland Club, 67 (Edinburgh 1835). More detailed consideration of farm amalgamation is given in Chapter 7.
31 Lebon, J. H. G., 'Old maps and rural change in Ayrshire', *Scottish Geographical Magazine,* **68,** 104–9 (1952); Gailey, R. A., 'The evolution of Highland rural settlement', *Scottish Studies,* **6,** 155–77 (1962); MacSween, M. D., 'Transhumance in north Skye', *Scottish Geographical Magazine,* **75,** 75–88 (1959).
32 McKerral, A., *Kintyre in the seventeenth century,* 78 (1948).
33 Glasscock, R. E., 'The study of deserted medieval settlements in Ireland' in Beresford, M. W. and Hurst, J. G. (eds.), *Deserted medieval villages,* 279–301 (1971).
34 Wedel, W. R., 'Dust Bowls of the past', *Science,* **86,** supplement, 8–9 (1937).
35 Woodbury, R., 'Climatic changes and prehistoric agriculture in the south-western United States', *Annals of New York Academy of Sciences,* **95,** 705–9 (1961); Griffin, J. B., 'Some correlations of climate and cultural change in eastern North American prehistory', *Annals of New York Academy of Sciences,* **95,** 710–17 (1961).
36 Beltzner, K. (ed.), *Living with climatic change,* Proceedings Toronto Conference Workshop, November 11–22, 1975, 41 (1976).
37 Beltzner, K. (ed.), *ibid.,* 39 (1976).
38 Tomanek, G. W. and Hulett, G. K., 'Effects of historical droughts on grassland vegetation in the central Great Plains' in Dort, W. and Jones, J. K. (eds.), *Pleistocene and recent environments of the central Great Plains,* 203–210 (1970).
39 Baerreis, D. A. and Bryson, R. A., 'Climatic change and the Mill Creek culture of Iowa, Pt. I', *Journal of Iowa Archaeological Society,* **15,** 1–358 (1968).
40 Wedel, W. R., *Prehistoric man on the Great Plains,* 286–87 (1961).
41 Griffin, J. B. *op. cit.,* 710–17 (1961).
42 Baerreis, D. A. and Bryson, R. A., 'Climatic episodes and the dating of the Mississippian cultures', *The Wisconsin Archaeologist,* **46,** 203–20 (1965).
43 Baerreis, D. A. and Bryson, R. A., *op. cit.,* 22 (1968).
44 Baerreis, D. A. and Bryson, R. A., *op. cit.,* 24 (1968).
45 Wedel, W. R., 'Environment and native subsistence economies in the central Great Plains', *Smithsonian Miscellaneous Collections,* **101,** 1–29 (1941).
46 Wedel, W. R., 'Some aspects of human ecology on the Great Plains', *American Anthropology,* **55,** 499–514 (1953).
47 Wedel, W. R., *ibid.,* 507 (1953). (Reprinted by permission of the Smithsonian Institution Press.)

48 Wedel, W. R., *op. cit.,* 25 (1941).
49 Wedel, W. R., 'Some environmental and historical factors of the Great Bend Aspect' in Dort, W. and Jones, J. K. (eds.), *op. cit.,* 131–40 (1970).
50 Wedel, W. R. (personal communication 1977), and in forthcoming papers.
51 Krause, R. A., 'Aspects of adaptation among upper Republican subsistence cultivators' in Dort, W. and Jones, J. K. (eds.), *op. cit.,* 103–15 (1970).
52 Lehmer, D. J., 'Climate and culture in the Middle Missouri Valley' in Dort, W. and Jones, J. K. (eds.), *op. cit.,* 117–29 (1970).
53 Lehmer, D. J., *ibid.,* 129 (1970).
54 Bryson, R. A., Baerreis, D. A. and Wendland, W. M., 'The character of late and post-glacial climatic changes' in Dort, W. and Jones, J. K. (eds.), *op. cit.,* 53–74 (1970).
55 Wright, H. E., 'Natural environment and early food production north of Mesopotamia', *Science,* **161,** 334–39 (1968); for references to other studies see Van Zeist, W., Woldring, H. and Stapert, D., 'Late quaternary vegetation and climate in S.W. Turkey', *Palaeohistoria,* **17,** 53–143 (1975).
56 Wright, H. E., *ibid.,* 38 (1968).
57 Waterbolk, H. T., 'Food production in prehistoric Europe', *Science,* **162,** 1093–1102 (1968).
58 Carpenter, R., *Discontinuity in Greek civilisation,* (Cambridge 1966).
59 Dickinson, O., 'Drought and the decline of the Mycenae: some comments', *Antiquity,* **48,** 228–30 (1974).
60 Lamb, H. H., 'Review of Carpenter, R., Discontinuity in Greek civilisation', *Antiquity,* **41,** 233–34 (1967).
61 Wright, H. E., 'Climatic change in Mycenaen Greece', *Antiquity,* **42,** 123–27 (1968).
62 Bryson, R. A., Lamb, H. H., and Donley, D. L., 'Drought and the decline of the Mycenae', *Antiquity,* **48,** 46–50 (1974).

Chapter 7: *Short-term fluctuations of climate*

1 Postan, M. M., 'Die wirtschaftlichen Grundlagen der mittelalterlichen Gesellschaft', *Jahrbücher für Nationalökonomie und Statistik,* **166,** 180–205 (1954).
2 Parry, M. L., 'The significance of the variability of summer warmth in upland Britain', *Weather,* **31,** 212–17 (1976).
3 Hoskins, W. G., 'Harvest fluctuations and economic history, 1480–1619', *Agricultural History Review,* **12,** 28–46 (1964).
4 Smith, L. P., 'Possible changes in seasonal weather' in Johnson, C. G. and Smith, L. P. (eds.), *The biological significance of climatic changes in Britain,* Symposia of the Institute of Biology, No. 14, 187–91 (1965).
5 Jones, E. L., *Seasons and prices,* 58 (1964).
6 Kershaw, I., 'The great famine and agrarian crisis in England, 1315–22', *Past and Present,* **59,** 1–50 (1973). This paper is the main source for the subsequent discussion.

7 Britton, C. E., *A meteorological chronology to A.D. 1450,* Meteorological Office Geophysical Memoirs No. 70, 132 (1937).
8 Britton, C. E., *ibid.,* 133 (1937).
9 Titow, J. Z., 'Evidence of weather in the account rolls of the Bishopric of Winchester', *Economic History Review,* **12,** 360–407 (1960).
10 Titow, J. Z., *ibid.,* 403 (1960).
11 Kershaw, I., *op. cit.,* 17 (1973).
12 Kershaw, I., *op. cit.,* 32–3, 41–2 (1973).
13 Kershaw, I., *op. cit.,* 47 (1973).
14 Kershaw, I., *op. cit.,* 42, 46 (1973); Lucas, H. S., 'The great European famine of 1315, 1316, and 1317' in Carus-Wilson, E. M. (ed.), *Essays in Economic History* Vol. 2., 49–72 (1962).
15 Le Roy Ladurie, E., *Times of feast, times of famine,* 367–8 (1972).
16 Hoskins, W. G., *op. cit.,* 28–46 (1964).
17 'The Chronicle of Fortirgall' printed in Innes, C. (ed.), *The Black Book of Taymouth,* Bannatyne Club (1855), 124, quoted by Lythe, S. G. E., *The economy of Scotland, 1550–1625,* 16 (1960). The following discussion is based upon Lythe, S. G. E., *ibid.,* 16–23 (1960).
18 Troels-Lund, Denmarks og Norges Historie i Sluttningen af det 16de Aarhundrede, 1, 44 (1879), quoted by Utterström, G., 'Climatic fluctuations and population problems in early modern history', *Scandinavian Economic History Review,* **3,** 3–47 (1955).
19 Friis, P. C., *Samlede Skrifter,* (ed.) G. Storm, 57 (1881) quoted by Utterström, G., *ibid.,* 28 (1955).
20 Utterström, G., *ibid.,* 3–47 (1955). The following discussion is based upon this source.
21 Baker, T. H., *Records of the seasons, prices of agricultural produce and phenomena observed in the British Isles,* 147 (1884).
22 McKerral, A., *Kintyre in the seventeenth century,* 78, (1948).
23 Fiars prices drawn for 1643–1810 from Mitchinson, R., 'The movements of Scottish corn prices in the seventeenth and eighteenth centuries', *Economic History Review,* **18,** 278–91 (1965); and for 1811–1900 from Symon, J. A., *Scottish farming: past and present,* Appx. 3 (1959). The fiars prices were those struck annually at Candlemas by the sheriff courts as a basis for settlement of various fixed payments such as feu duties and rents. They were based on the average price of the previous crop.
24 Quoted by Baker, T. H., *op. cit.,* 159–60 (1884).
25 Quoted by Baker, T. H., *op. cit.,* 161 (1884).
26 Transactions of the Banffshire Field Club, 50 (1932–35), quoted by Walton, K., 'Climate and famines in north-east Scotland', *Scottish Geographical Magazine,* **68,** 13–22 (1952).
27 Manley, G., 'Central England temperatures: monthly means 1659–1973', *Quarterly Journal of the Royal Meteorological Society,* **100,** 389–405 (1974); Baker, T. H., *op. cit.,* 169–70 (1884).
28 Quoted by Walton, K., *op. cit.,* 14 (1952).
29 Quoted by Walton, K., *op. cit.,* 15 (1952).
30 Walton, K., *op. cit.,* 15 (1952).
31 *Statistical Account of Scotland* (ed.) Sir John Sinclair, XVI–32, 482 (1791-9).

32 Walton, K., *op. cit.,* 15 (1952).
33 (Anon.) 'Comparative view of East Lothian husbandry in 1778 and 1810', *The Farmer's Magazine,* **11,** 51–68, 204–23, 343–53, 515–23 (1811).
34 A.B.C. (Hamilton, John: 2nd Baron Belhaven), *The country-man's rudiments: or, an advice to the farmers in East-Lothian how to labour and improve their ground,* 2nd edn., 36–7 (Edinburgh 1713).
35 Parry, M. L., 'The mapping of abandoned farmland in upland Britain', *Geographical Journal,* **142,** 101–10 (1976).
36 Boislisle, A. M. de, *Correspondance des contrôleurs generaux des finances avec les Intendants des provinces* (Paris 1864–97); quoted by Le Roy Ladurie, E., *op. cit.,* 69–70 (1972).
37 Jutikkala, E., 'The great Finnish famine in 1696–7', *Scandinavian Economic History Review,* **3,** 48–63 (1955).
38 Jutikkala, E., *ibid.,* 48–63 (1955).
39 Thorarinsson, S., *The thousand years' struggle against ice and fire,* 39 (Reykjavik 1956).
40 Manley, G., 'Central England temperatures: monthly means 1659 to 1973', *Quarterly Journal of the Royal Meteorological Society,* **100,** 389–405 (1974).
41 Pearson, M. G., 'Snowstorms in Scotland, 1782–1786', *Weather,* **28,** 195–201 (1973).
42 Quoted by Pearson, M. G., *ibid.,* 195–201 (1973).
43 N., 'Account of the district of Lammermuir, in East Lothian, drawn up in 1794, from the communications of several farmers', *The Farmers Magazine,* **4,** 507–11 (1803).
44 *Statistical Account of Scotland, op. cit.,* I, 8, 76 and I, 8, 76. (1791–9).
45 Dunglass Estate MSS, Reading University Library, 1/2/25–30; Biel MSS, Scottish Record Office, GD 6.
46 Low, D., *Report relative to the Lordship and Estate of Marchmont,* Scottish Record Office GD 158/20 (1819).
47 Peirce, J., 'Cultural sensitivity to environmental change: II, 1816, the year without a summer', Centre for Climatic Research, Institute for Environmental Studies, IES Report No. 15, University of Wisconsin, (Madison 1974).
48 Wood, D. J., 'The complicity of climate in the 1816 depression in Dumfriesshire', *Scottish Geographical Magazine,* **81,** 5–17 (1965).
49 Calculated from data in Manley, G., *op. cit.,* 389–405 (1974).
50 Wood, D. J., *op. cit.,* 5–17 (1965).
51 Desbordes, J. M., *La chronique villageoise de Vareddes,* (Paris c. 1969) quoted by Le Roy Ladurie, E., *op. cit.,* 66 (1972).
52 *Connecticut Gazette* (26 June, 1816) quoted by Peirce, J., *op. cit.,* 7 (1974).
53 Jones, E. L., *The development of English agriculture, 1815–73,* Studies in Economic History, 24 (1968).
54 Perry, P. J., *British farming in the Great Depression, 1870–1914,* 40 (1974).
55 *Royal Commission on the Depressed Condition of Agricultural Interests (the Richmond Commission),* XVI, 394 (Cmnd. 2778) (1883); quoted by Orwin, C. S. and Whetham, E. H., *History of British agriculture, 1846–1914,* 2nd edn., 245 (1971).
56 Thorarinsson, S., *op. cit.,* 40 (1956).

57 Glasspoole, J., 'The rainfall over the British Isles of each of the eleven decades during the period 1820 to 1929', *Quarterly Journal of the Royal Meteorological Society,* **59,** 253–60 (1933); Goldie, A. H. R. and Carter, H. E., 'The trend of annual rainfall in Scotland', *Transactions of the Institute of Water Engineers,* **44,** 93–7 (1940); Glasspoole, J., 'Variations in annual, seasonal and monthly rainfall over the British Isles, 1870–1939', *Quarterly Journal of the Royal Meteorological Society,* **67,** 5–14 (1941).

58 *Royal Commission on Agriculture* (1895), Reports from the Commissioners, XVII, 24–6, Cmnd. 2742.

59 *The Richmond Commission, op. cit.,* Reports of the Assistant Commissioners, XVI–II, 516 (1883).

60 *The Richmond Commission, ibid.,* 528 (1883).

61 Perry, P. J., *op. cit.,* 57 (1974).

62 See for example Orwin, C. S., *The reclamation of Exmoor* (1929), and M'Caw, L. S., 'The Black Mountains' in Stamp, L. D. (ed.), *The land of Britain: Pt 37, Brecon,* 394–416 (1941).

63 Ministry of Agriculture, Fisheries and Food, parish summaries of the June acreage returns. These figures are approximate because of changes in the accuracy and comprehensiveness of the acreage returns.

64 Parry, M. L., *Mapping moorland change: a framwork for land-use decisions in the Peak District,* Peak Park Planning Board (Bakewell 1977).

Bibliography

A.B.C. (Hamilton, John: 2nd Baron Belhaven), *The country-man's rudiments: or, an advice to the farmers in East-Lothian how to labour and improve their ground,* 2nd edn., (Edinburgh 1713).

Angot, A., 'Etude sur les vendages en France', *Annales du Bureau central météorologique de France,* (1883).

[Anon.], 'Comparative view of East Lothian husbandry in 1778 and 1810', *The Farmer's Magazine,* **11,** 51–68, 204–23, 343–53, 515–23, (1811).

Arakawa, H., 'Fujiwhara on five centuries of freezing dates of Lake Suwa in central Japan', *Archives für Meteorologie, Geophysik und Bioklimatologie,* series B 6, (1955).

—— 'Twelve centuries of blooming dates of the cherry blossoms at the city of Kyoto and its own vicinity, *Geofisica pura e applicata,* **30,** 147–50 (1955).

—— Climatic change as revealed by blooming dates of the cherry blossoms at Kyoto, *Journal of Meteorology,* **13,** 599–600 (1956).

Atherden, M. A., 'The impact of late prehistoric cultures on the vegetation of the North York Moors', *Institute of British Geographers,* New Series 1, 284–300 (1975).

Bannatyne Club, *Liber Sancte Marie de Calchou 1113–1567,* Bannatyne Club, Vol. 82 (Edinburgh 1846).

Bannatyne Club, *Liber Sancte Marie de Dryburgh,* Bannatyne Club, Vol. 83 (Edinburgh 1847).

Bannatyne Club, *Registrum Sancte Marie de Neubotle, 1140–1528,* Vol. 84 (Edinburgh 1849).

Baerreis, D. A. and Bryson, R. A., 'Climatic episodes and the dating of the Mississippian cultures', *The Wisconsin Archaeologist,* **46,** 203–220 (1965).

—— and Bryson, R. A., 'Climatic change and the Mill Creek

culture of Iowa, Pt. I', *Journal of Iowa Archaeological Society*, **15**, 1–358 (1968).

Baker, A. R. H., 'Evidence in the "Nonarum Inquisitiones" of contracting arable lands in England during the early fourteenth century', *Economic History Review,* **19**, 518–32 (1966).

Baker, T. H., *Records of the seasons and prices of agricultural produce and phenomena observed in the British Isles* (London 1884).

Barger, G., *Ergot and ergotism* (London 1931).

Barry, R. G. and Chorley, R. J., *Atmosphere, weather and climate,* 2nd edn. (London 1971).

Bean, J. M. W., 'Plague, population and economic decline in England in the later Middle Ages', *Economic History Review,* **15**, 424–37 (1963).

Beltzner, K. (ed.), *Living with climatic change,* Science Council of Canada (Ottawa 1976).

Beresford, G., 'The medieval clay-land village: Excavations at Goltho and Barton Blount', *Society for Medieval Archaeology,* Monograph Series No. 6 (1975).

Beresford, M. W., 'The lost villages of medieval England', *Geographical Journal,* **117**, 129–149 (1951).

—— *The lost villages of England* (London 1954).

—— 'Medieval settlement', in Raistrick, A., *North York Moors,* National Park Guide (London 1969).

—— and Hurst, J. G. (eds.), *Deserted medieval villages* (London 1971).

—— and St. Joseph, J. K., *Medieval England: An aerial survey* (Cambridge 1958).

Bergthorsson, P., 'An estimate of drift ice and temperature in Iceland in 1000 years', *Jökull,* **19**, 94–101 (1969).

Bessell, J. E., 'The measurement of managerial efficiency in agriculture', *Journal of Agricultural Economics,* **21**, 391–401 (1970).

Beveridge, W. H., 'British exports and the barometer–I', *The Economic Journal,* **30**, 13–25 (1920).

—— 'British exports and the barometer–II', *The Economic Journal,* **30**, 209–13 (1920).

—— 'Weather and harvest cycles', *The Economic Journal,* **31**, 429–52 (1921).

Birse, E. L. and Robertson, L., *Assessment of climatic conditions in Scotland, 2: based on exposure and accumulated frost,* Macaulay Institute for Soil Research (Aberdeen 1970).

Bourke, P. M. A., 'The forecasting from weather data of potato blight and other plant diseases and pests', World Meteorological Organisation, Technical Note No. 10 (1955).

Bove, F. J., *The story of ergot* (New York 1970).

Brandon, R. F., 'Late medieval weather in Sussex and its agricultural significance', *Transactions of the Institute of British Geographers,* **54,** 1–17 (1971).

Britton, C. E., *A meteorological chronology to A.D. 1450,* Meteorological Office, Geophysical Memoirs, No. 70 (1937).

Britton, D. K., *Cereals in the United Kingdom – production, marketing and utilisation* (London 1969).

Brooks, C. E. P., *British floods and droughts* (London 1925).

—— *Climate through the ages,* 2nd edn. (London 1949).

—— and Glasspoole, J., *British floods and droughts* (London 1928).

Brückner, E., *Klimaschwankungen seït 1700* (Vienna 1890).

Bryson, R. A., 'Airmasses, streamlines and the Boreal Forest', *Geographical Bulletin,* **8,** 228–269 (1966).

—— *World climate and world food systems III: The lessons of climatic history,* Institute of Environmental Studies, University of Wisconsin, IES Report 27 (Madison 1974).

—— 'Heyuppskera: An heuristic model for hay yield in Iceland', *Research Institute Netri Ås,* Bulletin No. 18 (Hveragerti, Iceland 1974).

—— 'A perspective on climatic change', *Science,* **184,** 753–60 (1974).

—— Baerreis, D. A. and Wendland, W. M., 'The character of late- and post-glacial climatic changes', in Dort, W. and Jones, J. K. (eds.), *Pleistocene and recent environments of the central Great Plains,* 53–75 (Lawrence, Kansas 1970).

—— Lamb, H. H. and Donley, D. L., 'Drought and the decline of the Mycenae', *Antiquity,* **48,** 46–50 (1974).

—— and Murray, T. J., *Climates of hunger* (Madison 1977).

—— Ross, J. E., Hougas, R. W. and Engelbert, L. E., *Climatic change and agricultural responses,* Institute for Environmental Studies, University of Wisconsin, IES Report No. 20 (Madison 1974).

Buchinsky, I. E., *The past climate of the Russian Plain,* 2nd edn., in Russian (Leningrad 1957).

Caporael, L. R., 'Ergotism: The Satan loosed in Salem', *Science,* **192,** 21–26 (1976).

Carpenter, R., *Discontinuity in Greek civilization* (Cambridge 1966).

Cass, H. J. and ApSimon, A., *The neolithic and early bronze ages in the north of Ireland* (Belfast 1970).

Connell, K. H., 'The colonization of waste land in Ireland, 1700–1845', *Economic History Review,* 2nd series, **3,** 44–71 (1950).

Cooke, R. U. and Reeves, R. W., *Arroyos and environmental change* (Oxford 1976).

Dansgaarde, W., Johnsen, S. J., Miller, J. and Langway, C., 'One thousand centuries of climatic record from Camp Century on the Greenland ice sheet', *Science,* **166,** 377–81 (1969).

—— Johnsen, S. J., Reek, N., Gundestrup, N., Clansen, H. B. and Hammer, E. U., 'Climatic changes, Norsemen and modern man', *Nature,* **255,** 24–8 (1975).

Dickinson, O., 'Drought and the decline of the Mycenae: some comments', *Antiquity,* **48,** 228–30 (1974).

Dort, W. and Jones, J. K. (eds.), *Pleistocene and recent environments of the central Great Plains,* (Lawrence 1970).

Douglass, A. E., *Climate cycles and tree growth,* Carnegie Institute, Pubn. No. 289 (Washington 1919).

Duchaussoy, H. B., 'Les bans de vendages de la region Parisienne', *La Meteorologique,* 111–88 (1934).

Dudley, D. and Minter, E. M., 'The medieval village at Garrow Tor, Bodmin Moor, Cornwall', *Medieval Archaeology,* **8,** 272–94 (1963).

Eyre, S. R., 'A consideration of the factors limiting land improvement and settlement on the upland east of the Derbyshire Derwent', unpublished Ph.D. thesis, University of Sheffield (1954).

Fenton, A., 'Early and traditional cultivation implements in Scotland', *Proceedings of the Society of Antiquaries of Scotland,* **96,** 264–317 (1962–3).

Finch, T. F., 'Cultivation limits in the Dublin Mountains', *Irish Geography,* **2,** 206–10 (1953).

Fjellbygdenes Økonomiske Problemer (Economic problems of the mountainous areas), *Innstilling fra komiteen til undersøkelse av,* argitt 1 Mars 1958, Landbruksdepartement (Oslo 1958).

Fleming, A., 'Bronze age agriculture on the marginal lands of N.E. Yorkshire', *Agricultural History Review,* **19,** 1–24 (1971).

Fox, A., 'A monastic homestead on Dean Moor, South Devon', *Medieval Archaeology,* **2,** 141–57 (1958).

Fridriksson, S., 'The effects of sea ice on flora, fauna and agriculture', *Jökull,* **19,** 146–57 (1969).

Fritts, H. C., 'Tree rings and climate', *Scientific American,* **226,** 93–100 (1972).

Gailey, R. A., 'The evolution of Highland rural settlement', *Scottish Studies,* **6,** 155–77 (1962).

Gibson, R., *An old Berwickshire town: history of the town and parish of Greenlaw, from earliest times to the present day* (Edinburgh 1905).

Glasscock, R. E., 'The study of deserted medieval settlements in

Ireland', in Beresford, M. W. and Hurst, J. G. (eds.), *Deserted medieval villages,* 279–301 (Cambridge 1971).

Glasspoole, J., 'The rainfall over the British Isles of each of the eleven decades during the period 1820–1929', *Quarterly Journal of Royal Meteorological Society,* **59,** 253–60 (1933).

—— 'Variations in annual, seasonal and monthly rainfall over the British Isles, 1870–1939', *Quarterly Journal of Royal Meteorological Society,* **67,** 5–14 (1941).

Gloyne, R. W., 'Wind as a factor in hill climates', in Taylor, J. A. (ed.), *Hill climates and land usage with special reference to the highland zone of Britain,* Memo. No. 3, University College of Wales (Aberystwyth 1960).

Godwin, H., *The history of the British flora* (Cambridge 1956).

Goldie, A. H. R. and Carter, H. E., 'The trend of annual rainfall in Scotland', *Transactions of the Institute of Water Engineers,* **44,** 93–7 (1940).

Gould, P. R., 'Man against the environment: a game theoretic framework', *Annals of the Association of American Geographers,* **53,** 290–7 (1963).

Gregory, S., 'Accumulated temperature maps of the British Isles, *Transactions of the Institute of British Geographers,* **20,** 59–73 (1954).

Gribbin, J., *Our changing climate* (London 1975).

Griffin, J. B., 'Some correlations of climate and cultural change in eastern North American prehistory', *Annals of the New York Academy of Science,* **95,** 710–17 (1961).

Guise, J. W. B., 'Factors associated with variation in aggregate average yield of New Zealand wheat, 1918–67', *American Journal of Agricultural Economics,* **51,** 866–81 (1969).

Harrison, S. J., 'Problems in the measurement and evaluation of the climatic resources of upland Britain', in Taylor, J. A. (ed.), *Climatic resources and economic activity,* 47–63 (London 1974).

Heckscher, E. F., 'Sveriges befolkning från det stora nordiska krigets slut till Tabellverkets borjan (Sweden's population from the end of the Great Northern War to the beginning of the Board of Statistics), 1720–50', *Ekonomiskhistoriska studier,* 255–85 (1936).

Hennig, R., 'Katalog bemerkenswerter Witterungsereignisse von den altesten Zeiten bis zum Jahre 1800', *Abhundlungen Preussichen Meteorologische Institut,* **2** (4) (Berlin 1904).

Hines, C. O. and Haley, I., 'On the reality and nature of a certain sun-weather correlation', *Journal of Atmospheric Science,* **34,** 382–404 (1977).

Hoinkes, H., 'Glacier variation and weather', *Journal of Glaciation,* 3–21 (1968).

Holmsen, A., 'Desertion of farms around Oslo in the late Middle Ages', *Scandinavian Economic History Review,* **10,** 165–202 (1962).

Hoskins, W. G., 'The making of the agrarian landscape', in Hoskins, W. G. and Finberg, W. P. R., *Devonshire Studies,* 294 (London 1952).

—— 'Harvest fluctuations and economic history, 1480–1619', *Agricultural History Review,* **12,** 28–47 (1964).

—— 'Harvest fluctuations and economic history 1620–1759', *Agricultural History Review,* **16,** 15–31 (1968).

Hovgaard, W., 'The Norsemen in Greenland, recent discoveries at Herfoljness', *Geographical Review,* **15,** 615–16 (1925).

Hudson, J. P., 'Agronomic implications of long-term weather forecasting' in Johnson, C. G. and Smith, L. P. (eds.), *The biological significance of climatic changes in Britain,* 129–34 (London 1965).

Hunter, H., *Oats: their varieties and characteristics* (London 1924).

Huntington, E., *The pulse of Asia* (Boston 1907).

—— *Civilization and climate,* 3rd edn. (New Haven 1925).

—— *Earth and sun: An hypothesis of weather and sunspots* (New Haven 1923).

—— and Visher, S. S., *Climatic changes – their nature and causes* (New Haven 1922).

Jager, H., 'Die Ausdehnung der Wälder in Metteleuropa über offenes Siedlungsland', *Geogr. Hist. Agraires,* 300–11 (Nancy 1959).

Jennings, B. (ed.), *A history of Nidderdale* (Huddersfield 1967).

Jones, E. L., *Seasons and prices* (London 1964).

—— *The development of English agriculture, 1815–73,* Studies in Economic History (1968).

Jones, G. R. J., 'Agriculture in north-west Wales during the later Middle Ages' in Taylor, J. A. (ed.), *Climatic change with special reference to Wales and its agriculture,* Memo. No. 8, 47–53 University College of Wales (Aberystwyth 1965).

Jutikkala, E., 'The great Finnish famine in 1696–7', *Scandinavian Economic History Review,* **3,** 48–63 (1955).

Kershaw, I., 'The great famine and agrarian crisis in England, 1315–1322', *Past and Present,* **59,** 1–50 (1973).

King, J. W., Hurst, E., Slater, A. J., Smith, P. A. and Tamkin, B., 'Agriculture and sunspots', *Nature,* **252,** 2–3 (1974).

Krause, R. A., 'Aspects of adaptation among upper Republican susbsistence cultivators' in Dort, W. and Jones, J. K. (eds.), *Pleistocene and recent environments of the central Great Plains,* 103–115 (Lawrence 1970).

Kutzbach, J. E., 'Fluctuations of climate – monitoring and modelling', *WMO Bulletin,* 155–63 (July 1974).

Labrijn, A., 'Het Klimaat van Nederland gedurende de laatste twee en een halve eeuw' (with English summary), *Meded en Verhandelingen,* Koninklijk Nederlandsch Meteorological Institute, **49,** No. 102 (1945).

La Marche, V. C., 'Plaeoclimatic inferences from long tree-ring records', *Science,* **183,** 1043–48 (1974).

Lamb, H. H. 'What can we find out about the trend of our climate?', *Weather,* **18,** 194–216 (1963).

—— 'Trees and climatic history in Scotland: a radiocarbon dating test and other evidence', *Quarterly Journal of the Royal Meteorological Society,* **90,** 382–394 (1964).

—— *The changing climate* (London 1966).

—— '[Review of: Carpenter, R.] Discontinuity in Greek civilization', *Antiquity,* **41,** 233–34 (1967).

—— 'Climatic variation and our environment today and in the coming years', *Weather,* **15,** 447–55 (1970).

—— *Climate: past, present and future,* Vol. 1 (London 1972).

—— 'Climatic change and foresight in agriculture: the possibilities of long-term weather advice', *Outlook in Agriculture,* **7,** 203–10 (1973).

—— 'Climatology 1: The need to make up for lost time', *Times Higher Educational Supplement,* IV (21 January 1977).

—— *Climate: present, past and future,* Vol. 2 *Climatic history and the future* (London 1977).

—— Lewis, R. P. W. and Woodruffe, A., 'Atmospheric circulation and the main climatic variables between 8000 and 0 B.C.: meteorological evidence', in Royal Meteorological Society, *World climate from 8000 to 0 B.C.,* Proceedings of the International Symposium 18–19 April, 174–217 (London 1966).

Larrson, L-O, 'Settlement in Finland. A review of Suomen asutus 1560-luvulla', *Scandinavian Economic History Review,* **23,** 171–5 (1975).

Lebon, J. H. G., 'Old maps and rural change in Ayrshire', *Scottish Geographical Magazine,* **68,** 104–9 (1952).

Lehmer, D. J., 'Climate and culture in the Middle Missouri Valley' in Dort, W. and Jones, J. K. (eds.), *Pleistocene and recent environments of the central Great Plains,* 117–29 (Lawrence 1970).

Le Roy Ladurie, E., 'Histoire et climat', *Annales,* 3–24 (1959).

—— *Times of feast, times of famine* (New York 1972).

Libby, L. M., *Final technical report on historical climatology,* Defense Advanced Research Projects Agency, ARPA No. 1964–1 (Santa Monica 1974).

Liestol, G., 'Glaciers of the present day', in Holtedahl, O. (ed.), *Geology of Norway,* 482–90 (Oslo 1960).

Liljequist, G. H., 'The severity of winters at Stockholm, 1757–1942', *Geografiska Annaler,* 81–97 (1943).

Linehan, C. D., 'Deserted sites and rabbit-warrens on Dartmoor, Devon', *Medieval Archaeology,* **10,** 113–44 (1966).

Lliboutry, L. A., *Traité de glaciologie* (Paris 1965).

Lucas, H. S., 'The great European famine of 1315, 1316, and 1317' in Carus-Wilson, E. M. (ed.), *Essays in Economic History,* Vol. 2, 49–72 (London 1962).

Lysgaard, L., 'Recent climatic fluctuations', *Folia geographica danica,* 5, supplement (1949).

Lythe, S. G. E., *The economy of Scotland, 1550–1625* (London 1960).

M'Caw, L. S., 'The Black Mountains' in Stamp, L. D. (ed.) *The Land of Britain: Brecon,* 394–416 (London 1941).

MacGrigror, A., *Reports on the state of certain parishes in Scotland (1627),* Maitland Club (Edinburgh 1835).

McKerral, A., *Kintyre in the seventeenth century* (Edinburgh 1948).

McQuigg, J. D., *et al., The influence of weather and climate on United States grain yields,* National Oceanic and Atmospheric Administration, United States Department of Commerce (1973).

MacSween, M. D., 'Transhumance in north Skye', *Scottish Geographical Magazine,* **75,** 75–88 (1959).

McVean, D. N. and Ratcliffe, D. A., *Plant communities in the Scottish Highlands,* Monographs of the Nature Conservancy, No. 1 (1962).

Manley, G., 'The effective rate of altitudinal change in temperate Atlantic climates', *Geographical Review,* **35,** 408–17 (1945).

—— 'The range of variation of the British climate', *Geographical Journal,* **117,** 43–68 (1951).

—— *Climate and the British scene* (London 1952).

—— 'The mean temperature of central England, 1698–1952', *Quarterly Journal of the Royal Meteorological Society,* **79,** 242–61 (1953).

—— 'Possible climatic agencies in the development of post-glacial habitats', *Proceedings of the Royal Society,* B **161,** 363–75 (1965).

—— 'Problems of the climatic optimum: the contribution of glaciology' in Royal Meteorological Society, *World climate from 8000 to 0 B.C.,* 34–9 (1966).

—— 'Central England temperatures: monthly means 1659–1973', *Quarterly Journal of the Royal Meteorological Society,* **100,** 389–405 (1974).

Mason, B. J., 'Towards the understanding and prediction of climatic variations', *Quarterly Journal of the Royal Meteorological Society,* **102,** 476–98 (1976).

Matthews, J. A., 'Little Ice Age palaeotemperatures from high altitude tree growth in S. Norway', *Nature,* **264,** 243–45 (1976).

—— 'Glacier and climatic fluctuations inferred from tree-growth variations over the last 250 years, central southern Norway', *Boreas,* **6,** 1–24 (1977).

Maunder, W. J., *The value of the weather* (London 1970).

Mitchell, J. M., 'Recent secular changes of global temperature', *Annals of the New York Academy of Science,* **95,** 235–50(1961).

—— 'Causes of climatic change', *Meteorological Monograph* No. 8, 155–59 (1968).

Mitchell, V. C., 'A theoretical tree-line in Central Canada', *Annals of the Association of American Geographers,* **63,** 296–301 (1973).

Mitchinson, R., 'The movements of Scottish corn prices in the seventeenth and eighteenth centuries', *Economic History Review,* **18,** 278–291 (1965).

Moodie, D. W. and Catchpole, A. J. W., *Environmental data from historical documents by content analysis,* Manitoba Geographical Studies No. 5, University of Manitoba (Winnipeg 1975).

Mossman, R. C., 'The meteorology of Edinburgh', *Transactions of the Royal Society of Edinburgh,* **1,** 63–207 (1896–7).

N. 'Account of the district of Lammermuir, in East Lothian, drawn up in 1794, from the communications of several farmers', *The Farmer's Magazine,* **4,** 507–11 (1803).

Nuttonson, M. Y., *Wheat-climate relationships and the use of phenology in ascertaining the thermal and photothermal requirements of wheat,* American Institute of Crop Ecology (Washington D.C. 1955).

Ohlin, G., 'No safety in numbers' in Floud, R. (ed.), *Essays in quantitative economic history, 59–78* (Oxford 1974).

Oliver, J., 'Problems in agro-climatic relationships in Wales in the eighteenth century', in Taylor, J. A. (ed.), *Climatic change with special reference to the Highland zone of Britain,* Memo No. 3, 6–14, University College of Wales (Aberystwyth 1965).

Ollerenshaw, C. B., 'Climate factors and liverfluke disease' in Taylor, J. A. (ed.), *Climatic factors and diseases in plants and animals,* Memo. No. 5, University College of Wales (Aberystwyth 1962).

Orme, A. R., *Ireland* (London 1970).

Orwin, C. S., *The reclamation of Exmoor* (London 1929).

—— and Whetham, E. H., *History of British agriculture, 1846–1914,* 2nd edn. (Newton Abbot 1971).

Parry, M. L., 'Secular climatic change and marginal land', *Transactions of the Institute of British Geographers,* **64,** 1–13 (1975).

—— 'Abandoned farmland in upland Britain', *Geographical Journal,* **142,** 101–110 (1976).

—— 'A typology of cultivation ridges in southern Scotland', *Tools and Tillage,* **3,** 3–19 (1976).

—— 'County maps as historical sources: A sequence of surveys in south-east Scotland', *Scottish Studies,* **19,** 15–26 (1976).

—— 'The abandonment of upland settlement in southern Scotland', *Scottish Geographical Magazine,* **92,** 50–60 (1976).

—— 'The significance of the variability of summer warmth in upland Britain', *Weather,* **31,** 212–17 (1976).

—— *Mapping moorland change: a framework for land-use decisions in the Peak District,* Peak Park Planning Board (Bakewell 1977).

Pearson, M. G., 'Snowstorms in Scotland, 1782–1786', *Weather,* **28,** 195–201 (1973).

—— 'The winter of 1739–40 in Scotland', *Weather,* **28,** 20–24 (1973).

—— 'Never had it so bad', *Weather,* **30,** 14–21 (1975).

Peirce, J., 'Cultural sensitivity to environmental change: II, 1816, the year without a summer', Centre for Climatic Research, Institute for Environmental Studies, IES Report No. 15, University of Wisconsin (Madison 1974).

Pennington, W., *The history of British vegetation* (London 1969).

Perry, P. J., *British farming in the Great Depression, 1870–1914* (Newton Abbott 1974).

Pittock, A. B., 'How important are climatic changes?', *Weather,* **27,** 262–71 (1972).

Postan, M. M., 'Die wirtschaftlichen Grundlagen der mittelalterlichen Gessellschaft', *Jahrbucher fur Nationolokonomie und Statistik,* **166,** 180–205 (1954).

—— *The medieval economy and society,* 2nd edn. (Harmondsworth 1975).

—— and Titow, J. Z. 'Heriots and prices on Winchester manors', *Economic History Review,* **11,** 392–411 (1959).

Proceedings of the Conference on the Climate of the Eleventh and Sixteenth Centuries, Aspen, Colorado, 1962, National Centre for Atmospheric Research, NCAR Technical Notes, 63–1 (1963).

Ragg, J. M., *The soils of the country around Kelso and Lauder,* Soil Survey Memoir (Aberdeen 1960).

Rahtz, P., 'Holworth, medieval village excavation, 1958', *Proceedings of Dorset Natural History and Archaeological Society,* **81,** 127–147 (1959).

—— 'Upton, Gloucestershire, 1959–64', *Transactions of the Bristol and Gloucestershire Archaeological Society,* **85,** 70–140 (1966).

—— 'Upton, Gloucestershire, 1964–68', *Transactions of the Bristol and Gloucestershire Archaeological Society,* **88,** 74–124 (1969).

Roberts, B. K., Turner, J. and Ward, P. F., 'Recent forest history and land use in Weardale, northern England', in Birks, H. J. B. and West, R. G., *Quarternary Plant Ecology,* 207–21 (London 1973).

Romanes, C. S. (ed.), *Selections from the records of the regality of Melrose, Vol. 3: 1547–1706,* Scottish History Society, Vol. 8 (1917).

Royal Commission for Ancient and Historical Monuments (Scotland), *Inventory of monuments and constructions in the county of Berwickshire,* (Edinburgh 1915).

Royal Commission on Agriculture, Reports from the Commissioners, Cmnd. 2742 (1895).

Royal Commission on the Depressed Condition of Agricultural Interests (*the Richmond Commission*), Cmnd. 2778 (1883).

Royal Meteorological Society, *World climate from 8000 to 0 B.C.* (London 1966).

Russell, J. C., *British medieval population* (Albuquerque 1948).

Saarinen, T. F., *Perception of the drought hazard on the Great Plains,* Chicago University Geography Department, Research Paper No. 106 (1966).

Salvesen, H., *Fra Landnåm til matrikelgård; studier framveksten av utkantgården Hoset* (Trondheim 1974).

—— 'The agrarian crisis in Norway in the late Middle Ages' in Dyer, C. C. (ed.), *Medieval Village Research Group Report,* No. 23, 1975, 58–60 (1976).

Sandnes, J., *Ødetid og Gjenreisning* (Oslo 1971).

Schneider, S. H. and Mass, C., 'Volcanic dust, sunspots and temperature trends', *Science,* **190,** 741–46 (1975).

Schulman, E., 'Tree-rings and history in the western United States', *Smithsonian Report for 1955,* 459–73 (1956).

Scola, P. M., 'The Lothians' in Stamp, L. D. (ed.), *The land of Britain,* Pts 16–18 (London 1944).

Sears, P. B., 'Climate and civilisation' in Shapley, H., *Climatic change: evidence, causes and effects,* 39–50 (Cambridge, Mass. 1953).

Shellard, H. C., *Averages of accumulated temperature and standard deviation of monthly mean temperature over Britain, 1921–50,* Meteorological Office Professional Notes No. 125 (Bracknell 1959).

Smith, L. P., 'Variations of mean air temperature and hours of sunshine on the weather slope of a hill', *Meteorological Magazine,* **79,** 231 (1950).

—— 'Possible changes in seasonal weather', in Johnson, C. G. and Smith, L. P. (eds.), *The biological significance of climatic changes in Britain,* 187–191 (London 1965).

—— 'The changing climate', *Agricultural Meteorology,* **7,** 361–2 (1970).

Sokolov, A., 'Reduction in duration of river ice with climatic warming' (in Russian), *Priroda,* 96–8 (1955).

Soulsby, J. A., 'Palaeoenvironmental interpretation of a buried soil at Achnacree, Argyll', *Transactions of the Institute of British Geographers* New Series 1, 279–283 (1975).

Statistical Account of Scotland, Sir John Sinclair (ed.) (Edinburgh 1791–99).

Steensberg, A., 'The archaeological dating of the climatic change about A.D. 1300', *Advancement of Science,* **9,** 31–3 (1952).

Symon, J. A., *Scottish farming: past and present* (Edinburgh 1959).

Tatham, G., 'Environmentalism and possibilism' in Taylor, G. (ed.) *Geography in the twentieth century,* 3rd edn., 128–62 (1957).

Taylor, J. A., *Weather economics* (Oxford 1968).

—— 'Climatic change as related to altitudinal thresholds and soil variables', in Johnson, C. G. and Smith, L. P. (eds.), *The biological significance of climatic change in Britain,* 37–49 (1965).

—— 'Upland climates' in Chandler, T. and Gregory, S. (eds.), *The climate of the British Isles,* 267–87 (London 1976).

—— (ed.), *Hill climates and land usage with special reference to the highland zone of Britain,* Memo. No. 3, University College of Wales (Aberystwyth 1960).

Teitsson, V. B. and Stefansson, M., 'Islandsk odegardsforskning' in Nasjonale Forskningsoverikter, *Det. nordiske pdergardsprojekt,* Pubn. No. 1, 111–48 (1972).

Thomas, M. K., 'Recent climatic fluctuations in Canada', *Climatological Studies No. 28,* Environment Canada (Ottawa 1975).

Thorarinsson, S., 'Tefrokronologiska studier på Island', *Geografiska Annaler,* **26,** 1–217 (1944).

—— *The thousand years' struggle against ice and fire* (Reykjavik 1956).

Thran, P. and Broekhuizen, S., *Agro-ecological atlas of cereal growing in Europe: Volume I, Agro-climatic atlas of Europe* (Amsterdam 1965).

Tomanek, G. W. and Hulett, G. K., 'Effects of historical droughts on grassland vegetation in the central Great Plains' in Dort, W.

and Jones, J. K. (eds.), *Pleistocene and recent environments of the central Great Plains,* 203–210 (Lawrence 1970).

Titow, J. Z., 'Evidence of weather in the account rolls of the Bishopric of Winchester, 1209–1350', *Economic History Review,* **12,** 360–407 (1960).

—— *Winchester yields: a study in medieval agricultural productivity* (Cambridge 1972).

Turner, J., 'A contribution to the history of forest clearance', *Proceedings of the Royal Society,* B 161, 343–54 (1965).

Utterström, G., 'Some population problems in pre-industrial Sweden', *Scandinavian Economic History Review,* **2,** 103–65 (1954).

—— 'Climatic fluctuations and population problems in early modern history', *Scandinavian Economic History Review,* **3,** 1–47 (1955).

—— 'Population and agriculture in Sweden', *Scandinavian Economic History Review,* **9,** 176–94 (1961).

Van Bath, B. H. S., *The agrarian history of western Europe, A.D. 500–1800* (London 1963).

Vanderlinden, E., *Chronique des evenements meteorologiques en Beligique jusqu'en 1834* (Brussels 1924).

Van Zeist, W., Woldring, H. and Stapert, D., 'Late quaternary vegetation and climate in S.W. Turkey', *Palaeohistoria,* **17,** 53–143 (1975).

Ventskevich, G. Z., *Agrometeorology,* Israel Program for Scientific Translations (Jerusalem 1961).

Walton, K., 'Climate and famines in north-east Scotland', *Scottish Geographical Magazine,* **68,** 13–22 (1952).

Waterbolk, H. T., 'Food production in prehistoric Europe', *Science,* **162,** 1093–1102 (1968).

Wedel, W. R. 'Dust Bowls of the past', *Science,* **86,** 2232, supplement, 8–9 (1937).

—— 'Environment and native subsistence economies in the central Great Plains', *Smithsonian Miscellaneous Collections,* **101,** 1–29 (1941).

—— 'Some aspects of human ecology on the Great Plains', *American Anthropology,* **55,** 499–514 (1953).

—— *Prehistoric man on the Great Plains* (Norman, Oklahoma 1961).

—— 'Some environmental and historical factors of the Great Bend Aspect' in Dort, W. and Jones, J. K. (eds.), *Pleistocene and recent environments of the central Great Plains,* 131–40 (Lawrence 1970).

Wood, C. A. and Lovett, R. R., 'Rainfall, drought and the solar cycle', *Nature,* **251,** 594–96 (1974).

Wood, D. J., 'The complicity of climate in the 1816 depression in Dumfriesshire', *Scottish Geographical Magazine*, **81,** 5–17 (1965).

Wood, K. D., 'Sunspots and planets', *Nature*, **240,** 91–3 (1971).

Woodbury, R., 'Climatic changes and prehistoric agriculture in the south-western United States', *Annals of the New York Academy of Science*, **95,** 705–9 (1961).

Wright, A. E. and Moseley, F. (eds.), *Ice ages: Ancient and modern* (Liverpool 1974).

Wright, H. E., 'Climatic change in Mycenaean Greece', *Antiquity*, **42,** 123–27 (1968).

—— 'Natural environment and early food production north of Mesopotamia', *Science*, **161,** 334–39 (1968).

Wright, S., 'Barton Blount: Climatic or economic change?', *Medieval Archaeology*, **20,** 148–52 (1976).

Index

Figures in *italics* refer to an illustration or table on the specified page. References to countries, states, counties and other localities are given only where these are discussed specifically. Reference to authors is made only where these are mentioned by name in the text.

D

E

T

U

V

W

X